ON DUBLIN'S DOORSTEP

EXPLORING THE PROVINCE OF LEINSTER

To Seamus Cashman

my former publisher

a person of vision and infinite patience

On Dublin's Doorstep

EXPLORING THE PROVINCE OF LEINSTER

Christopher Moriarty

WOLFHOUND PRESS

Published in 2002 by
Wolfhound Press
An imprint of Merlin Publishing
16 Upper Pembroke Street, Dublin 2, Ireland
Tel: +353 1 676 4373; Fax: +353 1 676 4368
e-mail: publishing@merlin.ie
www.merlin-publishing.com

British Library Cataloguing in Publication Data
A catalogue record for this book is available from the British Library.

ISBN 0-86327-892-2

5   4   3   2   1

Cover photographs: Christopher Moriarty
Cover design: Graham Thew Design
Book design: David Houlden
Typesetting: David Houlden
Printed by Colour Books Ltd, Dublin

Contents

Contents

Map of east Leinster

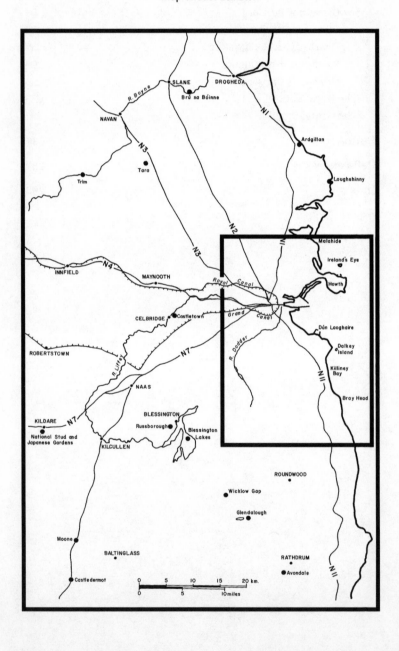

Map of Greater Dublin

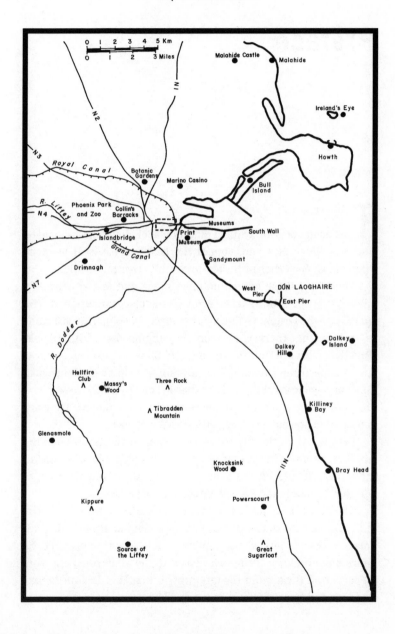

Preface

This book takes for granted that its readers have access to maps and bus timetables and, should the desire arise, will be close enough to a book shop or library to consult other publications.

Therefore, there are no detailed maps and few step-by-step instructions on how to explore any of the places mentioned. The quality of the Ordnance Survey *Discovery Series* of 1: 50,000 maps is so high that there is no point in copying them into a book. Together with the Dublin city map, OS Sheets 43, 50 and 56 cover most of the ground, and the few outlying spots are well signposted. The maps show everything that is needed on the longer routes, and the shorter ones are best wandered around at random. They are too small to present a risk of getting seriously lost.

References to the literature are given in the text under the author's name or, in the case of anonymous pamphlets, by the full title. The details of these are given in alphabetical order of authors' names in the References section (see p. 289).

The buses listed all go from various termini in the city centre, unless otherwise stated. Dublin Bus issues an excellent guide, with maps, to the city bus service, and its vehicles travel to many of the more distant places. Provincial buses to the other outlying spots depart from Busáras in the city centre. Tara and *Brú na Bóinne* need tourist coaches.

Introduction

The city of Dublin is more than the capital of Ireland — it lies in the centre of a wonderland of ancient and modern art, architecture and scenery. Moorland and wilderness overlook the green and fertile lowlands which nurtured a developing civilisation with its sacred places and castles. Increasing peace and tolerance in recent centuries have provided museums, parks and gardens. The seaside adds a further dimension.

This book was conceived as a source of inspiration for the citizen who is wondering what to do next Sunday — and there are fifty-two suggestions to ensure a year's supply. Sunday remains the day when the majority of citizens, with their offspring and dogs, are free to explore both city and wilderness with a minimum of competition for space. My first aim is to suggest places to visit, the second to attempt to share my own delight in going to see them.

The decision on what to do on a Sunday depends on many factors: mood, weather, time of year, ease of access, state of health and stamina. In and around Dublin the variety of activities on offer ranges from reasonably vigorous mountain walks to small and intensely concentrated museums, from places on somebody's doorstep to distant sites requiring an hour or so in the car.

This is an unashamedly self-indulgent book. The fifty-two places selected are favourites of mine. To my shame, the list includes a few that I have looked at only once. Some of these, such as the Collins Barracks Museum, have but recently come into existence. Others, like the Marino Casino, are places that I have been telling myself for forty years or more that I must go and see. But there are many, like Sandymount or Glenasmole, or the Zoo or Phoenix Park, that have welcomed me for many a month of Sundays, and which I long to see over and over again. Each time, every one of them offers something new and exciting: a bird or flower not seen before, a previously unnoticed detail in the Book of Kells or on a high cross, or on a hillside — features that have always been there but never noticed because there is so much more than can ever be absorbed on one visit.

One of the problems in compiling this book has been making the final selection of places to include. There are a great many more than fifty-two favourites of mine in Dublin and its surrounds, but that number seemed right for a Sunday book. The selection, in the end, did not derive from any logical process. Rather, it grew in its own way and simply comprises the places to which something propelled me on a particular occasion.

Excellent guidebooks or scholarly references exist for most of the places mentioned in this book, and many of these are included in the References section. My approach has been to attempt something of an essay rather than a comprehensive guide to each of the excursions; my hope has been to offer a little inspiration, or a revelation of some hidden detail, and to provide — what fascinates me more than anything — some explanation of why the scene, whether land-form or building, looks as it does.

Historic Sites

The entire city of Dublin is an historic site — but rather too big a meal for a single Sunday. Museums and galleries will be considered in another section. The five sites selected for this section vary in age — from five millennia at Brú na Bóinne to a mere thousand years at Castledermot — and in size from a few square metres at Moone to some ten square kilometres around Glendalough. Large or small, they contain elements that can be admired and understood without any knowledge of their history. In this approach, I part company with my illustrious predecessor, Patrick Weston Joyce, who could devote pages to an insignificant piece of stone wall because it was there when a particularly grisly murder was committed.

Four of the five provide guides or interpretative centres or both. Such facilities for visitors arouse controversy, with a great gulf between, one might say, purists and tourists. The purist feels that the sites should be the preserve of those who can appreciate their significance without such vulgar entities. The tourists are simpler folk, like myself, whose unashamed aim is to discover a little about a great many people, places, artefacts and living creatures. What is more, it rains in our beautiful country, and the visitor centre provides shelter and food in addition to scholarly information presented in digestible form.

Glendalough

It was St Kevin who first, unwittingly, initiated the over-exposure of Glendalough. Such was his sanctity that he had little chance of success as a hermit in search of solitude as crowds of pilgrims began to seek him out at an early stage of his career. The pilgrimage to Glendalough has never really ceased, although it becomes increasingly secular as time goes by. Meanwhile, miners in the nineteenth century and foresters in the twentieth exploited the valley's resources, and traffic congestion set in.

And, in spite of all that, Glendalough remains an enchanting place, even on a fine, summer Sunday afternoon. The valley is big enough and there are sufficient tracks and footpaths to accommodate great numbers of people. A short walk from either car park takes you away from the crowds. Much of the beauty and interest of Glendalough is rock solid, in the form of the valley itself, the ruined buildings of the monastic city and the traces of the mining settlement, which means that a visit in winter is every bit as rewarding as one in summer, with the added advantage of a minimum of cars.

Many people have written about St Kevin and Glendalough; there are pious books and story books and factual guidebooks.

Two of the latter deserve particular attention. The first is the official guide by H.G. Leask, giving an outline of the history of the monastery and a wealth of detail with excellent illustrations of the buildings that remain. The second is *Exploring Glendalough Valley*, an outstanding booklet published by the Office of Public Works in 1990, and compiled with the assistance of a very distinguished team of experts. It focuses largely on the marked trails in the valley and gives a comprehensive account of geology, flora and fauna but, very sadly, has been allowed to go out of print. Its successor *Exploring Glendalough* (1997), with bigger illustrations but less detail and scholarship, has the added attraction of suggestions for walks outside the immediate valley. These and many others are on sale at the Visitor Centre.

The Kildare and Wicklow geological map gives the rock in which the Glendalough Valley lies the pleasing designation of 'eastern inner dynamic aureole zone', but it may more conveniently be termed 'mica schist'. It is part of the aureole of metamorphic rock that surrounds the granite mass of the Wicklow Mountains and extends as far as 7 miles to the east of Glendalough, where it disappears along a fault system at the edge of much older rocks. The granite was extremely hot, and effectively cooked and crumpled the older sedimentary strata around it, creating the aureole. This aureole is of the greatest importance to Sunday folk because the forces of rain and ice break it down to produce far more impressive scenery than the gentle slopes of the weathered granite.

In Glendalough, an ancient river valley was invaded by a great glacier that flowed towards the south-east from the mountains. The original valley was V-shaped in section and the river zigzagged between mountain spurs. The glacier straightened out the valley, flattened its bottom and even excavated it in places — those now occupied by the lakes.

There was just one big lake when the ice receded ten thousand years ago, but the river carried sand down the hillside and deposited it as a delta. Eventually the sand — 20 million tons of it — divided the lake in two and formed a large patch of well-drained level land. That may well explain the presence of a wealthy community, capable first of welcoming and caring for a hermit and, subsequently, of supporting the great monastic settlement which arose in the course of the centuries after St Kevin himself died.

The predecessors of that community had occupied the valley for some thousands of years. The cave above the Upper Lake, known as St Kevin's Bed, is considered to have been excavated by Bronze Age people as a burial place. Similar tombs of that period are known in Sicily and Normandy. Copper is plentiful in the valley and it may well be that miners established themselves there and lived in affluence between the lakes. The *caher*, or stone fort, overlooking the Upper Lake is an Iron Age enclosure, likely to have been part of a settlement established before St Kevin's arrival in the sixth century.

The ruins of about ten stone churches remain to be seen in Glendalough. They range from the fragmentary cell perched high above the Upper Lake, to the charming St Kevin's Kitchen with its little round tower, to the great cathedral. Some are purely functional, with plain doorways and windows, while others are decorated with Romanesque sculpture. Dominating the whole scene is the great round tower, a very remarkable feat of engineering which has stood for a thousand years.

The archaeological record is of early building in the vicinity of the Upper Lake with later, and greater, structures on the delta. Tradition tells of the arrival of St Kevin in his search for solitude, in the sixth century. History relates many visits by prominent people and also the deaths there of some of them while on pilgrimage. There was a great flood in 1174 and a total of nine burnings, some of them accidental, in a period of nearly three hundred years between 775 and 1071. Unfortunately, no records have been passed down on such positive matters as the dates of major construction works in the area. The annalists, like the media of today, had little time for good news.

As its seaport increased in importance and Dublin became a cathedral city, Glendalough declined. Major building work,

A thousand years of stone at Glendalough

however, continued at least until the end of the twelfth century, giving the valley no less than six hundred years as a centre of worship of major importance. The great days may have ended in 1214 when the diocese of Glendalough was united with that of the growing city of Dublin. The final physical blow came when English forces devastated the monastery in 1398. But the spiritual power remained. The combination of the remote, somewhat austere, beauty of the valley with its tradition of worship and the charm of the fragmented churches continues to draw the crowds.

Footpaths lead all over Glendalough, several going up and away over the hills. Most of the trees in the valley are exotics, but there is a large and important area of oak to the south of the Lower Lake. This woodland, with its wonderful sequence of changing colours through the year, looks very much the same as the primeval forest which once covered the greater part of Ireland. Birch, holly, ash and hazel are all present and, like the oak, are native species which reached Ireland without assistance from human beings. Nearby, the Poulanass River cascades through the exquisite tree-shaded and fern-clad valley, its clear water dashing over the sparkling schist.

The Glendalough oak wood is one of very few Irish haunts of the redstart, a beautiful woodland bird, a sort of robin in reverse. It has the colours of the robin, brown and red, but the brown is in front and the red behind. Another rarity in the valley is the peregrine falcon which inhabits the cliff tops above the Upper Lake. Ravens live there too but, as everybody since Thomas Moore has known, the skylark is absent.

The path above the margin of the Upper Lake has been cut out along a scree slope. The opposite side of the valley is too steep for any sort of roadway. The scree is on the sunny, north side. The rocks, which form it, were broken off by the alternate freezing and thawing of water in cracks in the cliff face. Because of the warmth of the sun, thawing and freezing took place at more frequent intervals and did more damage to the rocks facing south. The opposite side was colder so that the ice stayed in place for longer and the cliffs remained steeper.

This path leads beyond the top of the lake, with its great, grassy alluvial fan, to the old mining settlement. The mines were a busy place through the greater part of the nineteenth century and were revived briefly from 1919 to 1920. They eventually closed when the value of the lead ore fell and extraction became uneconomical. The village, with its remains of works and dwellings, and its surroundings of enormous granite boulders, bubbling streams, and a great waterfall, is one of the most dramatic parts of the whole valley.

Grid 1296, Sheet 56. St Kevin's bus from the Royal College of Surgeons, St Stephen's Green. There are two car parks, one at the Visitor Centre, one between the lakes, and a fee is charged for parking. Do not attempt to go to the second one on a fine Sunday in summer as the approach road is frequently jammed and seldom, if ever, policed. The Centre, open daily, is excellent and its car park is convenient both to the main monastic ruins and to the lovely path between the oak wood and the Lower Lake. Guided tour including 17-minute audio-visual is available. Dog- and buggy-friendly, limited wheelchair access. Miles of well-surfaced level paths as wells as steep ones and steps for the energetic. Hotel with bar and meals, endless picnic spots. Beware of early closing of the car park at 5.00 p.m. in winter and 6.00 p.m. in summer, and the loos even earlier.

Moone and Castledermot

Historic sites

Two neighbouring villages on the Carlow–Kilkenny border offering three Celtic crosses (of which one is particularly outstanding) together with a selection of Romanesque and Gothic remains including a round tower. Suitable at any time of year, occupies half a day including drive from Dublin.

The great cross of Moone ranks among the highest achievements of Irish artists. Created by an unknown sculptor more than 1,000 years ago, it combines obvious skill in conception, design and craftsmanship with an element of charm, and perhaps even a sense of fun.

From the village of Moone, the approach by road to the cross is delightful: through a pair of noble gate posts to pass Moone Abbey, a small Palladian house with magnificent lime trees, and an old mill. In spite of recent excavation and general tidying-up of the surroundings, the situation of the cross itself is dismal. Nothing remains of the ancient Columban monastery, founded there in the sixth century, the ruined walls that still stand being those of a Franciscan friary of 1258. Sufficient to make a gloomy shade, they are unrelieved by any attractive architectural features.

But the cross more than compensates for its unprepossessing background. The design required something too tall to be hewn from a single stone, so the cross was made in three parts which were dismembered at some remote time later. The base and the top were discovered early in the nineteenth century and assembled to make an ill-proportioned entity. Then, in 1893, the centre piece was found and the cross was restored to its former glory. Fragments of a similar cross were also found and have been mounted in concrete nearby. What little remains of their sculptures are different in style, but delightful.

The great cross is made from granite: a beautiful stone, but because of its coarse crystalline structure, difficult to work. Sculptors using granite have to express themselves with bold outlines and little detail. The approach of the Master of Moone was to create a tall and slender cross and to decorate it with very stylised people and animals. Entirely in sympathy with the nature of the stone, they succeed in giving a vivid representation of the stories they illustrate. Comparison with other crosses dates the Moone work to the first half of the ninth century.

The base — at a convenient eye-level for the beholder — is the major part of the work and is decorated with the most important scenes. The high crosses for the most part are divided into panels, each illustrating a well-known story from the scriptures or from the lives of popular later saints. They have much in common with medieval art from all parts of Christian Europe. Many of the scenes are easy to interpret, being well-known stories from the Old and New Testaments. Others depict miracles relating to the anchorites who dwelt around Lake Mareoticus near Alexandria and whose lives were familiar to the Irish monks. Zoological and mythological beasts illustrate chapters from the bestiaries, and the artists elsewhere embellished their crosses with abstracts. Scholars, such as Peter Harbison, provide fascinating accounts of the sources.

At Moone, Adam and Eve appear, framed by a weeping tree which is festooned with tempting fruit; a fork-tailed serpent spirals around its trunk and whispers into Eve's ear. Below them Abraham, seated in a high-backed chair, prepares to sacrifice Isaac who bends obediently over an altar. Above Isaac stands a long-tailed ram and on Abraham's chair an angel perches. The scene nearest the bottom is of Daniel, resolutely standing surrounded by seven frustrated lions. The prophet's body is a simple rectangle and his head a somewhat triangular shape with enormous round eyes. What is particularly striking is the amount of expression that the sculptor has been able to give to these deceptively simple forms.

On other panels the Twelve Apostles are treated in a similar style, as is the Virgin Mary, seated on a donkey as she flees to Egypt. Above them, three equally rectangular Children of Israel stand in the burning fiery furnace, protected by a four-winged angel. Below the Flight into Egypt scene is the Feeding of the Five Thousand. Five circular loaves, two fat fishes and two thin ones fill the panel. Other scenes from the Scriptures mingle with the most wonderful beasts and abstract designs.

The narrow shaft of the cross bears a delightful bestiary while the head has a risen Christ at the centre of the east face, surrounded by a variety of beasts and people. The Christ figure has disproportionately large hands which fill the arms of the cross. The other sculptures are so skilfully executed that it is hard to believe that the exaggerated size of the hands is an error in design. Perhaps it illustrates some concept such as divine mercy.

The cross and its fragmentary neighbour are all that remain of the Columban monastery of Moone but the establishment of a Franciscan friary on the site in the thirteenth century implies that it continued to be a fairly important centre after the Columbans had left. The remains of a tower house nearby testify to the presence of a wealthy landowner but, since the times of the Anglo-Normans, Moone seems to have been overshadowed by the nearby settlement of Castledermot.

The Dermot of the name was an anchorite who died in 823. His hermitage became an important monastic centre and controlled offshoots as far away as Tullamore. Two high crosses, a round tower and the west doorway of a Romanesque church survive in the modern churchyard to tell of its former glories. The monastery was sufficiently wealthy to have been plundered by the Vikings twice in the ninth century, and by neighbouring clans — along with Moone — in the eleventh century.

The monastery was built of granite and, in the ninth or tenth century, the round tower was constructed using large,

Biblical scenes on the base of the
great cross of Moone

irregular blocks of the same stone. Its crenellated top was added considerably later. The crosses at Castledermot repeat many of the scenes of the Moone masterpiece and were probably influenced by it. However, the sculptors preferred traditional proportions and the crosses are lower and more solid in appearance. The style of the carving is naturalistic, but the crosses seem to be the work of two sculptors who had very different views as to where the various scenes from the scriptures and other writings should be placed. One feature they both share, and which can also be seen at Moone, is the shape of the heads of the people figured: little round, or almost triangular, faces with pointed chins.

The Castledermot crosses have many unusual features and perhaps the most remarkable is the position of Adam and Eve on the north cross. They occupy the central position between the arms — the place where you expect either a crucifixion or a scene of Christ in judgement. The logic, if there was any, apparently was to place the Fall of Man opposite to the Crucifixion which is the symbol of redemption. Perhaps the sculptor simply knew which scenes his patrons wanted and, ruled only by his own vision, made up his mind as to where they should go.

The most delightful scene at Castledermot is on the base of the south cross where Noah and one of his sons are driving the animals towards the ark. A duck and a stag obediently go in the direction indicated, while some small animal with a long tail and pointed ears — maybe a cat — is going its own, sweet way.

The presence, to this day, of a church close to the round tower and the crosses suggests that worship on the site of St Dermot's monastery may have continued without interruption since his time. But, as at Moone, the thirteenth century saw the establishment of a Franciscan friary in the town nearby, and of an Augustinian hospital. Under the Anglo-Norman de Riddlesford family, the importance of the Celtic monastery probably waned. The Franciscan ruins, in contrast to those at Moone, are well preserved and include a fine east window. Parts of the medieval town wall can also be traced in the vicinity.

Grid S7992 and S7885, Sheets 55 and 61. Moone is 36 miles from Dublin, and Castledermot (S7885) is 5 miles farther down the road. The quickest way takes the motorways M7 and M9, followed by the N9 for Carlow. But a much more attractive approach is through Blessington and Baltinglass which allows a picnic by the Blessington lake (see page 258) near Pollaphuca. There is a pleasant little park in Castledermot, on the line of the avenue that joined rectory and church in days gone by. Both villages are places in which to contemplate the beauties of early Christian art rather than to picnic or exercise dogs and children. Open all day, bumpy for wheelchairs, pub food available in villages.

Brú na Bóinne

Historic Sites

The Mecca of Irish archaeological sites, now embarking on its sixth millennium of tourism. Stone-Age art and architecture with outstanding twentieth-century visitor centre. Suitable at any time of year, occupies at least half a day.

Every time an archaeologist scratches at Newgrange, yet more wonderful mysteries are revealed. In the 1950s, when Frank Mitchell brought his students to visit the passage grave, the custodian supplied candles and we admired the art and the skill of the builders while wondering what the rectangular opening above the door, known as the roof box, was. Thorn trees grew and cattle grazed on the mound. Knowth was an untouched green hill nearby and those who wished could borrow a key and explore the passages of Dowth on their own.

Electric light and strictly-regimented tours have done little to impair the thrill of crawling down the passage at Newgrange, between the tall upright stones, and the wonder of the great cruciform chamber with its stone basins and abstract ornamentation. Speculation about the site has never ceased and much nonsense has been written about it. But this is a place where the facts can equal any fantasy.

Radio carbon dating pushed the origins of Newgrange farther and farther back in time, so that an age of about five thousand years is accepted; it therefore pre-dates the pyramids of Egypt by some centuries. The corbelled dome of the great burial chamber

Brú na Bóinne footbridge crossing the River Boyne

was considered a simple structure until it was realised that to balance the huge stones needed a very high degree of sophistication on the part of the designers. Moreover, the roof was so skilfully planned that rainwater runs off it and the chamber has remained dry throughout five millennia. The most impressive discovery was M.J. O'Kelly's demonstration that the mysterious roof box had been installed to allow the rays of the rising sun to penetrate the chamber at midwinter.

The monuments are the work of the neolithic people, the first farmers in Ireland. Many of the great stones bear elaborate abstract sculpture. Two of the finest are the spiral motif of the entrance stone at Newgrange and the decorated basin at Knowth. They are so beautifully executed that it is not easy to remember that the artists worked them with stone tools.

The engineering and organisational achievements of the Stone Age builders of the great temple are not immediately evident and were scarcely noticed by earlier generations of archaeologists. As time went by, those who had the privilege of taking part in major excavations became acutely aware of the logistical problems involved in shifting 200,000 tons of earth without a wheel, to say nothing of a JCB. The society which undertook the creation of these monuments had to be wealthy, well fed and highly sophisticated.

The many monuments of *Brú na Bóinne* — the Palace of the Boyne — are clustered in a bend of the river, the biggest and best of them standing on a ridge. The Big Three — Dowth, Knowth and Newgrange — are passage graves and the people who built them throughout Ireland favoured hilltop sites. Clearly, they wanted the monuments to be very conspicuous. Archaeologists, with due propriety, call these constructions tombs or graves; they contain human remains and there is no indisputable evidence that they were used for any other purpose. However, if present-day cathedrals had neither history nor tradition of use as places of worship, archaeologists would be forced to describe them as tombs since they also contain numerous burials.

It is hard to believe that the great passage graves were constructed as nothing more than monuments to the dead, and perhaps it is more reasonable to hold that they were temples rather than merely tombs. The archaeological record shows that Bronze Age people inserted their burials in the mounds of passage graves and that a Roman coin was found at Newgrange. The implication is that, whatever the original purpose of the passage graves, they certainly became shrines or places for pilgrimage as time went by. While the earliest written account of Newgrange, that of the seventeenth-century antiquarian Edward Lhuyd, is less than 400 years old, tradition goes back into mythological times, and *Brú na Bóinne* has long been associated with Aengus, the Danann god.

Having stood in a pastoral landscape with little disturbance for millennia, the past 50 years have seen greater and more rapid transformations of the monuments than ever before. It is not impossible that the builders of Newgrange used candles when entering the tomb, but very unlikely that they contemplated the insertion of electric light. Dowth, tragically, was desecrated and almost demolished in the nineteenth century. Fortunately, some of its underground passages and decorated stones survived. Newgrange became so popular a place for secular pilgrims that its passage needed re-enforcement. This led to the massive rebuilding of the 1960s and O'Kelly's discoveries of the sophistication of the builders.

In 1962, George Eogan began to excavate Knowth and continued the work for more than 30 years. He uncovered an incredibly complex assemblage of large and small monuments. Apparently, eighteen small tombs were constructed first, followed by the great mound. Round about, he found evidence of more or less continuous use up to the twentieth century. The farm, which surrounds the monument, inherits a tradition going back for 5,000 years. The viewing arrangements for visitors provide a new — or perhaps renewed — use for the site.

The greatest change of all has been the creation of the Visitor Centre at Newgrange and the shepherding of the ever-increasing numbers of visitors to the right bank of the Boyne. As late as the 1950s, relatively little damage was done to the monuments by the trickle of archaeologists, students and sight-seers who came. But thousands of pairs of feet, belonging to even the best-willed people in the world, can do untold damage to small areas of green fields which are likely to cover many more hidden treasures. Moving the centre across the river allowed for the creation of space for car parking and gave freedom for the development of the exciting modern building with its space for exhibition and refreshment.

The graceful suspension bridge which crosses the Boyne gives the river a degree of prominence that it lacked in the old days, when visitors parked their cars close to Newgrange but distant from the river. Below the bridge, the Boyne flows through a water meadow, bright with wild flowers in summer and probably looking very much the same as it did in ancient times. The neolithic farmers of the Boyne valley were cattlemen, and cattle continue to be the mainstay of the present-day inhabitants, as well as being the creatures that maintain the grassland. Salmon, easy to catch and plentiful in winter when other food was scarce, contributed to the leisure and sophistication of the Boyne people, allowing them to sit and think and plan great architecture.

Grid O0272, Sheet 42. Clearly signposted from the Finglas to Slane road. Numerous tour buses. Car parking, buggy-friendly paths and a pleasant spot to walk around — though not particularly welcoming for dogs. Food and books in the Visitor Centre, plenty of space for picnics. Newgrange Farm nearby is also well worth a visit on another Sunday. Access only through Visitor Centre, fee charged. Food and wheel-chair facilities at Centre. Open: 9.30 a.m. to 5.00 p.m. in winter, 9.00 a.m. to 7.00 p.m. in summer.

Tara

The first impression of Tara is of an undistinguished hill, little more, indeed, than a slightly elevated roll in the rolling country-side of County Meath. The next impression is but marginally better: a green plateau interrupted by a scattering of earthen mounds and ridges. But this is *Teamhar na Rí*, Tara of the Kings, the site of the halls where Moore's 'Harp that once ... the soul of music shed', where Fionn Mac Cumhaill defeated the ogre Aileen, son of Midhna and where St Patrick converted the High King, Laoghaire. Legend, myth and history combine to make Tara the most famous of all the ancient places of Ireland.

Even if the traditions did not exist, Tara would be worthy of a visit. Two features in particular make it unique. One is the sheer size of the level hilltop and the extent of the remains there — the complex could have catered for thousands of people at a gathering. The other is its strategic position — on the edge of an immense fertile plain to the west, and commanding distant views over the hills in all other directions.

On a clear day, it is possible to see a great deal of Ireland and let yourself imagine how it felt to be high king. Slieve Gullion and the Mournes stand out to the north, and the Wicklow Mountains to the south. Closer to hand, the white stone face of Newgrange is visible, a reminder of the possibility that passage graves were deliberately sited to be in view of each other. To the north is the Hill of Slane where tradition tells that St Patrick defiantly ignited his Paschal fire. Not too clearly visible because it is below the skyline, the hill can be identified by the ruined monastery on the summit.

The archaeologists who excavated on the hill of Tara came up with facts that were even more remarkable than the legend or history. The Four Masters recount that, in the Age of the World 3502:

> *Tea, daughter of Lughaidh, son of Ith, whom Eremhon married in Spain, to the repudiation of Odhbha, was the Tea who requested of Eremhon a choice hill, as her dower, in whatever place she should select, that she might be interred therein, and that her mound and her gravestone might be thereon raised, and where every prince of her race should dwell.... The hill she selected was Druim-Caein, i.e. Tara. It was from her it was called, and in it she was interred.*

Tea made her choice in 1698 BC, but Seán P. Ó Ríordáin excavated the Mound of the Hostages in the 1950s, revealing a passage grave which pre-dated that of the good queen by hundreds of years. Perhaps she selected the hill because it was already a sacred place. Medieval scholars attached more or less historical kings to Tara, but generally failed to place any of them earlier than the first few centuries of the Christian era. Meanwhile, the archaeologists showed that, a thousand years and more after the Mound of the Hostages was built, Bronze Age people buried their dead on its slopes. Then in the Iron Age, during the centuries before and after the birth of Christ, the great works whose traces still remain were undertaken.

Tradition tells of great feasting taking place at Tara, presided over by the High King and his druids. It also conjures up the idea of the king actually living there in a permanent palace. There is little reason to doubt the first part; all the evidence is that Tara was a great gathering place, centred on shrines to the old gods. The idea of a royal residence, however, is questionable and the archaeologists have found practically no traces of dwelling places, large or small. It would seem that the site, rather than being an administrative centre, was one where important rituals took place.

The Iron Age people were mostly herdsmen and much of Ireland at that time was covered in forest. Small communities were isolated from each other and one or more annual gatherings would have been a very welcome means of meeting friends and relations.

In the Dark Ages, Tara's religious position became more and more important. Powerful kings associated themselves with the hill and, whatever the facts of the tradition of the conversion there of King Laoghaire, taking a stand of some kind at such an important shrine would have been a logical part of St Patrick's mission.

Tara began to fade away some time after the arrival of the saint. It seems that no important monasteries were established there. The religious centre of Ireland, under the Christians, moved to Armagh, formerly *Emain Macha*, another Iron Age gathering place of the highest sanctity. Nevertheless, Tara retained its magic and was the site of important ceremonial events from time to time. Daniel O'Connell held one of his most successful monster meetings there in 1843. Well-intentioned desecration took place late in the nineteenth century, first in the form of a search for the Ark of the Covenant by the British Israelites, and subsequently with the erection of a concrete statue of St Patrick.

Today there is a pleasant shop close to the entrance to the Hill which is open all the year round. It serves tempting snacks and has an excellent stock of guidebooks — including two outstanding ones: *Tara*, by Edel Breathnach and Conor Newman, published in 1995; and *The Book of Tara* by Michael Slavin, which was published the following year. Tara deserves good books and both of these are models of their kind. They combine the facts as revealed by archaeologists and the more objective historians, with an account of the legends and traditions, as well as a collection of really helpful illustrations.

The only building on the hillside is the neat, white-painted church, built in 1831 and surrounded by beech trees. Standing on the site of a twelfth-century church of the Knights Hospitallers, its fabric contains some remnants of their original foundation. However, its great claim to fame is the possession of Evie Hone's Pentecost window.

Tara, the Stone of Destiny

The church was deconsecrated and, in 1991, sold to the Office of Public Works who renovated it to serve as an interpretative centre. It is open daily from early May to the end of October when a dramatic audio-visual display is shown. This is especially helpful as it presents aerial views of Tara, and also artists' impressions of life in the past. These give a good idea of the scale of the site and its buildings.

Outside the gate of the church stands an uncompromising statue of a thin-faced St Patrick, garbed as an earnest nineteenth-century bishop, crozier in one hand and a dubious shamrock in the other. Within the churchyard, to the west of the church, a rather worn sheela-na-gig can be made out, carved on a plinth that stands about 6 feet high. Grey and green lichens make her immodest form even more difficult to discern.

The path through the churchyard leads towards the Mound of the Hostages and to the great, green plateau. The earthworks, large and complex, have more or less irregular boundaries which evidently were constructed so as to embrace pre-existing shrines. A pleasing point made by the archaeologists is that the great circular mounds, ditches and embankments were not conceived as military defences: they were created as places of worship and ceremony rather than for warfare.

To savour Tara to the full, you need to have been reared on tales of Fionn Mac Cumhaill, the High Kings of Ireland and other heroes who lived, loved and fought there in Celtic times. But the hilltop is breathtaking anyway.

Grid N9260 Sheets 42 and 43. Clearly signposted off the Navan road, 24 miles from Dublin. Good car-parking. Dog- and buggy-friendly, the earthworks are eminently climbable and fun for children who may not be totally carried away by their cultural significance. Passable for wheelchairs. Fee charged. Food and books year round, quite good for picnics. Visitor Centre open: May to October, 10.00 a.m. to 6.00 p.m.

Trim Castle

Trim, *Baile Átha Troim*, the Ford of the Elder Tree, a crossing place on the river Boyne, was sufficiently important to induce St Patrick himself to found a monastery there. More than seven hundred years later, the ford retained its strategic importance and was the place chosen by the Anglo-Norman warlord, Hugh de Lacy, for his headquarters. In the course of the next few centuries, Trim flourished as a great administrative and religious centre and the land around it is dotted with the mortal remains of monasteries of a pleasing variety of religious orders. It remains a busy place retaining, thanks to its narrow streets, the atmosphere of a medieval centre. Few towns in Ireland can compare with it for the assortment of charming eighteenth- and nineteenth-century houses. If this were not enough, the beautiful modern garden of Butterstream is just a few outside.

All this would give plenty to do on a Sunday afternoon, but the central object of a trip to Trim is de Lacy's magnificent castle. More than any other medieval fortress in Ireland, this one really looks the part. A great curtain wall, with circular towers at intervals along it, protects the tall grey keep on high ground within. The Boyne flows by to the north, adding to the security of the Castle. This part of the river also provided a ford which the Castle served to control.

In places, outcrops of limestone form the foundations of the Castle walls, and this rock is also the reason why the ford and the surrounding land were worthy of occupation by the invaders. Limestone weathers to form the finest pasture land, the soil draining easily and providing lush green grass throughout the year. Strong and healthy cattle were the mainstay of life in Ireland from neolithic times to the twentieth century. The Celtic people fought each other for the possession of the animals while the Anglo-Normans, more practically, seized the land on which cattle could be most successfully reared. The Boyne itself had the added attraction of providing plentiful salmon, especially in winter when other food became dull, if not scarce.

A Norman-French poem, 'The Song of Dermot and the Earl' tells how, in 1172, Hugh de Lacy fortified a house at Trim by excavating a ditch and surrounding it with a wooden palisade. Excavations in the 1990s identified the ditch together with traces of the palisade, as well as revealing horseshoes and arrow heads. Threatened by the High King, Ruairí O'Connor, Trim was burned and abandoned by its defenders before he could reach it. The destruction of this, his first stronghold, encouraged de Lacy to try his hand at something more durable, and so began the Castle that has survived for more than 800 years.

Determining the date of the construction of a castle is always problematic. Written descriptions of the event are very rarely preserved, and the experts have to study the style of architecture and relate it to buildings of known age. They seldom have quite enough information to go on and sometimes make mistakes. In the case of Trim, H.G. Leask, one of the leading authorities, believed that work began in 1190. Other authorities put it even later, but one, Tom McNeill, believed that the great central tower or 'keep' began to rise from the ground in the mid-1170s.

That would certainly be logical. After his defeat by the Connaughtmen, de Lacy would have been in a great hurry to build a more secure headquarters. No doubt the experts would have

Trim Castle: the keep and part of the curtain wall

continued to argue about the date but the problem was eventually laid to rest by the discovery of 'putlog' timber in holes in the walls of the tower. These timbers were scaffolding beams used while construction work was in progress. The beams were sawn off after the building was completed, and the stumps left in the holes where they remained until the modern archaeologists found them.

Ancient timber is particularly interesting in archaeology because the rings, laid down every year while the tree was growing, can be seen, measured and counted. In good years for tree-growth, the rings are wide apart, and in bad years they are narrow. The succession of years of slow, medium or fast growth makes a unique pattern for any particular sequence of dates. Dendrochronology, as the study is called, allows the experts to tell with great confidence the year in which the tree was felled. So the wood from Trim was sent to Queen's University, in Belfast, for examination. The team there came back with the answer that some of the pieces of wood in the lower part of the keep dated to the 1170s.

The dating of the timbers shows that there were two phases in building the keep: the first two storeys were begun in the 1170s, while the third was added ten or twenty years later. The keep at Trim has also a very unusual shape, it is basically square, but each of the four walls has a square turret jutting out in the middle, so that the overall plan is cross-shaped. The most remarkable point about these turrets is that they have relatively few windows from which the defenders could fire on their enemies. As a piece of military architecture, the keep at Trim would have been something of a failure. This leads to the conclusion that de Lacy felt reasonably secure within the strong curtain wall, and wanted a magnificent house with a great many rooms, rather than a strong place of refuge.

The curtain wall once surrounded the entire fortress and it encloses no less than three acres. It has been damaged and rebuilt in places and much of the stretch that ran along the river has disappeared. The remaining parts of the wall, to this day, give a sense of impregnability. The barbican-gate on the south side was an outer defence of the drawbridge that spanned the moat which, though filled in over most of its length, is still visible.

David Sweetman, in his *Medieval Castles of Ireland*, describes the phases of construction of Trim Castle. The great keep, at the beginning of the thirteenth century, had a public hall on the third floor — an inconvenient position both for the public and for the owner of the Castle. A century later, a new and more accessible hall was built at the north-east corner of the curtain wall. This was a gracious building, with big windows giving a view out over the Boyne. Beneath this were cellars and a slipway providing access to the Castle for boats.

Trim Castle flourished for two hundred years until, in 1403, the Privy Council in England declared that it was on the point of falling into ruins — a faint miscalculation as much of its fabric has continued to stand for a further six centuries. It saw warfare for the last time in Cromwellian days, though it resounded to the roar of battle once more in 1994 — as a film set for *Brave Heart*.

Today, Trim Castle stands as a place of peace and beauty rather than an expression of military supremacy. The keep is surrounded by green lawns which slope down to the river bank and are protected from modern life by the curtain wall.

 Grid N8056, Sheet 42. Trim is clearly signposted from the Navan Road from Dublin, and the Castle can't be missed. Good car-parking. Buggy-friendly, tolerable for dogs, and wonderful to explore, with battlements to walk and spiral stairs to climb. Wheelchairs confined to ground level. Fee charged. Variety of food and drink available in the town, lovely picnic spots.

Mountain Walks

The Gospels tell that Jesus escaped to the wilderness for 40 days of meditation. In the early centuries of Christianity a whole community of saints retired from the busy world to the desert around Lake Mareoticus. Irish Christians thought so highly of them that they carved their images on most of the Celtic crosses. Latter-day Christians and others continue to seek the wilderness – though in most cases a Sunday afternoon, rather than a lifetime, suffices. No matter what the degree or the period of isolation from the crowd, the urge is the same – but even the Desert Fathers left their hermitages at regular intervals. The wilderness is always wonderful, provided that there is a way of escape.

The Dubliner is endowed with a marvellous expanse of moorland which is truly remote from civilisation and yet visible from the very centre of the city. The seven suggestions in this section are all in the form of gentle walks which can be completed within an hour or two. Nonetheless, they offer isolation amidst wonderful scenery: on the grand scale as in Kippure and the Sugarloaf, or in miniature, as at the Source of the Liffey.

Mexico City and Addis Ababa are on land twice as high as the highest Irish peak and are themselves surrounded by lofty mountains. Where the Dublin and Wicklow highlands truly qualify as mountains is in their inhospitality. Climate and soil decree that nobody can live there. So they offer the world-weary citizen a haven of peace and an element of solitude.

Great Sugarloaf

Mountain Walks

One of the most satisfactory summits in Ireland, rewarding a manageably short climb with an unsurpassed view of coast and mountains. Suitable at any time of year, occupies half a day.

In one sense, the ascent of Great Sugarloaf is a simple climb up one of the lower mountains that surround Dublin. On the other hand, small though it may be, this is no mere hill walk. It ends in a scramble up a really treacherous scree to a peak which makes a fair claim to be amongst the most spectacular in any part of Ireland, capable of holding its head high in the company of such giants as Errigal and Croagh Patrick.

Metrication has saved the Sugarloaf from dismissal as a very small mountain. In the good old days, its summit stood 1,654 feet above sea level — therefore, it was substantially below the magical height of 2,000 feet. Nowadays it appears on the map at 501 metres — thereby gaining admission to the over-500-metre club. But it has always looked taller than its companions, thanks in part to its isolation beyond the main mass of the Wicklow Mountains and, also, to its steep sides and sharp point.

Old cookery books tell you to use loaf sugar. Before modern methods developed, sugar was crystallised in conical vessels from which it was turned out in the form of sugar loaves. Steep quartzite mountains in many parts of the world, with their white crystalline tops, have been given the name.

The two Wicklow Sugarloaves — Great and Little — owe this prominence mainly to their composition. In spite of appearances, they are not volcanic, never were, and never will be. The bed rock is quartzite, derived over an immense period of time from a sea bed of clean sand. The sand was deposited more than 500 million years ago, during the Cambrian era. This sea was part of the Iapetus Ocean which was to be squeezed out of its existence at the time that the Wicklow granite was formed, about 100 million years later.

The sand consolidated to form sandstone, but the pressures generated by the moving continental plates changed its crystal structure to quartzite, one of the hardest rocks in the land. The sand was deposited by currents from the east, and occurs in

The south face of the Great Sugarloaf, from the Callary car park

isolated patches. The greater part of the sediments came from the north. They were muddy and solidified to form greywackes. Greywackes are relatively soft and were worn away, leaving the quartzites standing out as the peaks or ridges of the Sugarloaves, the Rocky Valley and Bray Head.

The lower slopes of the Sugarloaves were covered by the Midlandian ice sheet and, to some degree, smoothed by its movement. But the peaks stood out above the ice and were subjected to a seasonal alteration of freezing and thawing. Water trapped in crevices expanded as it cooled, and shattered the rock — in the same manner as freezing water bursts pipes to this day. This brutal treatment explains both the sharp point of the mountain and its coating of scree. Scree is a mass of rocks which has settled at its angle of rest — the point of balance which is achieved over time by any heap of solids, from sugar to boulders. Disturbance of the balance by an outside force, such as a hill-walker, sends the stones, and sometimes the climber, rattling downwards to find a new place of repose.

The car park, in the townland of Glencap Commons South, is marked on the map, but, in the absence of any signposting, needs careful navigation to find. It is on the edge of the Calary plateau, which, at round about the 280-metre contour, extends for miles southwards to the Roundwood Reservoir. According to the maps in William Warren's book, somewhere in the region of this car park, two glaciers met. One came from the Irish Sea basin, the other from Kippure. This may possibly explain why there is tillage to the east of the car park and pasture to the west.

Sadly, the land around the car park has long been used as an illegal rubbish tip, and the last remains of cars and houses, which scatter the ground, require careful negotiation. A patch of land with parallel ridges to the west of the hill path shows where lazy beds were cultivated once upon a time. Gorse is trying to take over the sheep pasture on the lower slopes. Higher up the slope, where the soil becomes more acid, heather begins to dominate, and patches of gorse with occasional clumps of heather are replaced by heather interrupted by prickly cushions of gorse. Where the hill-walkers have worn a path, neither gorse nor heather can thrive and close-cropped grass makes a pleasant green carpet.

The underlying rock on the green pasture is greywacke and the geological boundary between it and the quartzite is clearly indicated where the hill slope increases abruptly and the serious climb commences. The path becomes more and more stony, with the heather having a difficult time and being gradually reduced to scattered patches once more. It is mostly the small-flowered, pale-coloured ling that grows here but there are occasional clumps of the deep purple bell.

Much of the scree is nearly black in colour. These are the stones that have lain undisturbed at least for decades, perhaps for centuries. They are encrusted with dark-coloured lichens, but these can grow only in daylight. The stones which have been dislodged by sheep and climbers are pale-coloured and almost bare. Of these, the ones that have enjoyed the light of day for longer periods have little patches of green or yellow-green lichen which will ultimately cover the exposed surfaces.

For the final 40 metres, the climb is almost vertical in parts — hands-and-knees stuff rather than a hike. The vegetation is even thinner, except for lovely little patches of a pink-flowered stonecrop, one of the great survivors in dry places. Immediately below the summit, however, there are patches of level ground where grass grows and some frochans make their appearance. The very top of the mountain is solid rock, standing out above its mantle of scree.

The view from the summit is magnificent: north, to the Mournes, east, across the sea to Snowdonia on clear days, and west, to the long line of the flanks of the Wicklow Mountains. The geographer Anthony Farrington always insisted on calling this range the Leinster Chain, since it extends from Dublin to Wexford and even to Carlow and Kilkenny.

Closer at hand, to the north-west, the green copper domes of Powerscourt House can be seen two and a half miles away. The superb formal gardens were carefully designed to use the Sugarloaf as a backdrop. Powerscourt Waterfall appears as a white thread on the hillside between Djouce and Maulin.

To the north, the quartzite extends as far as the Rocky Valley, which follows an east–west fault line. The barren, heathery slopes are commonage. while below them, the more fertile land was fenced in during the eighteenth century. A modern development has been the removal of many of the hedges, which divided the richest fields. The older meshwork of hedges has been allowed to survive on the poorer land.

 Grid O2312, Sheet 56. Approached either from the Wicklow (N 11) or the Roundwood (R 755) road. St Kevin's Glendalough bus goes across the Calary Plateau and can stop on the main road half a mile from the car park; the return journey might be made on foot to Kilmacanogue where there is a more frequent bus service. Good for picnics — but no facilities or shelter. Sheep have right of way on lower parts, so dogs need to be fully under control. Utterly unsuitable for wheelchairs or buggies.

Hellfire Club

Mountain Walks

Rivals Great Sugarloaf as a Dubliner's most popular mountain walk, having similarly magnificent views of sea and mountain — with the city thrown in for good measure. Suitable at any time of year, occupies half a day or a summer evening.

Hellfire is a pleasing name for the best-known landmark in south County Dublin, a two-storey building carefully placed on the skyline — as seen from the lowlands around Rathfarnham. Built in or about 1725 by Speaker Conolly, owner of Rathfarnham Castle, it seems likely that he wanted to be able to see his hilltop lodge from the more comfortable surroundings of the lowlands. Another explanation for the choice is that he wanted the greatest possible numbers of his fellow citizens to see and admire his works. Whatever the origin, the ruins of the lodge remain, as they deserve to, one of the most popular goals for the mildly energetic Dubliner of today.

While history confirms that the Hellfire Club held its meetings in the more accessible Eagle Tavern in Cork Street, tradition has much to say about the occasional visits of its members to Mr Conolly's hunting lodge. Much of the stone used in the building was quarried from the adjacent neolithic passage grave. This may have been the lair of the black cat which took up residence in the house, where it was held in great reverence by the satanic members of the club. One stormy night, a priest making his way across the mountains sought shelter there. Immediately discerning the diabolical nature of the beast, he denounced it. In a frenzy of rage, the cat paced up and down the table, eventually levitating and taking the roof with it.

That was not the end of the story. Over a period of 50 years in the twentieth century, a monstrous black cat, the size of an Airedale dog, materialised from time to time in the eighteenth-century Killakee House, on the edge of the hillside below the Hellfire Club. The artist Tom McAssey saw this creature in 1968 and painted the portrait which now hangs in the House.

The Hellfire Club from the west

While some parts of the tale may be doubted, history confirms others. It would seem, for example, extremely unlikely that a priest, or anybody else, would have set off across the hilltops on a dark and stormy night in those days. But the house did indeed have a slate roof which was demolished by natural or supernatural forces. It was replaced by the massive barrel-vaulted stone roof which survives to this day and seems to be more than equal to demonic cats, or other elements.

The main apartments of the house were on the first storey and their great windows opened to the north, commanding a view of sea and city, rather than mountains. The south wall is unrelieved grim stonework. The house stands a little way below the summit, lending credence to the idea that it was deliberately placed to appear to be at the hilltop when viewed from the lowlands. Beside it, the foundations of the desecrated passage grave can still be seen: an oval bank with traces of a surrounding ditch, 24 paces by 30, four or five granite boulders protrude, and one of bluish dolerite.

When the Forest Service acquired the land and planted conifers in the 1950s, the gently sloping ground round about the summit was left free from trees, thus saving the traditional view of the landmark and the wonderful panorama that it commands. Occasional grazing by sheep and cattle preserves a beautiful green sward, so that Hellfire remains a perfect spot for a picnic.

A large car park was laid out in the 1970s between Killakee House and the plantation, and a gently rising path zigzags up the hillside through the trees. This leads around the higher slopes to the summit or away south or east towards the Dodder valley. At an age of 50 years, the conifers, now mature, have been thinned several times and they form a delightfully open woodland, completely shaded by the canopy of their leaves but with plenty of space between them. The shade prevents the growth of brambles or practically any other plants so that the ground is pleasant to walk on. The principal trees are Norway spruce, with soft, green needles; Douglas fir, with smooth, almost shining, grey bark; and the stalwart sitka spruce, with prickly, bluish needles. Power lines run though the woods and, as this necessitates frequent harvesting of the trees long before they approach maturity, noble fir is planted below them as a crop of Christmas trees.

Besides the trees of the forestry plantation, many older inhabitants of the hillside survive and there are fine specimens of oak, beech, sycamore and larch to be seen. Within the forest, occasional holly, birch and rowan have established themselves, and gorse and foxglove add splashes of colour along the way.

The southern extremity of this path leads almost to the edge of the forest and looks down from a height of 350 metres, over a steep-walled but virtually dry valley. This is the Piperstown Gap, scoured out by the torrential rivers that flowed in the latter years of the glaciation when the snowfields melted in summer. The gap was eventually left dry when the neighbouring rivers, Owendoher and Dodder, cut their ways down into the valleys that lie to the east and west.

From the summit of the hill, a track leads straight down the eastern slope back to the car park. Energetic people use it for the ascent, but they miss most of the delights of the woodland. About half way down, on the 310-metre contour, the large granite boulder is marked on the map as a 'standing stone'. So, indeed, it is, but the designation implies that it was stood by human rather than glacial energy. Such stones are notoriously difficult for archaeologists to date, but others elsewhere in the country belong to the Bronze Age. This one may therefore be a contemporary of the wedge tomb in Massy's Wood lower down the same slope (see p. 157).

The Hellfire mountain is called Mount Pelier, which in turn is called after the eighteenth-century mansion of the same name on its lower slopes. The Gaelic name of the hill seems to have been forgotten. The bedrock of the greater part of Mount Pelier is mica schist, but the eastern quarter is granite; the two merge with each other so that there is no obvious boundary on the hillside. The summit of Lugnaquilla is also underlain by schist and has a similarly pleasant green sward, in contrast to the heather moor which granite usually produces and which, in the case of Mount Pelier, is disguised by the forest.

Grid O1123, Sheet 50. Bus 15C, 15X to Ballyboden, 2-mile walk by road to the car park. Buggy-friendly with sheep-free footpaths — a lovely playground for dogs. Lower slopes passable for wheelchairs. Good for back-pack picnics. An hour's unhurried walk by the path gains the summit. Car park closes at 6.00 p.m.

Kippure

Mountain Walks

Kippure is the highest of the Dublin Mountains. In spite of its wilderness setting, there is a footpath to the TV mast on the summit. Suitable at any time of year, occupies half a day or a summer evening.

Kippure is a most distinguished mountain and, at 757 metres, its summit is the highest in County Dublin. In the good old days of Imperial measurements, it was measured as 2,481 feet, and only three other peaks in the county — Seefingan, Seahan and Corrig Mountain could exceed the magical 2,000 feet barrier. Metrication, happily, has enhanced Kippure's status and, in Dublin county, only it and Seefingan top the 700-metre mark. Such elevation might not matter so much were Kippure not also out on the edge of the Leinster Mountain chain, making it visible from an enormous area of lowland and thereby also making it a marvellous viewing point.

This position made Kippure the obvious site for the television transmitter which receives a beam from Donnybrook and can distribute waves of modern culture, not only to homesteads throughout the midlands, but also to masts on far-distant hilltops. It can also exchange electronic greetings with antennae across the Irish Sea. A mast was first erected here in 1962 for the newly-created Telefís Éireann, and this was replaced in 2000. Its height, according to a notice at the gateway, is 110 metres, thus making the highest point in Dublin a great deal higher again.

Where there is a busy transmission mast, there must also be a service road, and Kippure is no exception. A well-built track snakes its way up the mountain from the Military Road. It represents a very considerable feat of engineering because it has to be capable of bearing construction cranes and other exceedingly heavy loads. Building such a road over a substrate of peat bog is a formidable problem, and the slope has to be fairly gentle so that the heaviest of vehicles can climb the mountain. The qualities of the track combine to make the ascent of Kippure a pleasant and not unduly arduous expedition. There are, of course, much more difficult ways of reaching the summit — such as a climb up the cliffs of Lough Bray. But we will leave these to the delectation of athletes.

The gateway to the track is on the 520-metre contour, some way down the slope from the ridge which separates the valleys of the Liffey and the Glencree River. This small topographical factor means that the view in all directions is of mountain and moorland — an expanse of wilderness with not a house in sight. The granite bedrock here is thickly covered with peat in places, and the banks and pools left by hand-cutting of turf are a feature of the bog. To the south, tractor-driven sausage machines have been exploiting the peat at a greater rate, for the moment leaving swathes of bare brown cut-away. Provided that the uncut remnant is not swept away by floods, the bog plants will eventually grow up again.

Around Kippure the moorland is brown, even in summer. The damp, low-lying parts are covered by deer grass with some bog cotton — lovely to look at in late summer, each stem with its little tuft of white. Where the slopes are steeper and the rain water runs off quickly, heather grows, most of it ling heather, with tiny pale mauve flowers. Amongst the ling, the straggly, cross-leaved heath appears in places, its conspicuous pink bell-flowers adding tiny splashes of brightness to the brown surroundings. Crowberry can also be found by the side of the track and over the moorland; this is a heather-like mountain plant with bright shiny leaves, unknown in Dublin at an elevation of less than 300 metres. The best of the peatland flora is the bog asphodel which blooms in late summer in damp patches. It is a grass-like plant, but distinguished by its spike of beautiful, star-like yellow flowers.

A little way to the south of the track, there are pools of clear water, usually covering bright green moss. These are relatively rare entities, their existence threatened by peat cutting and drainage. In view of this, the National Park people have been building little dams of peat to make sure that they survive. This is a welcome strategy as, aside from the ecological interest of the pools, they add to the beauty of the scenery in their mirror-like reflections of blue sky and cloud.

A little group of planted conifers struggles for survival at the gate, and the importation of limestone gravel for the roadway has allowed another alien to appear. This creates just enough alkalinity and drainage to allow occasional gorse bushes to grow. One more little group of conifers, pines and firs stands by the riverside where the track takes a bend a little more than a mile up the hill. After that, the hillside is left to the native vegetation of heathers, mosses and deergrass.

The river that runs near the track is no less than Anna Liffey herself. The bridge is above the 600-metre contour, and the stream comes down from a point 50 metres above the bridge. This would not be so remarkable if the Source of the Liffey were not marked on maps as being nearby, but at a height of 525 metres. Why geographers made this error remains a mystery — though it must be said that the Source, as indicated on the map, is easier to reach and is very beautiful with its tiny lake and chasm through the peat (see pp 64–68). My school geography book also claimed that the Liffey rises on Kippure, and few people would disagree. Nevertheless, the highest point in the middle distance is the beautiful mountain of Mullaghcleevaun, and that is where the King's River rises at 700 metres. Paradoxically, the King's River is considered to be a tributary of the Liffey, but this is a serious abuse of the term. The King's River is bigger and begins much higher in the mountains than the Liffey itself. Strictly speaking, the Liffey is a tributary of the King's River, but it seems that the name 'Liffey' was first applied to the part of the river that flows by the Curragh of Kildare. Anna Livia Plurabelle is a wayward river and it is pleasant indeed to think that her official source is so very much lower than all contenders for the true title.

Close to the summit, the peaty soil is slowly being carried away by wind and rain. Peat hags stand out, where the water has carved gullies and removed the soft peat, while little patches of soil and heather remain on top, preventing the peat from being removed completely. Unless the climate changes quite significantly, all the peat will be removed and the mountain top will revert to the way it looked at the end of the last glaciation: white quartz gravel in places, bare granite in others. Patches of this kind of landscape can be seen already. The good news is that nineteenth-century Geological Survey maps show that the peat was being eroded then — indicating that this process is slow.

Kippure summit in 1997 with the original 1960s TV mast and its 1990s replacement

Near the summit of Kippure, a sort of frochan grows which has the romantic name *Vaccinium vitis-idaea*, 'Vine of Mount Ida'. It is even more rarified than the crowberry and is seldom seen below 700 metres. In winter its yellow-green leaves stand out against the darker background of the heather, giving some relief to the blanket of brown. A little way downhill from the summit, on the northern slopes, the highest tributaries of the Dodder trickle down from great brown gulleys in the peat. Liffey and Dodder nearly meet in their headwaters but then swing off in different directions — the Liffey taking a long tour and the Dodder a short one — before they meet once more in Dublin Bay.

The sense of isolation from the outside world, so strong at the beginning of the ascent, diminishes with height. More and more of Ireland comes into view until, at the summit, there are wonderful views of far-away places: to the south-west, the Blessington Lakes and then, in the distance, the Bog of Allen with its power stations and cooling towers. To the north there is Dublin and, on a good clear day, the Mountains of Mourne. Towards the east and south-east, Bray and the Sugarloaves, the Irish Sea and — when the air is exceptionally clear — Snowdonia across the water.

Utterly breathtaking!

Grid O1115, Sheet 56. A long hike (8 miles) from Ballyboden bus 15C, 15X, but a delightful drive over the Featherbed on the Military Road. Car-parking at gateway to TV mast, good for picnics. Fine for dogs in winter when sheep are absent, otherwise control is essential. Buggy-friendly for parents seriously into weight-training (2 miles of unrelenting ascent), also manageable — at least in theory — by wheelchair. Bring a small-scale map and have fun identifying all the distant features.

Three Rock

Three Rock, besides offering one of the finest views anywhere in Dublin, is an ideal walk for traditional Sabbatarians: there is comfortable time to gain the summit between Church and Sunday Lunch. Thus, having nurtured the soul, the body may be prepared for its sustenance in a salutary manner. The mountain-top bristles with radio antennae which demand regular attention and therefore a serviceable approach road. This makes Three Rock one of few mountain tops which may be approached in relative ease with a buggy.

The Ticknock Road, bounded by stone walls and by hedges of hawthorn and sycamore, climbs the hill to a *Coillte* sign, announcing Ticknock Wood. Cars can travel some distance farther up the hill within the forest until the way is eventually blocked by a barrier, around which there are also many spaces for parking. The way from the barrier is simply onwards and upwards. The first forestry planting took place here in the late 1950s, and Norway spruce is plentiful on the lower slopes. Sitka spruce has been much more successful, however, since the Norway species prefers a drier soil. The woodland is old enough to support a rich variety of fungi, including the beautiful, but toxic, fly agaric — the really traditional fairy toadstool, bright red with white spots. There are also big clumps of sulphur tuft which grows on old tree stumps and is said to have an unpleasing bitter taste.

Looking west, out of the wood, the view is of Kilmashogue and the Little Dargle valley. The bright green and well-tended turf of Stackstown golf course makes a striking contrast with the dark-coloured higher slopes of the hills. The change in colour marks the boundary between the local granite soil and the lime-rich glacial till deposited by the Midlandian ice sheet. During the last glaciation, the view to north and west would have been of a sea of ice. Closer to hand, and of rather more recent origin, are the remains of an abandoned military firing range.

Granite tor on Three Rock

On bends in the path, the ground has been excavated to display a profile with peaty soil at the top overlying the glacial till which is 2 metres deep in places. The till is made up mainly of granite, but contains grits and the pale blue, lightly-speckled dolerite which was carried from the Glenasmole hills by a mountain glacier.

As you progress further up the mountainside, Dublin Bay appears, and the panorama widens as the 'rocks' at the summit are approached. On a particularly clear day, the mountains of Snowdonia can be seen, while the Mournes are visible 60 miles to the north except in very hazy conditions. Three Rock, on close inspection, turns out to be little more than a spur of the higher Two Rock, but, from the lowlands, it gives the impression of being a mountain in its own right.

The 'rocks' are granite tors, which provide welcome shelter from the wind on a wild day, or comfortable picnic spots in better weather. The slow dissolving away of the granite along the lines of ancient crevices give the tors their uneven shape with steps, slopes and ledges. Take stock of the radio masts: they lend a certain character to the spot but, more importantly, will probably be obsolete within a decade or two and will take their places amongst the relics cherished by industrial archaeologists.

The tors are certainly the most striking features of Three Rock and its companion hills. Frank Mitchell describes the process of how these are formed and why they are there. Their creation began after the Munsterian glaciation, during which ice covered the greater part of Ireland, including the Dublin Mountains. This period was followed by the Glenavian warm stage, which lasted for many thousands of years and during which the granite was exposed to the weather. Earth movements crack the granite allowing rain water to penetrate into the crevices and dissolve the less resistant minerals, creating a porridgy mass. Indeed, the porridge analogy is particularly apt because the quartz crystals from the granite provide the sparkle of sugar. This weathering begins at the outer edges of great blocks of rock bounded by the crevices so that large masses of solid rock are left within the matrix.

When the next, and final, cold stage, the Midlandian, came, Three Rock stood above the glaciers, but, as the water in the porridge alternately froze and thawed, the loose material crept down the hillside, leaving the solid tors behind. When the climate improved, soil formed and peat grew up to cover and protect the rock surface and the rubble above it. So, to this day, the tors stand out from the surrounding landscape to form a notable mountain feature that is visible from the city, several miles away.

The moorland above the forest is covered with heather on its drier parts and with sedges in the damp places. Ravens fly over Three Rock at any time, but, in winter, bird life is very limited. There is more activity in summer, when meadow pipits and sky-larks come to nest in the area.

The return journey to the car park can take the same path, but as it zigzags and the forest is well-grown and relatively open, there are pleasant short-cuts to be taken between the trees. Several alternative tracks lead over the flanks of Three Rock in many directions, with a western path to Kilmashogue and a northern one to Two Rock and the Wicklow Way.

Grid O1625, Sheet 50. The Grange Road bus (No. 16) goes to Taylorsgrange cross-roads. The road leading south goes for a mile up the Little Dargle valley, around Ticknock Hill with its covering of granite boulders, to Ticknock Road and the car park. Car park to summit and back takes less than an hour. Dog- and buggy-friendly, just possible for wheelchair users. Good picnic places, hotel food at Taylorsgrange.

Tibradden Mountain

Mountain Walks

A hill walk through forest and heather, leading to an antiquarian anachronism with a pleasant view of hills and valleys. Suitable at any time of year, occupies half a day.

Tibradden is the triangular-looking hill that stands out amongst the smooth-topped hills on the northern side of the Dublin Mountains. In common with its companions, it has a long ridge with a gentle slope to the tors at the summit. But Tibradden has steep-sided valleys on both sides, and these give it the triangular appearance. Glencullen, the valley to the south, follows the line of the major geological fault which runs from Woodtown in the west to Enniskerry in the east.

The north-western slopes of Tibradden, together with those of its neighbour, Cruagh Mountain, constituted the Pine Forest which was planted there in 1910. Some of the old Scots pine and beech still survive and more were planted in the 1930s together with Norway spruce. In the 1960s, extensive planting of the slopes with European larch and sitka spruce took place and the wood began to develop possibilities as a public amenity. In 1970, together with several other forest properties on the northern slopes of the mountains, Tibradden Wood was provided with a car park and footpaths. Today, with the functional roads that are required to admit machinery, the woods offer a variety of enticing walks.

The car park is 320 metres above sea level — an elevation of great significance. The Midlandian ice field, which covered the northern part of Ireland and filled the Irish Sea, reached a height of about 300 metres on the slopes of the Dublin Mountains. It deposited lime-rich soil, carried from the limestone of the plains, and this is the basis of the green pasture that can be seen today on the lower slopes. The upper slopes were covered by glaciers from the mountains which dumped granitic material along them. This forms a poor acid soil which is good for pine trees, bracken, heather and sitka spruce which is a more recent addition to the area. Of paramount importance to wandering persons is the fact that nobody bothered to create fenced fields on such poor land. Moreover, it wasn't even considered worth holding for sheep grazing, so the owners sold it to the State for forestry. Geology, more than any other factor, explains the marvellous extent of wilderness close to the city of Dublin.

Much of the older forestry plantation has been clear-felled and replaced with a new generation of spruce and larch. Pines on the higher slopes failed to thrive; the combination of poor soil and exposure to wind proved too much for them and this part will probably not be planted again. Above this tree line lies an expanse of delightful, springy heather — pale mauve ling with small flowers and purple bell heather with larger ones. Scattered amongst them, in damp patches, is cross-leaved heath with pink bell flowers, while bog cotton makes its presence felt in the patches which are too damp for heather.

Amongst the heather, the firmly-constructed path within the plantation gives way to one that is less than comfortable for walking. As relatively little rain water drains into the peaty soil, most of it runs in the form of minor torrents down steep slopes and along the line of where a path has been cut. The peat is thus eroded quickly and so is the gravelly soil. Nothing is left but loose stones and uneven pieces of outcropping granite.

Fortunately, higher on the hillside the slope becomes very gentle and the path much more attractive, both to look at and to walk on. Here, the rainwater dissolves the feldspar crystals from the granite and leaves the much tougher grains of quartz. The path is thus covered not with uncomfortable stones, but with a bright, clean, soft gravel. Grouse live amongst the heather here, but are seldom disturbed or seen by those who keep to the paths.

The most convenient path runs a little way below the summit of Tibradden and it is easy to walk past the highest point of the mountain and its very remarkable cairn without noticing either. The cairn of Tibradden was excavated in the nineteenth century and found to contain two 'food vessel' burials. Food-vessel pottery implies a Bronze Age ritual, some time in the second millennium BC. The excavators were enthusiastic restorers of ancient monuments and built the neat circular stone wall, about nine paces in circumference, with a narrow entrance passage. Thereby, they created a Neolithic passage grave of the kind used some 2,000 years before the Bronze Age burials on Tibradden took place.

Tibradden Wood

Past efforts to explain the name of the mountain may have been equally misleading. Patrick Weston Joyce perpetrated the pleasant idea that the word means the house of the chieftain, Bradden, whose last mortal remains were consigned to one of the food vessels found in the cairn. Nothing is impossible, but the fact that there is a word *tiobraid*, meaning 'a well', suggests that the mountain may have been named after one of its many wells rather than in honour of a gentleman whose name is otherwise unrelated to the area.

Anyway, the fake passage grave makes a pleasant place to sit and contemplate the view of the very fine scenery. To the south is the aptly named

Glendoo, the dark glen, the ridge which forms Cruagh and Glendoo Mountains, and Prince William's Seat. To the west, the Hellfire Club has, unfortunately, been hidden from view by the growth of sitka spruce around it, and the sharp profile of Piperstown Gap has been blunted by the same forest.

At Tibradden's summit, close to the cairn, granite tors stand out above the heather, though these are not as big as the ones nearby on Three Rock and Two Rock which lie a mile and a half towards the south-east. In 1835, G.V. Du Noyer correctly identified the tors as part of the bedrock rather than blocks moved by the glaciers. Rain and frost, acting on the bare granite before it received a protective covering of peat, carried the rock away from around the summit, and the tors represent the last remnants of the rock which stood at a higher level (see Three Rock, pp 56–59). Gabriel Béranger, writing in the late eighteenth century, had a far more romantic view of the tors, taking them 'to be altars on which sacrifices were offered'.

Grid O1422, Sheet 50. Rockbrook bus No. 161 terminus is about a mile down the hill. Buggy and wheelchair utterly unfriendly — lovely for dogs, sheep being fenced out from the forest property. From the car park it takes an hour or so to reach Tibradden summit and that makes a very pleasant Sunday afternoon excursion (the lower slopes are good for frochans in autumn). Car park closes at 6.00 p.m.

The Source of the Liffey

In defiance of the convention that a river's source is its highest point, the official Source of the River Liffey has, for a great many years, been marked on Ordnance Survey maps at the head of one of its tributaries. However, the location of the true source of Anna Livia Plurabelle is every bit as enigmatic and as open to varying interpretations as is *Finnegans Wake*. The highest point on the Liffey is actually between the 620- and 630-metre contours, half a mile east of the summit of Kippure (see pp 51–55) while the official Source is 100 metres lower than this. But the real confusion lies in the fact that the Liffey is a mere tributary itself. The main stream in the upper reaches is the King's River which rises on Mullaghcleevaun at 720 metres and is joined by the Liffey further down.

To avoid further confusion, we will accept as the objective of this Sunday the 'Source of River Liffey', as named on the map. It is a most delightful stream of dark, peat-stained water that makes its way down a shallow valley in the peat of Liffey Head Bog. The approach is from Liffey Head Bridge, which carries the Military Road across the valley. Strategically placed on the edge of a small plateau at 620 metres, the bridge is more of a causeway, built of large granite boulders collected from the river banks. Some traces remain, on the upstream side, of a neatly-built abutment, but the general appearance is of a random collection of stones. The original bridge, constructed in 1802 was, in common with its companions on the road, probably a true arch. But this has been replaced by an ignominious structure comprising three superimposed concrete sewerage pipes. They make a remarkably high opening for the bridge, necessitated by the infant Liffey's propensity for an occasional torrent of rage.

The surrounding mountain slopes are all underlain by granite which is covered by a blanket of bog, some 2 metres or more in depth. The mountain glaciers, which finally melted some 10,000 years ago, left the slopes strewn with granite boulders, large and small. As the climate improved, lichens and mosses and other small plants grew amongst them, and various species of soft, spongy sphagnum moss predominated. When they died, their remains accumulated, filled the spaces between the stones, and then went on to build up the blanket bog. Liffey Head Bog is of particular interest. In the first place, having begun growing some 8,000 years ago, it is thousands of years older than many of the bogs of Ireland. What is more, while most peat — including the cover on the higher slopes round about — is being eroded nowadays, patches of sphagnum still thrive there, and the bog is actually growing in places.

One more special characteristic of this kind of bog is that drainage to a great extent takes place beneath the surface. The rain water, instead of running off, seeps down and has to carve out tunnels to escape. So, one more problem in semantics arises. The Liffey at its source is, in fact, a well-established underground stream — the point being that the official Source is where it finally emerges from the ground to enjoy the light of day, rather than where it becomes a singular flow of water.

Anyhow, from this point downwards, the stream began both to cut its way down through the peat to the bedrock and to meander to create a relatively wide valley — constricted in places by rock outcrops and also by the builders of the Military Road. This is the valley that we travel up for less than half an hour — the stream being small and the ascent short, all of 800 paces. But it's a very rugged way, and full of things of beauty, so it takes time to reach our destination.

The peatland is at its brightest and best in July and August. Because of the extreme acidity of both the peat and the underlying granite, few species of plant can grow there, and those that do grow very slowly, flowering only late in the season. The drier parts of the bog are clothed with ling, the heather with minute, pale-coloured flowers. Two other heathers are scattered here and there also: the bell heather with bigger, deep purple flowers and the cross-leaved heath which usually grows as single sprigs and has pink bells. One of the most rewarding plant finds along the stream is the crowberry, a heather with bright green, shiny leaves, to be found only by intrepid mountaineers who attain the dizzy heights above 300 metres.

In the damper parts of the bog, the heather is replaced by bog cotton and by the most beautiful of all the wild flowers of the region: the bog asphodel. Small, yellow, star-like flowers with red tips to the stamens cluster around the tip of a slender green stem. Sometimes they grow isolated from others, and sometimes in patches of bright yellow. This plant acquired a curious Latin specific name: *ossifragum*, the bone-breaker. The belief was that sheep or cattle which ate it developed weak bones. The more plausible explanation is that stock feeding on the poor pasture, where the bog asphodel grows, have mineral deficiencies which do indeed weaken their skeletons.

The infant Liffey has cut its way down through the peat which forms a cliff, all of two metres high, on each side of the valley. Between the peat cliffs lies a miniature flood plain where all is green in contrast to the brown of the heather and the red of the bog-cotton leaves. Nutrients are still scarce in the gravelly soil which remains, but it drains more freely and this allows grasses to grow above the usual flood level, while sedges, rushes and mosses thrive in the damper parts. One of the most pleasing to the eye is the bulbous rush which grows in dense tufts of brilliant green, but whose stems are too weak to stand up, so that they spread outwards to form cushions. The river gravel is white and sparkling, formed of quartz and mica crystals released from the granite rock.

Ten minutes' walk along the valley floor leads out of sight of the road and gives a wonderful feeling of wilderness and isolation — the only signs of humanity being the television mast on Kippure and an occasional aircraft making its way to Dublin Airport. On the left bank there are two little caverns in the peat face, each about a foot in diameter. The mouth of the first is guarded by fronds of bracken, while within is a delicate, pale green fern. These caverns are the mouths of tributary streams that run beneath the peat, in the same way that the Liffey itself does before emerging at its Source.

The infant river at Liffey Head Bridge

Finally, you attain the Source itself. Ten years ago, I described it as a little amphitheatre in the peat, with a dark pool at its floor — and so it was, and I have photographs to prove it. But nothing stays still in the life of a stream, and the Liffey has obliterated its amphitheatre and replaced it with a chasm — undoubtedly dark with its black walls, and, indeed, quite romantic in its way. A mother duck and four ducklings were there on my last visit.

Above this lies a broad pan of water. In dry weather it is reduced to a shallow pool but a good rainfall fills it and produces a waterfall which is gradually extending the chasm upstream. This is the point where the Liffey finally issues from its subterranean channel. You can follow its line upstream, because the plants are greener along its course. In places the stream is fairly firmly roofed over, in others the roof has collapsed and you can hear it gurgling down below. The lines of two such streams can also be clearly seen on the hillside.

That is the source of the Liffey: everything is on a small scale and you can walk it in 20 minutes or less, but it has all the beauty of a miniature painting and is a haunting place to visit.

Beyond it, the hill slopes are gentle and you can climb Tonduff both for the distant view and to see at close quarters the granite tors and the glistening white gravel that lies where the peat has been eroded. And if that isn't enough and you want more river sources, the Dargle and the Cloghoge Rivers rise nearby.

Grid O1313, Sheet 56. Attained by the Military Road R115. Car parking space at the entrance to the TV mast 700 paces to the north or space for one car 500 paces to the south. Sheep graze nearby, though mostly on the lower slopes so dogs need to be fully controlled. Buggy- and wheelchair-unfriendly. Very uneven ground, slightly dangerous in places because of the bog holes. Good for back-pack picnics.

Wicklow Gap

Mountain Walks

A remote, fairly rugged and very beautiful mountain pass — apart from a power station, one of the most lonely roads in Wicklow. A trip for a fine summer's day.

Wicklow Gap is the highest point on a road that nowadays seems to lead nowhere. It was a pilgrims' way in early Christian times, has subsequently been a busy route to nineteenth-century mines, and is now an access to one of the most remote and remarkable of the ESB's power stations. It is known by the majority of explorers who use it as a picturesque route to Glendalough, or as a good place to go for a day's enjoyment of the incomparable scenery.

The Gap is the dividing point between the catchments of the King's River and the Glendasan River. The former is the main tributary of the Liffey while the latter ultimately joins the Avoca River to reach the sea at Arklow. The highest points of both of these rivers — and, indeed of the Liffey — lie above the 700-metre contour on the slopes of Mullaghcleevaun. The approach road to Wicklow Gap, from the west, follows the King's River which takes a gentle, meandering path along the wide floor of the valley. The stream that flows — according to the map and to tradition — from the Source of the Liffey is, in fact, the smaller of two tributaries of Dublin city's main river. The King's River, which meets the Liffey near Blessington, is the main stream but, surprisingly, loses its name there. One possible explanation is that the inhabitants of the two upper valleys were less than hospitable to English surveyors in the seventeenth century, and so the cartographers opted to name the less remote of the two tributaries as the source of the Liffey.

There is a school at Granabeg in the lower part of the valley and, on the left bank of the river, a road which runs to an end on the lower slopes of Carrig Mountain and which serves a scattering of farmsteads. After a cluster of houses which lay beyond that at Ballinagee Bridge, there are no dwellings for 6 miles. A ruined church might mark the site of a stopping place on the pilgrims' way to the shrine of Glendalough, but otherwise the upper valleys were far too inhospitable to allow anyone to think of living there. Spruce plantations now cover much of the King's River valley, but they give way to sheep pasture after the Gap.

Two car parks are marked on the map at Wicklow Gap, and there is a third one a little way down the road towards Lough Nahanagan. There are mountains or hills in all directions, giving a feeling of complete isolation from the outside world. The first of the car parks is overlooked by huge blocks of granite that were dumped by the local glacier. A concrete path goes down the hill from them to the point where a big black cable emerges from the ground. This then enters a forest of man-sized insulators, before dividing in two and climbing the majestic pylons which march down the hill and along the valley. Notices tell that one branch of the cable heads for Maynooth and the other for Dunstown. By the side of the path, water draining off the bog keeps the sur-roundings moist and maintains a small stream and little patches of white-flowered water crowfoot. There are also big patches of the beautiful moss, *Polystichum*, which looks like forests of miniature pine trees, as well as cushions of pale green or pinkish *Sphagnum*, one of the most important progenitors of peat.

The source of the underground cable can be approached from the second car park where a road leads down through the heather to Turlough Hill power station. A huge enclosure, which might be more appropriate as a set for a *Star Wars* sequence, contains the switching gear for controlling 270,000 volts. Close by are an office block and an enormous tunnel leading into the mountainside. The office block was brilliantly designed and fits in remarkably well with the rocky cliffs above it. The tunnel leads to the turbines of the 'pumped storage' generators.

The basis for this intrusion to the mountain fastness is Lough Nahanagan, a corrie lake occupying a hollow scooped out by a local glacier. No less an authority than Robert Lloyd Praeger, in *The Way that I Went*, recounts the behaviour of the *piast*, or water monster, that lived in this lake — and may still survive, having evidently avoided the attention of the slayers of monsters, St Patrick and Finn Mac Cumhaill. Even if the monster fails to appear, and in spite of major interference by the ESB, Lough Nahanagan remains a place of wonder and beauty. Camaderry Mountain towers above it with its steep cliffs standing out amongst the heather.

Granite boulders dumped in Wicklow Gap by a mountain glacier

The generating system uses surplus power to run the turbines in reverse and pump the lake water to the reservoir built at the top of the neighbouring hill. At busy times, the water flows down from reservoir to lake, turning the turbines and sending the electricity back along the power lines. The shoreline of the lake has been rock-strewn since the ice age and when the lake level is low, its stony sides are revealed. The granite is whitish rather than grey because the lake water has prevented the growth of the lichens which cover the exposed rock.

The mountain to the north is Tonelagee, a lovely gentle climb over dry heather slopes. Like Camaderry, Tonelagee has a corrie lake, Lough Ouler, on its northern slopes. The map marks the site of 'St Kevin's Road' but this is not easy to discern and the modern road takes an easier, though slightly longer, curving way. The view to the south-east is down into the Vale of Glendasan.

The long straight valley is associated with a geological fault line which runs from near the car parks to Laragh. The most conspicuous features on its flanks are three great grey mounds, faintly reminiscent of reclining dinosaurs. These are the spoil heaps of the mines that flourished in the valley for the greater part of the nineteenth century and produced, according to the Geological Survey, some 46,000 tons of lead and 330,000 ounces of silver. The spoil still contains an appreciable quantity of lead ore and this is sufficiently toxic to prevent the growth of plants that would normally cover such heaps. Two miles down the valley there is a car park beside some of the old mine buildings and, a little way upstream, a bridge helps you to get to the old mine workings in comfort.

The ore was extracted by blasting with gunpowder, and the broken rock was taken by a railway down to the cobbled floors of the ruined buildings. There the rock was broken up by hand and the metallic ores were separated. These were then sent off by horse and cart for smelting at the Lead Mines of Ballycorus, near Dublin. The lead ore — galena — is grey and shiny, and small pieces of it can easily be found attached to stones in the tip heaps. Some of the mine shafts are still open and stand at the top of the spoil heaps. One or two have been blocked up and at least one of them is slightly dangerous where the safety fence suffered from long neglect.

From these upper mines, the river plunges steeply — not quite making a waterfall — down to the long, flat-bottomed Vale of

Glendasan, where there were more mine workings. These were revived for some years in the 1950s but fell into disuse again. Extraction of heavy metals is expensive and the survival of a mine depends to a great extent on the world price of the ore. Major discoveries anywhere in the world can bring the value down abruptly and put existing mines out of business. As in the upper valley, the spoil from the ore extraction defies the growth of vegetation, but here it is spread out on the level ground rather than appearing in heaps. The ruins of a line of mine-workers houses along the riverside are being replaced by modern bungalows.

To the south-east of the mines, the first turn off the valley leads westwards into the Vale of Glendalough, while the main road towards Laragh passes the headquarters and information centre for the Wicklow Mountains National Park. Here there is shelter and an exhibition of the wildlife.

Grid O0800, Sheet 56. St Kevin's bus to Glendalough passes the mouth of Glendasan from which it is 2 miles by road to the mine workings and 4 miles to Wicklow Gap. Wonderful country for hill-walking in any direction but the presence of sheep demands fully-controlled dogs. No buggies, wheelchairs, food or shelter, heavenly picnic spots.

Museums

The ideal refuge on a wet weekend, the best museums are those that offer refreshments for the body as well as for the mind. Great strides in this direction have been taken by the National Museum of Ireland which, not so very long ago, took pride in its austerity not only in scholarly though stultifying exhibitions, but also in offering few facilities — even chairs were scarce. Times have changed and, of the seven recommended institutions listed here, all except two provide excellent food in pleasant surroundings. Of these two, the exhibition space in Trinity College Colonnades is too limited and well filled to leave room for a cafeteria. This is remedied in summer by the proximity of the Arts Block student café, and at all times of year by Bewley's and others a little farther away.

The Natural History Museum is the other defaulter. Its problem is not lack of space, but a happy accident of a history of neglect. The exhibition of animals, from whales to microscopic animals, was arranged early in the twentieth century, altered slightly in the 1920s and then left as it was. While properly-funded museums modernised, with more and more audio-visuals and fewer and fewer stuffed animals, the collection in Merrion Street was left to rest in peace. Late in the 1980s, distinguished scientific visitors realised that Dublin's museum was just about the last of its kind in the world — in effect a museum of a museum. To introduce a tearoom to such an entity would be an act of desecration.

The three buildings of the Kildare Street/Merrion Street complex were planned as museums. The others demonstrate great skill in adaptation: Collins Barracks from the home of a garrison, the Colonnades from a library, and the Print Museum from a chapel — not inappropriately in view of the title 'father of the chapel' held by printers' shop stewards. The Chester Beatty galleries have risen from what was first a stable yard and then an office of the tax-collectors.

Whatever about their origins or amenities, the museums of Dublin hold their heads high as places of wonder and delight, with so much to see that they can fully occupy not just a month, but a lifetime of Sundays.

National Museum
Kildare Street

The portable archaeological heritage of Ireland is the responsibility of the Irish Antiquities Division of the National Museum, and quaint as the terminology sounds, it is most appropriate. Overcrowded and seriously understaffed for most of its life, the Museum building on Kildare Street enters the twenty-first century as a brighter, and very much more attractive, entity than at any other time in its distinguished history.

The site was originally part of the property of the town house built by the twentieth Earl of Kildare in 1744, to the design of Richard Cassels. The house was sold by the Duke of Leinster to the Dublin Society, in 1814. Leinster House, as its name was then, remained the headquarters of that body until 1924, when, it is said, Michael Collins made, the — now 'Royal' — Dublin Society an offer for the property, which it could not refuse. Decades before independence, in 1877, the British Government had bought all the buildings on the site but allowed the Society to continue to use Leinster House. Later, the Government commissioned Thomas Newenham Deane and his son, Thomas Manley Deane, to design the complementary museum and library buildings that now flank the house.

The Museum was completed in 1890. Built mainly of durable granite, it suffered from an unfortunate choice of sandstone for the doors and windows. This pleasant, buff-coloured, stone from Mountcharles in County Donegal was promised by geologists to be safe from weathering. They had not reckoned with Dublin air pollution and, as early as the 1930s, damage became apparent. Major repairs began in the 1960s, entailing the replacement of most of the decorative work.

The entrance to the Museum is a splendid rotunda, with a gallery supported by pillars of many varieties of Irish marble. It opens into a spacious main hall, decorated in classical style and with a fine mosaic floor — now mostly concealed by the exhibition cases.

The collection of portable archaeological material begins with misplaced objects: Palaeolithic stone axes, the sole Irish remnants of the great civilisation whose people included the cave-artists of France and Spain. Although these flints are genuine, it is considered that they were carried to Ireland by a glacier, rather than being the tools of local communities. The first undoubted Irish people were the Mesolithic hunter-gatherers, whose arrow heads and other implements of Antrim flint are widely distributed around the country. These people travelled, hunted and traded, but left few traces of their dwellings besides rubbish tips — and the skilfully-made stone implements. Studies of present-day hunting communities allow archaeologists to make good guesses as to how our most remote ancestors lived.

Far firmer conclusions can be drawn from the abundant remains of the first farmers, the Neolithic people. Builders and brilliant sculptors of great monuments such as Newgrange, their artefacts are plentiful and often very well preserved. Besides the tombs or temples, sufficient traces of their homes remain to provide detailed information about their way of life. Neolithic pottery and stone implements are thrilling to archaeologists but rather unimpressive to others — except for the sense of awe that is generated by being in the presence of objects that were made and used 5,000 or more years ago. The great achievements of the neolithic people in Ireland, however, cannot by any stretch of the imagination be classed as portable (see *Brú na Bóinne* pp 25–29).

This situation is dramatically reversed in the case of the Bronze Age civilisation which succeeded the users of stone. Bronze resists corrosion and gold is almost indestructible so we have a wealth of objects from the period between 2000 and 700 years BC. What is most striking is the modern appearance of so many of them. Perhaps there is not much room for variation once a successful cooking pot, sword or trumpet has been designed, nor room for improvement in abstract works of art. What does impress is the level of skill and originality of the objects' creators.

The Iron Age, which followed the Bronze Age and dates to about 500 BC, effectively introduced many of the comforts of life as it was enjoyed until the nineteenth century. Iron implements are very much tougher and more efficient than those of bronze. However, from the viewpoint of archaeology, they have a serious disadvantage in their propensity to rust and disappear. Invaluable in the short term, they leave little for posterity, and much of the Iron Age material that survives today is made from stone.

The Rotunda at the National Museum, Kildare Street

The triumph of Irish sculpture developed some centuries after the Christians introduced not only their religion, but also the use of the Roman alphabet. While builders and sculptors in stone left their mark on the countryside in earlier periods, Christian metal workers produced the most exquisite vessels and shrines for churches and monasteries, together with brooches and other ornaments for secular use. The Tara brooch, the chalices of Ardagh and Derrynaflan and the cross of Cong are possibly the finest. However, as the Museum 'treasury' puts them in the context of an abundance of beautiful work, this means that worthy, but less notable, artefacts are slightly overshadowed by the more famous pieces. A video is screened regularly and is something not to be missed. Besides giving a good account of the background to the collection, it is also able to show the finest details of the most delicate works.

In the middle of the twentieth century, no Irish school child was taught much about Viking civilisation. The Vikings were bad and the native Christians good. Perceptions change and the archaeologists of the past fifty years, many of them still employed within the Museum, have made a notable contribution to our understanding of the positive contribution of the 'foreigners' to the Irish way of life. Above all, the Vikings were the founders of Dublin's fair city and the developers of our international trade. The Museum's exhibition of Viking Ireland brings home the similarities that exist between their life and ours.

The Irish material in the Museum takes a time leap from Viking times to the 'Road to Independence'. This uses personal memorabilia, graphics and video to illustrate the rise of nationalism from the 1800s to its culmination in the events of the first quarter of the twentieth century. Photographs, weapons and clothing conjure up the heady times of the Volunteers and the achievement of independence.

Upstairs, the Egyptian collection makes a dramatic contrast to all the Irish material. The exhibition covers the period from 5500 BC to 400 AD, which roughly corresponds to the time from our meso-lithic era to the Iron Age. However, the fact that it rarely rains in

Egypt partly explains the difference between the condition of Irish and Egyptian artefacts, which is striking. It is unlikely that even the very best Egyptian embalmers could have preserved a body that would withstand thousands of years of Irish weather. Cloth, wood and other organic materials decay in Ireland but survive in Egypt so that there is a scarcely credible wealth of archaeological material in the valley of the Nile. Fortunately for the Dublin museum, prior to independence, British collectors were bringing home large quantities of artefacts and these were distributed amongst the major museums of the then United Kingdom.

The Egyptian collection is fully representative of the great civilisation which flourished for 6,000 years by the banks of the Nile. Thanks to its excellent state of preservation, the material shows how weavers, graphic artists, scribes and sculptors of stone and metal worked. The enthusiasm of the Egyptians for representational art means that the very features of their dead remain for us to wonder at.

Grid 14L, OS Dublin City Map (16th ed.) in Kildare Street. Buses 5, 7, 10, 11, 45 among others pass close by. Car parking is available on Merrion Square, otherwise multi-storeys available off Molesworth Street. Egyptian mummies and the odd Viking skeleton thrill even very young children. Good videos and conducted tours, delicious tea, coffee and snacks. Open: 2.00 p.m. to 5.00 p.m. Free admission, wheelchair-friendly.

National Museum
Collins Barracks

In the old days, the authorities considered that a great many
soldiers were required to keep the Irish in their place. Since
Independence, the combination of peaceful citizens and a more
mechanised and centralised army has led to the abandonment of
many a barracks. Inspired thinking, by persons associated with
the National Museum, led to the commandeering of Collins —
formerly the Royal — Barracks, which had been abandoned by the
military. In 1997, following some excellent restoration work, it was
opened as a section of the National Museum of Ireland.

The original construction of the building, to the design of
Surveyor-general Thomas Burgh, began in 1701. According to
J.W. de Courcy, who gives an outline of its architectural history, the
Royal Barracks was substantially complete by 1709 and, with
accommodation for 5,000 fighting men, claimed to be the biggest in
Europe. Many of the original buildings were demolished or built
over; however, the central block which overlooks the Liffey has
survived, and with it the great barrack square behind, with its
surrounding buildings. The south and west ranges form the
nucleus of the new Museum.

All but the most determined of Dubliners used to walk or drive past the barracks, admiring it at a small distance across the playing fields which used to extend over Croppies' Acre. This is the mass grave of an unknown number of un-named insurgents executed after the Rebellion of 1798. A more dignified treatment of the burial ground, with the addition of an enhanced memorial, was put in place for the Rebellion's bicentenary, in 1998. The military had not encouraged tourists or citizens to invade their privacy, so the barrack buildings remained rather unknown and received scant attention in books about Dublin.

The barracks stands on a terrace above the Liffey from where the visitor gets a fine view across Croppies Acre and the river, to the Guinness brewery which is dominated by a copper-domed windmill tower — the only one in Dublin to have survived the advent of steam. On the south side of the terrace, an arched entrance gives access to the parade ground, named Clarke Square in honour of Tom Clarke, the senior signatory of the 1916 Proclamation.

The impression of space within is breathtaking. There are bigger enclosed squares in Dublin, but they lack the austerity required for military purposes: no trees, no statues, just a great level courtyard, surrounded on all sides by well-proportioned ranges of four-storey buildings. Each side of the square has an entrance arch surmounted by a pediment and, all the way round, there are arcades on the ground storey which have been glazed over in some places and left open in others. Like the Natural History Museum in Merrion Street, the fabric of Collins Barracks itself constitutes a museum piece — even though it has yet to admit to it.

The entrance to the Museum is through an arch on the west range; on the left is an enticing restaurant, with tables at the ready to be set out in the open in the colonnade in warm weather. To the right, the colonnade has been glazed and forms the reception area. The collections are contained on the next three floors. A poster exhibition on the first outlines the history of the contents, for the most part an amalgamation of the nineteenth-century collections

The entrance to Collins Barracks

of the Royal Dublin Society, Royal Irish Academy and the Museum of Irish Industry.

One of the most satisfying aspects of Collins Barracks is the generous space that is available, making it possible for the designers of the exhibitions to give the treasures an uncrowded setting. This is seen at its best in the remarkable collection called 'Curator's Choice', comprising twenty-five favourite objects selected by senior museum staff. Each piece has a story — sometimes quite an unexpected one — for example, an opulent cabinet, embellished with faintly erotic illustrations of Ovid's *Metamorphoses*, was a wedding present from Oliver Cromwell whose public image was far removed from such delights.

The gallery where the Curator's Choice exhibition is displayed leads to a special corner which presents the Fonthill Vase, a beautiful fourteenth-century Chinese porcelain piece whose remarkable journey across continents and centuries ended in Ireland. Together with those of a great many of the other exhibits, the story of this vase is explained at the touch of a nearby video screen.

Entire galleries are devoted to Irish silver, period furniture, scientific instruments and Irish country furniture. Each has notable collections of beautiful and, often, unique objects. Besides these, which are the stock-in-trade of most great national museum collections, Collins Barracks has three special and very remarkable exhibitions.

The first, with the title 'Out of Storage', is a two-storey gallery with a dazzling assortment of ornaments and models, large and small. Brought together from all parts of the world and created over many centuries, this material had languished for generations in cellar storage or in closed-off, overcrowded rooms in the Museum in Kildare Street. Unobtrusively-placed video screens provide the background details, and the collection — ranging from tableware through model steam engines to sedan chairs — provides a little something for everyone; it also invites more than just one Sunday's viewing. Classification is minimal, perhaps because there is not quite enough of any one class to make a meaningful exhibit, and items stand arranged in order of date of acquisition. The great achievement has been in rescuing these beautiful objects from the eternal darkness of the Museum's storage drawers.

The second exhibition, 'The Museum at Work', illustrates brilliantly the skills — mental and manual — of restorers, in the Museum itself and in other places such as libraries. One of the crowning restoration achievements is the work that has been done on the seventeenth-century Cloyne Harp. Destroyed long years ago, it had been known in the form of two large fragments of a decorated frame of a dark-coloured wood. Combining knowledge of contemporary harps with chemical analysis of the minute traces of paint which were still present, the restorers have produced an instrument in bright primary colours with painted relief figures of the denizens of a medieval bestiary — indeed, the very frame of the harp is a sea monster in pursuit of lesser creatures. The audio-visual display not only presents the story of the reconstruction but also allows the harp's voice to be heard.

The third special exhibition whets the appetite for more, by displaying items which will be moved to other positions as the development of the Museum proceeds. It also demonstrates the variety of new technology that goes to make a modern museum. Above all, the combination of video screens and headsets has transformed appreciation of the objects on display. Their value lies in the possibility of listening to a commentary and seeing details, both of the object itself and of its background — and all without disturbing other visitors.

 Grid K12 OS Dublin City Map (16th ed.) to the north of Benburb Street. Buses 90 from Aston Quay, 25, 25A, 66, 67 from Wellington Quay and museum shuttle bus from Kildare Street. Free car park within the museum campus. But why take a bus from the city centre when a delightful riverside walk from O'Connell Bridge beckons? Open: 2.00 p.m. to 5.00 p.m., admission free, good wheelchair access, pleasant café.

The Chester Beatty Galleries

A world of beauty and thought farther from everyday life than anything within a Dubliner's usual ambit. Take an hour or two and come back for more.

Since 1954, when it was opened to the public by An Taoiseach, Éamon de Valera, this marvellous exhibition has always been a welcoming place. But its previous location, discreetly hidden amongst the trees and affluent houses of Shrewsbury Road, discouraged all but the most dedicated collectors and lovers of oriental art from enjoying its wonders. All of this changed in February 2000, when the exhibition was re-opened within the grounds of Dublin Castle. Now, in the very centre of the capital, it attracts both citizens and foreign tourists in a way that was never possible before.

Alfred Chester Beatty was a mining engineer of such rare ability that his natural love for minerals helped him to become immensely wealthy. Possibly the same urge that led him to seek for buried treasure explained his enthusiasm and skill in collecting manuscripts and books which were rare or beautiful, or both. The result was a treasure-house of oriental art, together with a range of printed books, from the early years of printing right up to the twentieth century.

What matters more than anything is that Beatty's urge to collect was equalled by his wish to display the collection and share it with everybody. This led not only to the foundation the library, but also to making public access without charge a condition of his bringing it to Ireland. The choice of Ireland was prompted partly by his ancestry — his grandparents were Irish — and partly because, in 1950, at the age of seventy-five, he considered the pace of life in Ireland to be more agreeable than in any of the numerous other countries where he had lived and worked.

In 1992, the Director of the Library, Dr Michael Ryan, together with the Chairman of the Trustees, Dr Tom Hardiman, and other distinguished people, set to work on finding a more worthy home for the collection.

During the course of their search, they discovered that the eighteenth-century Clock Tower Building in Dublin Castle had been abandoned by its previous occupiers — the Revenue Commissioners. The Government agreed to extend the Clock Tower for a gallery, and also to make the restored older parts of the building available, in order to provide all of the office and study space that such a great collection deserved. They also arranged to provide substantial funding to maintain the institution.

The Clock Tower itself was topped with a new weather vane in the form of a peacock — the work of Rachel Joynt. The peacock's name is Harry and, at the time of writing, he is still alive and well at his home in Rathfarnham. An image of one of his feathers is the motif of the fountain occupying the ground floor of the Gallery.

The original building was a range of three-storey blocks surrounding an open courtyard. This has now been covered with a glass roof, transforming outdoors to indoors and giving the whole complex a great feeling of space. The old rooms now serve as offices, library, laboratory and photo studio as well as lecture theatre — with the all-important addition of restaurant and souvenir shop on the ground floor. The galleries themselves have been added on at the southern end of the building and are approached by a modern stairway.

While the hall outside is brightly lit, the Gallery doors lead into a darkened space. Daylight is forbidden in the interests of conserving the colours of the ancient works, and the exhibits are changed frequently so that none will be exposed, even to the subdued light of the Gallery, for too long. Besides fulfilling the demands of conservation, this practice means that every visit to the Gallery will reveal something different — not that any human being could possibly assimilate all the offerings at one time.

Harry the Peacock, custodian of the Chester Beatty Galleries

The first-floor exhibition is largely of secular manuscripts and printed books, while the second floor is devoted to works inspired by the major religions of the world. Each subject is introduced by a poster, and the posters themselves are outstanding examples of how to explain great subjects with a minimum of words. The individual exhibits have concise descriptions in small print and, to honour the latest developments in communication, there are many video screens giving more detailed background explanations. Thus you have the choice of taking a quick walk-about to gain a kaleido-scopic impression of the entire world of written knowledge, or of spending an indefinite amount of time to make a close examin-ation of some small part of it.

In some ways, the most important items at this gallery are also the least impressive in appearance. The collection contains some of the very earliest texts of the Gospels, dating back to some 200 years after the birth of Christ. The originals are generally considered to have been written more than 50 years after the Crucifixion, so there is a gap of only a century between the first writing of the Gospels and the Chester Beatty papyri. But the fact that even these copies are mere fragments of text, worn at the edges, is a reminder of how great was the risk of complete destruction of any writing. However fragmentary they may be and incomprehensible to most of us, it is inspiring just to be in the presence of manuscripts which have been passed down from hand to hand and venerated for the greater part of two thousand years.

The opposite extreme to the pale brown papyrus fragments lies in the exquisite books and scrolls from countries ranging all the way from Europe and Egypt, across Asia to Japan. Many are manuscripts, illuminated in a variety of styles and brilliant with colour. Others are more representational pictures — often on a grand scale — of religious themes or of ancient stories or historical events. The decorated manuscripts of the Koran have their own special appeal because the artists were forbidden to represent people or animals and, therefore, developed marvellous abstract styles.

Besides the manuscripts, the collection presents a history of printing from the earliest times: beginning with Chinese wooden blocks and moving on to the movable type whose introduction revolutionised the world of thought. Some of the oldest printed books are there, and with them are beautiful volumes from every century of printing — books in which appearance is as important as the text.

Grid 13L OS Dublin City Map (16th ed.) Buses 49, 50, 121, 150 among others. Ideal for a wet Sunday, equally good on a sunny day when you may enjoy the roof garden and its views and wander though the beautiful new gardens in the Castle Grounds. Open: 1.00 p.m. to 5.00 p.m., admission free, wheelchair access, good restaurant.

Trinity College Library

Copied nobody quite knows where, venerated for centuries at
Kells in County Meath, buried for a while and finally rescued in
the seventeenth century, the *Book of Kells* makes a fair claim to be
one of the world's great survivors.

For generations, it was displayed in austere, though magnificent, surroundings in the Long Room of Trinity College Library.
The public were freely admitted and welcomed to view it, as one
page was ceremonially turned every day. Both the hours and days
of exhibition were restricted until the 1990s when the College
authorities realised that the great Gospel manuscript could be
made to pay for its keep. A very positive step taken with this
discovery was the decision to open the exhibition on Sundays.

The Long Room has a wonderful atmosphere and is in itself
something well worth visiting, but maintaining its integrity made
it impossible to give the *Book of Kells* the sort of exhibition that it
so richly deserves. The inspired solution to the problem was to
take the book downstairs and display it in a special museum
created within the Colonnades.

The Library, as designed by Thomas Burgh at the beginning of
the eighteenth century, was a granite-clad building of two storeys,

supported by a colonnade. The ground floor was completely open, a device which ensured that the books up above were safe from damp. The present-day appearance of the library, with its ground floor of limestone, dates to the nineteenth century when the space for book storage on the upper storeys had run out and the colonnade was bricked in to provide some more. For the greater part of the twentieth century the Colonnades had a drab, but serviceable, interior packed with books arranged by size rather than by content, so that the greatest possible numbers could be fitted in.

Trinity College Library

Transformation began in the 1980s when some of the book stacks were removed from the Colonnades and an entrance was provided on the south flank; a gallery and souvenir shop were also created at that time. The final development came in 1999 with the opening of the magnificent permanent exhibition. This introduces the *Book of Kells* and also includes a number of lesser manuscripts from those dark ages when the Celtic church shone so brightly.

The *Book of Kells* was the work of four calligraphers and painters, working, probably as monks, in one of the many monasteries that followed the rule of St Colmcille. No information on its production exists in the surviving monastic annals. It may have been written and illustrated on the Scottish island of Iona, where Colmcille lived in self-imposed exile and where a community flourished for centuries after his time. Viking raids led the monks to seek refuge in another great Columban monastery at Kells, in County Meath. One theory is that they brought the precious Gospel manuscript with them and it became one of the greatest treasures of Kells. The possibility that it was written there rather than on Iona, however, is far from being ruled out.

The book follows the style of many contemporary works. The essential part is the manuscript of the Gospels, together with some aids to their study. It is written in exquisitely formed and regular letters, and would be a joy to look at even if it had not been embellished with ornaments and full-page illustrations. Each Gospel has a 'portrait' of its evangelist, and each begins with a few words on a magnificently decorated page; there are also some 'carpet pages' filled with abstract ornament. Then there are the ornaments on the plain pages, where attenuated people and animals surround letters and coil themselves into intricate patterns. Most of these figures and creatures are stylised, but there are occasional cats, birds, hounds and wild animals which are more realistic. While the letters of the text are boldly painted, the ornamentation contains details of scarcely credible intricacy.

All this was apparent to the monks who saw the new book for the first time in the eighth century, and has been to everybody who has admired it since. But the monks probably did not have magnifying glasses and, until the nineteenth century, nobody had the chance to see the enlarged images which really bring home the skill of the original artists. That has been the great achievement of the exhibition in the Colonnades. The best pages have been reproduced as man-sized posters and, for the first time in the life of the book, it is possible for admirers to stand back and comfortably see the details of the fine work. The *Book of Kells* has always been good to look at but the modern exhibition has really added a new dimension to the whole experience.

After the detail in the reproductions has been admired, the book itself takes on a new life and makes the high point of the visit. People with strong backs can enjoy several hours studying it, while weaker mortals need to come back again and again. Besides the riot of colour and detail in the posters, the exhibition presents the background of life in Ireland at the time the manuscript was copied, and excellent videos give an indication of the techniques used in making it.

The way out of the exhibition leads upstairs to the Long Room. This is an eighteenth-century gallery that was actually improved in the nineteenth century when Benjamin Woodward did away with the original low ceiling and opened up the present vista with its arched roof of pitch-pine. The Long Room shares with the *Book of Kells* the atmosphere of a shrine. The ancient stacks display the spines of many thousands of books which contain a large proportion of the knowledge acquired by the human race up to the early decades of the nineteenth century. Impressive though the collection is, it contains only a relatively small proportion of the books in the library.

The Old Library is the most majestic of the buildings of Trinity College, but it is just one of many distinguished elevations. On a Sunday, elevations are about as much as the casual visitor may hope for — other than the *Book of Kells*. A Sabbath calm pervades the college, which is transformed from a frenetic seat of learning to a quiet place inhabited mainly by visitors. Most of the buildings are closed, but their exteriors are delightful. Front Square with its eighteenth-century classical symmetry takes life seriously, while the Museum Building, a mid-nineteenth-century creation, combines dignity with a sense of the absurd. For example, every one of the hundreds of medallions that surround it has a different design. Then there is College Park, with its old trees and a lovely expanse of green, sometimes scattered with athletes, but safely cut off from vigour of the outside world.

Grid L14 OS Dublin City Map (16th ed.) Most of the city buses pass nearby, 5, 7, 10, 11, 45, 46A among others. Dogs and buggies not welcome. Open: 12.00 noon to 4.30 p.m. year round (mornings in summer), admission charge, wheelchair access to Colonnades. Restaurant across the lawn in the Arts Block, May to September, otherwise nearest food is in Grafton Street.

The National Gallery

A collection including some of the greatest paintings in the world and many of the finest in Ireland, in splendid surroundings old and new. Occupies an hour or two at a time over several visits.

The extension to the gallery, opened in 2002, is stunning. The doorway, opening off the mundane pavement of Clare Street, leads to an explosion of space. Walls in Portland stone give a feeling of brightness, and stairways beckon the visitor onwards and upwards. Food and shopping at the beginning of the trail present a welcoming earthly touch, in preparation for the heavenly creations within. Those who have known the gallery for long years will meet their old friends in new surroundings and the uninitiated will benefit from the excellent background information provided beside the paintings and sculptures.

This 'Millennium Wing' was designed by the architects Benson and Forsyth and complements the second of a symmetrical pair of pavilions built on the lawn to the east of Leinster House. To the south of the lawn stands the Natural History Museum, completed in 1857 (see pp 100–105). The Gallery, designed by Francis Fowke, opened its doors just three years later. To some degree, the National Gallery was the offspring of the Dublin Exhibition of 1853 which took place in temporary buildings on Leinster Lawn. The man behind the Exhibition was William Dargan who insisted that the industrial exhibits must be accompanied by pavilions for painting and sculpture. A brilliant railway engineer and entrepreneur, he had written at some length on the place of the fine arts in industry. The following extract shows his preoccupation with the theme:

It is not easy often to draw the line of demarcation between objects which come within the strict limits of the Fine Arts, and those Arts which are purely utilitarian in their character. There are few of the latter which do not, to a greater or less extent, include or intimately ally themselves to the former; and, therefore, were the boundary to be defined with a scrupulous determination to exclude every article whose object is not solely utilitarian, the result would be to reject from the Exhibition much that now finds a place within it. When the mere necessities of life have been satisfied, civilization superadds to the useful the ornamental, and soon learns to recognise it as a necessity of life also; for the perception of the beautiful is innate to the mind of man, and when the useful has been achieved, the cravings for the beautiful will seek to be satisfied. Hence Sculpture, in the most extended acceptation of that term, enters into the composition of a vast proportion of the articles designed for utilitarian purposes. The same may he said of Painting. In truth it is difficult, when once we have emerged from the rudest and most elementary state of society, to deny that the Fine Arts are themselves utilitarian. The desires of the eye for that which is beautiful in form and colour, if not essential to mere existence, assuredly are so to the enjoyment of life; and hence Sculpture and Painting, in the abstract, may, it is presumed be fitly exhibited without transgressing the strict limits which should be assigned to an Industrial Exhibition.

After the Great Exhibition, friends and admirers of Dargan subscribed to a testimonial, and his suggestion that the money should go to found a picture gallery was accepted. The RDS provided the land, and the National Gallery was opened to the public in 1864. A statue of Dargan stands in front of the Gallery and an inscription on the foundation stone, to the left of the main doorway, tells of his contribution.

The Gallery has a marvellous nucleus of paintings from most of the great European schools from the sixteenth century onward. Larger and wealthier galleries of the world are able to exhibit a number of works by each of the great masters, but Merrion Street provides for the people of Ireland a representative selection — you can see in Dublin the work of most of the greatest names, including even such exquisite rarities as a Vermeer.

William Dargan and the National Gallery

What the National Gallery of Ireland offers above all is the achievement of centuries of Irish painting. Part of the pleasure of this is the presentation of familiar views and village scenes — with the difference that people, trees and even whole landscapes have changed since the artists committed them to canvas.

Perhaps the crowning glory of the National Gallery is the Yeats Room, a delightful testimony to one of the most remarkable families ever to be raised in Ireland — three generations of distinguished painters, with poets and craft workers thrown in for good measure. Pride of place goes naturally to Jack B. Yeats. 'Riot of colour' is the phrase that springs to mind, though it might not be quite the right term to describe the artist's exquisite craftsmanship.

Perhaps at the other extreme is the Turner exhibition, based on the bequest, in 1900, of 36 'drawings' collected by Henry Vaughan. Quite apart from giving a view of the artist's work, it has something of an air of mystery in that it is open only in January — the darkest month of the year — and even then, is shown in a shaded room. The practical reason for this is that the pictures will last longer when kept away from bright lights. The joy of stepping into these gently glowing colours on a gloomy winter's day makes the visit a very special occasion.

Grid 14L, OS Dublin City Map (16th ed.) Entrances on Merrion Street and Clare Street, lots of buses including 5, 7, 9, 10, 45, 46A pass nearby, car parking on Merrion Square. Perhaps less fun for young children than the Natural History Museum. Very positive for adults in having seats, shops and refreshments. Open: 12.00 noon to 5.30 p.m., admission free except to special exhibitions, wheelchair access to most areas.

Natural History Museum

A treasured relic of early twentieth-century museum ideals and a delightful introduction to the concept of biodiversity. An hour or two covers most of the exhibits.

A quarter of a million people visit the Natural History Museum every year, making it one of the most popular of all Dublin's places of exhibition. This happens in spite the institution's being distinguished by its modesty, having a minuscule publicity budget, no restaurant, no connection with great historical personages and not a single exhibit that is unique by international standards. For these reasons, relatively few tourists cross its threshold. The majority of the visitors are, therefore, Dubliners, and the Museum may well qualify as being the most favoured cultural haunt of the citizens of the capital.

Sunday afternoons see it packed, particularly with parents or grandparents and children — the younger generation thrilled by their close encounters with birds and animals, the older equally excited by the memories of their own introduction to the wonders of nature. The most interesting indicator of the Natural History Museum's continued popularity is that, since the 1950s, television has brought superb wildlife material within reach of everyone. While much of this revels in fierce animals and gore, the work of luminaries such as David Attenborough, with an unashamedly scientific approach, is equally popular. In spite of this competition, the Museum still attracts people of all ages who have a desire to be in the presence of real animals — even if the creatures have been dead for more than a hundred years.

The late eighteenth century witnessed, amongst Europeans, a growing desire to collect and classify all sorts of objects. In Uppsala in Sweden, Carl von Linné was supreme in describing and naming thousands of plants and animals that he had either gathered himself or had received from correspondents all over the world.

In Ireland, the Dublin Society took the lead in making collections and displaying them for the education of the public. One of its leading members, the chemist Richard Kirwan, was responsible for the purchase of the great collection of minerals and insects made by N.G. Leske, in Marburg. This was first put on show, in 1795, at the Society's premises on Hawkins Street and was then moved to the organisation's new home at Leinster House, in 1815. There, the Society's entire natural history collection occupied four rooms on the first floor.

From here it grew. The owners, now exalted as the Royal Dublin Society, took a lease of land to the south-east, on Leinster Lawn, as a site for a new building. The Government made a substantial contribution to the cost and engaged the services of the architect, Frederick Villiers Clarendon of the Board of Works, to oversee the project. The foundation stone was laid in March 1856 and the Museum was opened in August of the following year amidst great celebrations. David Livingstone was a guest lecturer on the occasion. The main entrance was originally at the west end, but this has long since been engulfed in Government Buildings. The east façade is a stolid wall, relieved by three recesses still waiting to be occupied by statues of eminent naturalists. Above them, a little relief appears in the form of three rectangular panels beneath a leaf-scroll motif on the cornice. The left-hand panel has a serpent, the centre a deity flanked by dolphins, and the right a crocodile.

The Government contributed to the running costs of the Museum from 1863 and adopted it completely in 1877, employing a small but very distinguished group of staff members. While carrying out their scientific work of identifying and classifying creatures, they also became enthusiasts for making an attractive public display.

The present display, on the first floor and the galleries above it, was begun in 1881 under the direction of Alexander Goodman More. Beginning at the top, with small creatures of incredibly ancient ancestry, the exhibits descend through examples of increasing complexity to the birds and mammals which occupy the floor. The skill and artistry of a nineteenth-century taxidermist created a magnificent group of primates capable, after a hundred years, of giving children a satisfying thrill — even though they know from television and zoos that gorillas are peaceful family animals.

One of the most interesting exhibits in the galleries is the Barrington Collection of Irish birds. Most of these died accidentally, many by striking lighthouses while on migration. R.M. Barrington was a pioneer in the study of bird migration and published a major work on the subject early in the twentieth century; much of the basic information in this volume was obtained from the lighthouse-keepers of the time.

In the early years of the Museum, the ground floor was used for special exhibitions. But in 1895 most of the Irish material from the upper regions was brought together and displayed downstairs. For some time, it shared the space with an international display, illustrating geographical variation between animal groups. Then the Irish collection grew and took over the entire floor. On entering the Museum by the west doorway, the visitor was confronted by skeletons of three great Irish deer, excavated at Rathconnor in County Limerick, in 1824.

After Leinster House became the seat of government, the west door to the Museum was closed to the public for security reasons. The east door, opening to Merrion Square, became the main entrance, and the ground-floor exhibitions were turned around to face the east. And there they have stayed.

Subtle changes have since been made in the Irish exhibition — in particular, the reduction in the number of birds and other creatures on show. The enthusiasm of past curators to show examples of almost everything had led to an overcrowded and almost stultifying display. Other improvements have been the replacement of rank upon rank of birds' eggs with interesting and beautiful collections of fossils and minerals in the window and wall cases. The central space is occupied, as it has been for a century or more, by 'reconstructions' of birds and mammals. This is brilliant work and, quite apart from its antique appeal, continues to serve its original purpose of giving a close-up view of families of fox, otter and various birds.

The Natural History Museum and surgeon T.H. Parke

Skeletons of whales and a rather battered basking shark that hang from the ceiling never fail to impress because of their sheer size. There are monstrous fish, amongst them a sunfish 6 feet tall and a superb swordfish. Then there are smaller creatures, exquisite seashells, tropical butterflies and other insects of wonderful variety.

Most of the exhibits are originals: the stuffed skins of larger animals, the 'sub-fossils', such as the tusk of a mammoth which perished in Waterford Harbour in the ice age, and the true fossils.

Fossils are natural chemical replacements of the creatures which died when the rock was soft sediment, and the ones at the Museum include a specimen from Tipperary of *Cooksonia*, the oldest known land plant. It flourished in Silurian times, 420 million years ago. Nineteenth-century miners at the Jarrow colliery in County Kilkenny spotted various creatures in the coal and brought them to the attention of the authorities. These had the distinction of being examined by the great Thomas Henry Huxley, redoubtable defender of Darwin and his ideas. The finest of the fossil fish in the Museum were bought from a German dealer by the third Earl of Enniskillen, kept by him in Florencecourt, and then purchased by the RDS for its collection.

Finally, one of the most remarkable collections in the Museum is of models rather than actual organisms. Microscopic creatures are difficult to preserve and even more difficult to display. Larger, soft-bodied beasts such as sea anemones and slugs can be preserved but only in a condition that would please nobody but the most dedicated anatomists. An answer to the problem was developed by Leopold Blaschka in Bohemia in the 1870s. With his son, Rudolph, he made exquisite models of the organisms in coloured glass — the microscopic ones greatly magnified, the bigger beasts life-size. The lustre of the glass resembles to a remarkable degree the moist, gelatinous surfaces of the originals and these make a fascinating display.

Compared with modern exhibitions, such as the Chester Beatty Library and Birr Castle Science Centre with their excellent audio-visual material to explain the artefacts, the Natural History Museum is a restrained place. It was not planned that way and in its first 50 years was a state-of-the-art temple to scientific under-standing. Then it suffered some 60 years of neglect, when it just about maintained its fabric and was able to effect only the minimum amount of preservation work.

By the time the tide turned in the 1980s, most of the properly funded museums of the world had done away with the nineteenth-century image and made their collections very much more attractive. By accident, the Dublin museum was left as one of very few unaltered nineteenth-century 'cabinets'. The present-day custodians, fully aware of its unique value, persuaded the authorities to clean, paint and restore the structure but not to modernise the arrangements of the collections. The Natural History Museum contains more than a wonderful collection of the animals of the world. It preserves the atmosphere of excitement and discovery of the time of the revolution in thought that resulted from *The Origin of the Species*.

Grid 14L, OS Dublin City Map (16th ed.) Entrance on Merrion Street, lots of buses including 5, 7, 8, 9, 10, 45 at either end of the street, car parking on Merrion Square. Not a place for dogs or infants and slightly un-relaxing in its shortage of seating — but extremely popular with mobile children and their minders and an inspiration to all ages in revealing the beauty and variety of the world of animals. Open: 2.00 p.m. to 5.00 p.m., admission free, wheelchair access to ground floor only.

National Print Museum

Any writer above a certain age experiences a wave of nostalgia upon entering the new and charming National Print Museum. Here, for posterity, are the marvellous machines — intertype, linotype and monotype — which clattered away in the printing works of the world for a century or so. Then came the revolution of computers and desk-top publishing whereby writers, sitting by the fireside in their own homes, turn their creations into Times New Roman at the touch of a computer key.

Opened by President Mary Robinson in 1996, the Museum is housed in the garrison chapel of the former barracks of Beggars Bush — a site not unworthy of attention in its own right. The barracks was built in 1827 with the troops' quarters constructed in a pleasing classical style. Having being distinguished as the first British barracks to be handed over to the newly independent Ireland in 1922, it suffered years of neglect. Parts were used as government offices, but many of the buildings were allowed to decay. The fortunes of the site changed in the 1980s with the building of new government offices within. These include the Geological Survey with its brilliant museum which, alas, is not open on Sundays. Later on, the old residential buildings were thoroughly refurbished and now form a complex of extremely expensive-looking apartments.

The chapel was tucked away in a remote corner of the barracks and forgotten until Bertie Ahern, then Minister for Labour, helped Seán Galavan and other members of the Irish Print Group to take it over. Teams from FÁS worked to repair and restore the neglected buildings and they did a particularly good job on the roof beams. Collecting the exhibits had been a personal commitment of Seán Galavan since the 1980s. Happily, this coincided with case-room equipment from the *Irish Press* newspaper becoming available, and this now forms a major part of the collection.

The exhibition on the ground floor of the chapel gives an excellent impression of what a printing works was like during the century or so in which type was set mechanically. A video shows the machinery on exhibit actually in use. The most remark-

The doorway to the barracks chapel at Beggar's Bush — now the National Print Museum

able feature is that electricity was used only to drive the machinery and melt the type metal, which flowed into the mould as each line of type was set. For many years before hot metal was finally laid to rest, electric motors and relays could have been used to speed up and quieten the process. But the print shops preferred to use machines which rely on a marvellous array of cams and gear wheels as well as the force of gravity; this is what makes them so wonderful to watch — immeasurably cumbersome, but so much more fun to look at than the silent and motionless efficiency of the computer systems.

Many of the machines on show are nineteenth-century creations of cast iron which enjoyed very long lives. Beautifully restored with black paint and gold lettering, their big levers and occasional ornate decoration — such as the casting of an eagle for a counterweight in a proofing machine — add to the feeling that they are from another world. Development in printing takes place so rapidly that the exhibits include computers which look distinctly modern but are, in fact, genuine museum pieces as they have already been completely superseded.

Upstairs, the walls of the gallery have a collection of newspaper pages, selected to demonstrate the evolution of styles, or to show how past editors saw fit to announce world-shaking events. The days of the compositor's seven-year apprenticeship are recalled by original indentures from as late as the 1930s, with their strict moral code:

> *the youth was forbidden to commit Fornication or contract Matrimony, to play at Cards, Dice Tables or other unlawful Games, to haunt Taverns, Ale-houses or Playhouses.*

Hard times, indeed !

Grid15L, OS Dublin City Map (16th ed.) Beggar's Bush is at the north-east end of Haddington Road, accessible by innumerable buses: 5, 7, 45 among others. Car parking close to the museum. Coffee and snacks available in the bright new conservatory, even in midwinter. Be sure to buy their delightful little booklet Key events in the history of printing. Open: 2.00 p.m. to 5.00 p.m., admission charge.

Great Houses

The eighteenth century witnessed a considerable element of peace and prosperity for the people of Ireland. True, the penal laws were still in force and the Irish Parliament was singularly unrepresentative. But so were many other parliaments at the time. The categories of landlords included bad, very bad and remarkably good. Good and bad for the most part built beautiful houses in the classical style. It was a great leap forward from the previous centuries, when Gaelic, Norman and newly arrived landowners lived in fortresses.

Four of the five houses in this section were family homes into the second half of the twentieth century. The fifth, Marino Casino, was more of a summer house and, besides, ceased to be occupied more than a hundred years ago. Both Speaker Conolly and the Earl of Charlemont, who built Castletown and the Casino respectively, were deeply committed patriots. Conolly wanted his home to demonstrate to the outside world the skills of Irish artists and craftsmen. Lord Charlemont's aim was to create an architectural ornament set in surroundings which were free for all citizens to enjoy.

Malahide Castle, Drimnagh Castle and Russborough were equally designed to impress the people, but their owners had somewhat lower profiles. Russborough was the palace of the heir of a very successful brewer, while Malahide and Drimnagh were ancestral homes. The beauty of Russborough lies in the coherence of its design. The charm of the other two lies in their display of renovations, large and small, carried out in the course of more than seven hundred years.

Like the museums, the great houses are perfect for rainy days — but good for sunny summer visits, too, with such added attractions as gardens, parkland and scenery.

Castletown

Great Houses

The greatest of the great houses of Ireland, overlooking the Liffey and surrounded by woodland and green fields. Occupies half a day including the journey from Dublin and a snack.

Seething with history and romance, Castletown House can be described only in superlatives of grandeur and beauty. The great, grey house is approached by half a mile of avenue, shaded by ancient lime trees. The front lawns are sheltered by a yew hedge, itself protected by a line of sentinel Florencecourt yews. The view from the lawn is of an enormous expanse of parkland which is dotted with elderly, but still splendid, trees.

The backdrop is of woodland in all directions. The fact that some of it is a narrow fringe takes nothing from the general effect of a stately home safely screened from the busy outside world. A path across the grass leads straight down to the Liffey where it rushes over a low weir, succeeded by a long, calm pool. Beech and ash line the far side and mallard dabble peacefully. Blackthorn and brambles cover much of the ground on the near side and a particularly fine ancient willow leans across the water. Possibly this is a survivor of Lady Louisa Conolly's planting at the water's edge. The Doric temple on a ridge nearby is certainly her creation. Once it commanded a view of house and river — but bushes have grown up to conceal both. Fine old oaks abound in the demesne — a not uncommon feature. But young trees are plentiful, too, and they are unusual and more than welcome since oaks are not immortal. Not only is Castletown one of the first and finest of the great houses of Ireland, but its founder and his successors are well known from contemporary publications and the correspondence of Lady Louisa Conolly and other inhabitants. However, discovering details of the planning and construction of the House has required an element of detective work on the part of art and architecture historians. This process was delightfully described in *Country Life*, in 1969, in a series of articles by Maurice Craig and other experts. The articles were reprinted as a single booklet published by the Irish Georgian Society.

The builder of Castletown House was the remarkable William Conolly, a native of Ballyshannon, who made a fortune by buying and selling some of the many forfeited properties that were available following the turbulent times of William III. He was elected Speaker of the Irish House of Commons and clearly wanted to make a statement of his personal wealth and power. However, this was equalled by a patriotic view that his home should be a shining example of the resources and skills of the people of Ireland. The designers had to be amongst the best architects in the world and the House was to be a model to other landlords of how their dwellings should appear.

Planning began in 1719 when the Italian architect, Allesandro Galilei, was employed to design the general outline. Building began soon afterwards, perhaps in 1720, but Galilei had returned to Florence by that time and did not visit Ireland again. There is evidence, however, that the work was in progress in 1722, under the control of Edward Lovett Pearce. He had been closely involved in the planning, but was also in Italy for most of the time that the House was under construction. The entrance hall, the colonnades, the wings and, perhaps, much of the detail of the interior were his contribution.

Tragedy surrounded the builders of Castletown. Speaker Conolly died in 1729 in his town house and it seems that he did not enjoy very much time in his country seat. Pearce died just three years later, in his early thirties, after an amazing professional career that had been crammed into six or seven years. After the Speaker's death, his widow, Katherine, retired to Castletown where, besides leading a dazzling social life, she showed her enthusiasm for ebullient architecture. In the 1740s, she commissioned the Wonderful Barn near Leixlip and the 'Conolly Folly', the magnificent obelisk, which stands between Castletown and its stately neighbour, Carton.

The next phase in the construction of Castletown took place when the Speaker's grand-nephew, Tom Conolly, and his wife, Lady Louisa, moved there in 1759. The great staircase was completed n 1760 and the magnificent plaster work of the hall was added at about the same time. Lady Louisa was responsible for much of the interior design, in particular the gallery which was finished in 1775.

Many of the great eighteenth-century houses were substantially altered by their owners in the nineteenth century. One of the many joys of Castletown is that the interior remains very much the same as it was in 1821 when Lady Louisa died, peacefully, at the age of 78. Many of the rooms contain the furniture of her time. While the great front rooms downstairs have an air of formality and were used on state occasions, those in the rear and

Castletown

upstairs are very much more homely. One of the most interesting is the Print Room. Its walls are decorated with pictures cut out from magazines that were then embellished with specially printed borders. Many ladies in the eighteenth century papered rooms with their favourite pictures in this way, but the example at Castletown is the only one of its kind to have survived in Ireland. The charm of the collection is that it shows what appealed personally to the good lady, rather than what a design consultant thought was right.

In 1965, Castletown was put on the market, and the future of the great house stood in the balance. Much of the land was sold for building and, for some time, nobody wanted to buy the mansion. It was rescued by the Hon. Desmond Guinness who, in 1967, bought the House and 120 acres of parkland for £93,000. The purchase included the entrance gates and the avenue from the village, together with the fields that slope down to Anna Liffey and also some delightful pockets of woodland. In 1979, the property was acquired by the Castletown Foundation which initiated the major restoration work and, in 1994, house and grounds became the property of the people of Ireland. The restoration is being continued under the expert guidance of the architects of Dúchas, the Heritage Service. The Castletown Foundation continues to be involved as an adviser and is still the owner of the greater part of the contents of the House.

Grid O9834, Sheet 50. Bus 67 goes to the gate in the bustling village of Celbridge. Admission by guided tour only, quite good for wheelchairs. Restaurant inside and possibilities for picnics in the park. Open: 1.00 p.m. to6.00 p.m. Easter to September, 1.00 p.m. to 5.00 p.m. October and November. The parkland, which is not too friendly to buggies or wheelchairs, is sheer heaven for dogs and is open all the time. Car parking at the house.

Russborough

Russborough never thought of itself as a lakeside mansion. It was built a century and a half before the ESB embellished its outlook by adding a lake to the fields in front of the great house. Described by many writers as the most beautiful of the great country houses of Ireland, it also enjoys one of the finest settings. Like its senior relative, Castletown, it was built at a convenient distance from the Liffey, though Russborough is in the upper valley of that remarkable river while Castletown is in the lower.

Many, perhaps most, of the great houses of Ireland are well hidden from the plain people, often surrounded by high stone walls enlivened only by screens of beech trees. One of the owners of Russborough felt that his property deserved to be admired by the populace as they passed by on the road that leads through Blessington to the waterfall on the Liffey. With this in mind, he arranged for a low section of wall to be created so as to frame the lovely, Palladian-fronted house as it presides over its gently sloping green pasture.

Russborough, in the words of Desmond Guinness, 'is the jewel in the crown of all Richard Cassels' houses and the best preserved with every original feature still intact; stonework, statuary, inlaid floors, mantels and so on.' Like many of Ireland's fine houses, it owes its origin to the success of a family of Dublin brewers. Joseph Leeson, the heir to the founder of the family brewery, inherited a fortune on his father's death and decided to invest in a magnificent country house. Building began in 1741 using the beautiful silvery granite from a local quarry. Two years later, Leeson was elected to the Dublin Parliament, where he served until 1756, and remained an important public figure, ultimately becoming the first Earl of Milltown. Very little was done by successive owners to alter the appearance of Russborough, and the contemporary visitor enjoys much the same impression of opulent beauty that the first Earl did.

Russborough, the central block

Richard Cassels, who was still engaged in the building of Carton and Leinster House as well as Russborough, died in 1751, and Russborough was completed in 1756 by Francis Bindon. The approach to the House is from the side — as is the case in Castletown — and a granite arch opens on to a straight avenue of beech trees. This leads up to the House revealing more and more of the façade as it goes. The frontage of the building measures 700 feet in length, The family home at Russborough comprises a central block of three storeys, with the ceremonial entrance reaching to the second storey, its pediment supported on four Corinthian pillars. Lions rampant on the balustrade of the front steps hold the Leeson coat of arms. The central block is flanked on each side by a curved Doric colonnade with sculptured figures in niches. These colonnades are passages leading to a pair of two-storey wings. Each is pierced by an arch, the south one surmounted by a sundial, the north by a clock. The arches lead to stable yards and farm buildings. The great house of the time was self-sufficient — at least in transport, meat, poultry and vegetables.

At the south end of the range, tablets commemorate great horses which were buried there. These include Cruiskeen, who died in 1847, and is commemorated in these words:

Beneath this tree a mare is laid
Who never yet a friend betrayed.

Nearby stands a splendid wellingtonia, which was:

graciously planted by His Royal Highness The Prince of Wales
and Earl of Dublin September 1861.

Discreetly hidden from view behind the screens, the out-buildings are rather less beautifully finished. Persons of quality, presumably, never ventured to these nether regions. Rather, they stepped out from the front buildings to mount their steeds or enter their carriages which were presented to them by grooms, footmen or other lesser mortals. The north yard is now the car park and entrance for visitors, and also leads to a very remarkable indoor exercise yard for horses. Opposite its gate is the entrance to a pleasant, hidden garden.

While the exterior of the House derives its beauty from the severity of its form, the interior is very different. At the time Russborough was built, the fashion was for baroque plaster work and this has rarely been developed on such a lavish scale as in Russborough. The ceilings of all the important rooms are richly decorated and the main staircase has an incredible display. The work in the Saloon, the Library and the Music Room is believed to be that of the brothers, Paul and Philip Francini — although no documentary evidence of their employment there has been found. The stucco in these rooms is generally confined to the ceilings, but in the Drawing Room it extends down the walls and, in particular, forms four oval surrounds. These were made specially to frame four pictures of harbours and shipping, by Joseph Vernet, which were bought for the Earl, in Rome, in 1750. The most exuberant of the stucco covers the walls of the massive mahogany staircase and, as well as depicting hunting scenes, this includes a portrait of the first Earl. The first pictures, collected by the Earls of Milltown, were presented to the National Gallery where they form a very important part of the collection.

The first two of Lord Milltown's three wives died young. However, the third outlived both the Earl and his heir, and died in 1842 at the age of 100 years. Meanwhile, the second Earl inherited the estate and, at the end of the eighteenth century, Russborough suffered its first and only serious damage in its two hundred and fifty years as a family home. In 1798, first the United Irishmen and then the English troops occupied it. The Irish treated the buildings with respect, but the English pulled down some of the roofs for firewood and ruined the outer buildings.

Russborough remained in the ownership of the descendants of its builder for more than a century until the sixth Earl died in 1890. Following the death of his widow, in 1914, the property passed to a nephew, Sir Edmund Turton. The Turtons did not use the House much and sold some of the paintings, including the Vernet marine scenes. In 1931, Lady Turton sold the House to Captain Denis Daly. Once again, it became a family home and the Dalys were able to repair much of the damage that had occurred during the period of neglect. However, as far as the public was concerned, apart from being something to admire from the road, Russborough was essentially a private house,.

Then came the change which has transformed Russborough into one of the treasure houses of Ireland — one which welcomes anybody who is willing to pay a modest fee for admission. It was bought, in 1951, by Sir Alfred Beit who was looking for somewhere to live, which would also be worthy of housing his fabulous collection of paintings and sculpture that had been begun by his uncle.

Sir Alfred established the Beit Foundation, by which both house and paintings have become the property of the people of Ireland. Following two robberies, the most valuable of the paintings are now kept in the National Gallery. However, that still leaves a great many superb works in the House, including the four Vernets which Sir Alfred succeeded in finding and bringing back again.

Besides the wonderful details of eighteenth-century stucco and fixtures such as the marble fireplaces, the inlaid floor of the Saloon, the Genovese velvet wall covering and many others, Russborough has a special place, amongst the accessible great houses, in retaining its atmosphere as a home rather than a museum. Furniture, ornaments, candelabras — everything is of the highest quality, and many of the artefacts are rare and valuable as well as beautiful. There is a feeling that it was all brought together to be enjoyed and used rather than simply to be admired from a distance.

Grid 9610, Sheet 56. Bus 65. Although there is plenty of open space in front of the house, Russborough is more a museum excursion than a country place, not too good for buggies or dogs though there is plenty of play and picnic space by the nearby Blessington Lakes. There are craft workshops, a restaurant and shop and a children's play area. Access to the main rooms of the house is by guided tour only and entails a flight of steps — problematic for wheelchairs. Car parking in stable yard. Open: April to October, 10.30 a.m. to 5.00 p.m. Admission fee.

Malahide Castle

Great Houses

A castle full of history, an important garden, unique transport exhibition, wide open spaces — one of Dublin's most exciting parks. Occupies half a day including the journey from Dublin and a snack.

Seven hundred and ninety-one years is a respectable period for a family to enjoy its homestead. The previous owner of the demesne at Malahide, Hamund MacTurkill, the last King of Dublin, was slain by the Anglo-Normans. In 1185, they granted his demesne to Richard Talbot and, in 1977, the people of Dublin, as represented by their County Council, acquired it for the sum of £650,000. The last member of the family to have lived there, the Hon. Rose Talbot, was still visiting her old home from time to time, at the beginning of the twenty-first century; so the family connection with Malahide continued for more than 800 years.

There was a blip in Cromwellian times when the royalist Talbots were expelled in favour of Myles Corbet, one of the four signatories of the death warrant of King Charles I. His judgement was duly rewarded in 1661 when he was hanged and the Talbots were reinstated. Tragically, they once again took the wrong side in civil war and fourteen members of the family died fighting for the Jacobites at the Battle of the Boyne. The survivors, however, who were astute, promptly made their peace with King William and this time managed to retain their house and grounds.

With its assortment of circular and square turrets, and windows of varying shapes and styles, the Castle gives an impression of having happened rather than being the result of any particular architect's design. This was indeed the case, and evidence of construction work which took place at intervals in the course of six centuries may be detected in its fabric.

There are no visible traces left of the Talbot dwelling of the first few generations of their occupation. But in the fourteenth century, they built a tower house of the kind then in fashion, an uncompromisingly grim and grey fortress of limestone some three storeys in height. Its small windows made it easy to defend, though gloomy within. It did include, however, a spacious hall, and this — much embellished and greatly enlarged — has remained the centre of Malahide Castle to this day.

The walls of the present hall were built in the latter half of the fifteenth century. Repairs, refurbishments and modernisation were a continuing process in the course of the next four hundred years. The earliest work includes some of the oak panelling, including the lovely Flemish Coronation of the Virgin. The Gothic windows were inserted in the nineteenth century and they give the Castle its present day appearance

The most important rooms are visited by way of an organised tour, conducted mainly by a disembodied voice, but helpful and enthusiastic humans are never far away and they are always happy to answer questions. Not only is Malahide Castle a treasure house of fine furniture from many ages, it also displays a large number of paintings which have been supplied by the National Gallery. These include a collection of thirty-one Talbot family portraits, purchased by the Gallery at the time of the sale of the Castle. A picture of the Battle of the Boyne dominates the end wall of the great hall, and tradition — in this case, very credible — tells that the fourteen Talbots who fell in that engagement had their last family meal in this same room.

There is a small door in a turret where the family ghost used to appear and there is also a 'Margaret Thatcher Slept Here' room. The view from the upper windows of the house is magnificent:

gardens and green lawns in the foreground, then out across Dublin
Bay to the Wicklow Mountains.

Below the rooms that were enjoyed by the Quality in past times
— and now restricted to organised tours or banquets — are the
quarters of the Lower Orders. These have been developed in
various ways, and house a restaurant and craft shops. The
restaurant is in a delightful, vaulted ground-floor room with Gothic
windows and good reproduction furniture. It serves excellent
salads and other tasty morsels in a relaxed atmosphere. Outside,
the old stable yard and grooms' quarters have been converted to
craft shops. The Talbots, like the Powerscourts in the nineteenth
century, believed in providing at least some of their servants with
first-rate accommodation, and the buildings in the yards are
beautiful in themselves. A resident peacock is an appropriate
embellishment.

Close to the stables are two very remarkable features: the first,
a creation of the family, the second a new development made since
public ownership. The last male heir to the estate, Lord Milo Talbot
de Malahide, was a diplomat with a more than ordinary interest in
horticulture. On his worldwide travels, from 1948 until his death,
in 1973, he collected plants for his gardens which cover about
20 acres and, thanks to his efforts, contain about 5,000 varieties.
While the garden has been developing over a century or more —
and contains many fine old trees — its appearance is essentially
twentieth-century and the conception of the last Lord Talbot.

Every great garden is unique in its own way and there are
many of them in Ireland; the Fry Model Railway Museum, on the
other hand, is the only one of its kind in the country. In the 1930s,
Cyril Fry constructed beautiful gauge O models of the Irish
railways. His collection was brought to Malahide in the 1970s and
is now on display in a spacious hall, together with a selection of
the work of other model makers and a collection of railway
photographs. It's nostalgic stuff for visitors above a certain age
and a riveting experience for modellers, old and young.

So much for the Museum: in the next room is a magnificent
working layout of all forms of land- and water-based public

transport in Ireland. The tour and exhibition here are conducted under the direction of John Dunne. The display itself is a living entity which is constantly being added to and includes replicas of the latest in shipping and rolling stock. At the time of writing, work was still in progress on a section for the Ballinamore and Ballyconnell Canal. An excellent recorded commentary, enhanced with sound effects and spotlights, leads visitors around railway stations and harbours while the many trains and the odd tram, trolley bus and boat go about their business.

Malahide Castle, five centuries of building

All of these wonders are set in the middle of '268 acres of undulating fertile land', as the official guide booklet puts it. The demesne is roughly diamond-shaped, about a mile along its longer axis, and generously supplied with footpaths. Many of them lead through woodland to such features as a lime kiln, traces of an ice house and a covered spring of clear water. From the main entrance a path leads northwards across an immense lawn to the Castle, passing on its way a line of oak trees — some have fallen over the years, leaving gaps in the row, but one particularly fine specimen stands beside the path.

Its combination of history, variety and a sense of space and freedom, makes Malahide Castle truly a place for all seasons.

Grid O2145, Sheet 50. Bus 42, 43, DART and train station a short walk away. Dog- and buggy-friendly, very safe. Models, woods and lawns fun for all ages, the Castle itself more for restrained persons. Too many stairs in the Castle for wheelchair comfort — but gardens and other attractions are manageable. Delightful tearoom. Open: winter, 10.00 a.m. to 5.00 p.m. summer, 11.00 a.m. to 6.00 p.m. Admission charge to Castle.

Marino Casino

One of Ireland's architectural gems: ideal for a short Sunday afternoon, as visits are restricted to guided tours.

There was a song about 'a lonely little petunia in an onion patch'. It comes to mind when the Earl of Charlemont's Casino, almost dwarfed by large but unimpressive red-brick buildings, appears on the left of the busy road to Malahide. It doesn't quite fit in to a built-up suburb — nor was it meant to. However, a few acres of green surrounds have survived and provide just enough space to view this charming edifice from a reasonable distance.

Maurice Craig described the Casino as 'one of the most beautiful buildings of its kind anywhere' and few people would disagree. Its proportions, graceful pillars and charming sculptures all blend together to form an entirely satisfying unit. The pale Portland stone, imported from Derbyshire in England, contrasts pleasantly with the green lawns that sprawl around it.

The architect of the Casino, Sir William Chambers, worked closely with his client James Caulfield, first Earl of Charlemont. They had been close friends during the years that the Earl, as a young man, had spent in Rome on a greatly extended Grand Tour. Charlemont loved Rome and its architecture, but also loved his home country and decided to live and work there rather than relax in warmer foreign lands.

The Earl was Commander-in-Chief of the Volunteers in the years leading up to 1798, as well as being the driving force behind the foundation of the Royal Irish Academy, and the introduction of a classical summer house to his demesne was very much part of his patriotism. Like Speaker Conolly and Castletown, Charlemont wished not merely to provide luxurious accommodation for himself, but to bring the very best in architecture to Ireland, and to make it accessible to the people. The parkland around the Casino, part of an estate which extended all the way down to the sea, was deliberately kept open as a place for the public to enjoy.

Charlemont had spent lavishly on the Casino, on his country house in whose grounds it stood, and on his town house in Rutland Square — now the Municipal Gallery. His son, the second Earl, had to sell much of the property to clear the debts he inherited and, after his death, the estate went into decline. It was sold in 1881 and the Casino was abandoned until 1930 when legislation was enacted specially to allow the State to care for it. Essential repairs were carried out at the time and more work was undertaken in the 1950s and 1960s.

In the following decade things changed for the better and, to celebrate European Architectural Year of 1975, major restoration began in 1974. This was completed in 1984 and the Casino was finally re-opened to the public that year. The interior can be seen only in the presence of one of the excellent guides employed by Dúchas. However, the outside and the sadly reduced lawn around it have unrestricted access, as in the days of the good Earl.

The building is guarded by four stone beasts of leonine form. They are friendly creatures, with big smiles and lovely paws. What teeth and claws their models might have had are discreetly hidden. The books call them lions and it is not impossible that lions are what the sculptor intended to portray. But they have human ears and the musculature on their forearms bears little relationship to that of any known beast — although there is more than a hint of one of the inhabitants of the *Book of Kells*.

The initial impression that the Casino gives is of a building of classical simplicity: clean and pure lines together with Doric columns and stonework in the form of big rectangular blocks; the two burial urns on the parapets, which hide the chimneys, and the statues of deities, are the only obvious complications. However, this appearance is utterly deceptive. Chambers had in fact designed an extremely complex building, full of hidden surprises.

The biggest of them is that, in spite of the impression it gives of simply containing a single great hall by having only one big window on each of the four walls, the Casino actually has three storeys and many rooms. Each of the four elevations is unique. The enormous wooden door on the north face simply frames a very much smaller double door. This feature accommodates both a satisfying external appearance and an equally well-proportioned door giving access to the relatively small entrance hallway. The south and west faces have single windows, while the east has additional windows flanking the central wing.

Climbing the steps of the base reveals a sunken area on all sides and a door and windows to the lower storey. This was the kitchen and servants' quarters and it communicated by a tunnel to the big house nearby.

The ground floor is covered with parquet, made up from a variety of hardwoods to give a beautiful geometrical pattern. The rooms are tall and spacious with superb plaster work on the ceilings and door frames. Unfortunately, the original items of furniture, together with the Earl's collection of books and sculpture, have long since been dispersed and the rooms feel a little lonely; perhaps this gives an even better opportunity to admire the graceful proportions and the details of the decoration. All sorts of devices have been used to give

A pensive beast at Marino Casino

the required impressions of symmetry. For example, the doors in the apse of the hall are themselves curved to follow the semi-circular wall, and one of them leads nowhere: its sole purpose is to balance its companion which really does open.

A relatively small and simple stairway leads to the top storey. The centrepiece is the opulent State Room which has a screen of columns and a frieze with gilded details. In contrast, the other rooms at this level are relatively simple and comfortable. The windows offer good views of the sky, being concealed from outside view by the upper walls. Curious details of the placing of the windows are apparent at this level, some being used to light two rooms. In addition, and in order that the general appearance of the Casino would not be marred by unsightly downpipes or gargoyles, some of the great columns are hollow and bring the roof water down to the basement; at one time it went out through the smiling mouths of the lions.

The Casino's surroundings are less spacious than when it was built, but a visit today to a building so clearly cherished by its custodians still gives a sense of the elegant side of life in Georgian Dublin.

Grid 1736, Sheet 50. Well supplied with public transport: buses 20A, 20B, 27, 27A, 27B, 42, 42C, 123 Imp, and the DART to Clontarf Road Station. The access road is a little way past the building itself in the Malahide direction and is signposted from the main road. Sufficient space for exercise of undemanding dogs — but not ideal — and the Casino may not impress very young humans. Food is far distant and the car park is rather small and not inviting for picnics. Be sure to buy the excellent booklet by Seán O'Reilly with its beautiful illustrations old and new. Open: February to the end of November, 12.00 noon to 3.15 p.m. (longer hours in spring and summer). Admission — by guided tour only — for a modest fee on Sundays. Wheelchair access to ground floor only.

St Fiachra's Garden

The Liffey at Islandbridge

The Bronze Age wedge tomb in Massy's Wood

The rose garden of Ardgillan Castle

Blessington Lake

A classical scene in Avondale House

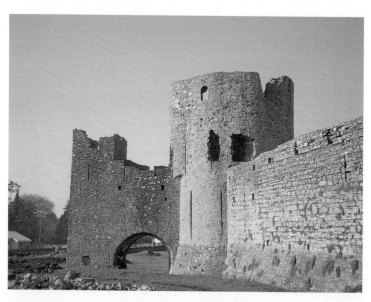

Trim Castle

On the Hill of Tara

Oystercatcher's nest on Ireland's Eye

The Martello Tower on Dalkey Island

Where the Grand Canal joins the Liffey

Pandora and Bella on the Great South Wall

Fern fronds opening in Massy's Wood

A heron fishing on the lower Dodder

Peat hag on Kippure

The official Source of the Liffey

Drimnagh Castle

The Longmile Road, a busy dual carriageway, flanked by a conglomeration of factories and retail parks, would seem to be low on the list of addresses for a delightful Sunday afternoon. Nevertheless, a very remarkable oasis waits in this industrial desert. A discreet signpost a quarter of a mile from the Naas Road junction indicates Drimnagh Castle. Behind the brick buildings of the Christian Brothers' school, the Castle stands. To this day it is protected by a moat, though the drawbridge was replaced by a solid stone structure in the eighteenth century.

The moat, a diversion of the nearby Bluebell Stream, is filled with clear water, flowing beside the tall stone walls of the gate-house and outer defences. An archway, closed by a great wooden door, gives access to the Castle across the bridge. The arch leads into a courtyard, surrounded on three sides by stone buildings, while the fourth opens into a well-kept garden. The oldest part of the complex is the keep, the rectangular building to the left of the gate tower, which dates to the thirteenth century when the Barnewall family first made it their headquarters.

The original front door is so low that most present-day visitors have to stoop to enter. People are much taller now than in the thirteenth century and, besides, a hostile visitor was much easier to deal with if he had to bend down. Inside the same door, there is a square opening in the ceiling — the 'murder hole' — through which a defender could, with a minimum of effort, dispatch an unwanted guest. The lowest storey of the Castle has a vaulted ceiling and is a gloomy room. Its purpose was mainly to store food for people and animals and also to provide shelter in times of attack.

The character of the next storey is completely different: a generously proportioned hall with a high ceiling. When the keep was built, it too would have been dimly lit within, because the original windows were narrow slits. For many generations, the descendants of the Anglo-Norman invaders felt far from secure, and their dwellings were planned for ease of defence rather than for comfort. The seventeenth century appeared to be more promising, and many wealthy landowners, including the Barnewalls, rebuilt their castles to incorporate big, bright, mullioned windows. This hall was the centre of life in the Castle, where the lord of the manor held court and entertained family, friends and neighbours.

Drimnagh Castle was continuously inhabited from the time it was built until 1954, when the last private owners, the Hatch family, departed. Subsequently, the Castle's fabric began to decay, and, by 1986, the hall was in ruins with no roof or upper floors. A variety of local and national organisations rallied to the latter-day defence of Drimnagh. Under the inspired leadership of the architect and historian Peter Pearson, restoration began, with much of the work carried out by FÁS trainees and local craftsmen. The great hall today is a worthy tribute to what can be achieved and clear evidence that modern Irish craft-workers are every bit as skilled as those of the remote past, besides being equal to the best in any country. Most of the tiles on the floor, 5,500 of them, are modern ceramics made in Dublin, in 1991, though those nearest the door come from St Andrew's Church in Suffolk Street.

The galleries, which surround the great hall, are made from Irish oak and constructed in the old style, using wooden pegs and joints rather than nails. The owners, in the seventeenth century, had imported an English sandstone for the fireplace, which contrasts with the local limestone used for the greater part of the Castle. Damage and decay over the centuries have been repaired with modern carving.

Any sculpture in wood that might have been present in the old building has long since disappeared. The roof line above the gallery, however, is richly decorated — but with completely modern work. The marvellous array of wood carving is the creation of Conor Rushe. As did his forbears in medieval times, the sculptor used his contemporaries for models, and the features seen here today are those of local residents, and people who were involved in the restoration work.

The old roof had also disappeared, but the type of structure used is known from surviving timbers in Dunsoghly Castle, near Finglas. Oak from County Roscommon was cut by hand and assembled with timber dowels to make a new ceiling for Drimnagh. The only concession to modern technology was to assemble the roof on the ground and use a crane to lift it into position.

All good castles have ghosts and Drimnagh is haunted by the Lady Eleanora, who lived there 500 years ago. She was a Barnewall but fell in love with Seán O'Byrne from the Wicklow Mountains. Eleanora was betrothed to a Barnewall relative and was on her way to be married in Dublin when the O'Byrnes ambushed the wedding party. Seán slew his rival, but was killed himself by the bride's father. Later, Eleanora slipped away from the Castle and was found dead on the grave of her true love.

The tower was added to the keep in the sixteenth century and the range of buildings to the left — where you can have tea and buy postcards — were built two hundred years after that. Together they made a very comfortable dwelling for a family of wealthy landowners.

Just outside the Castle courtyard, the old garden has been beautifully restored. It is laid out in the style of the seventeenth century with a geometrical arrangement of box hedges and a carefully pruned bay tree in each section.

Drimnagh Castle, the thirteenth-century gate tower and sixteenth-century additions

Grid O1132, Sheet 50. Bus 18, 58A, 210, car parking in castle grounds. Lovely for children, not good for dogs. The custodians, at the time of writing, were engaged in a brave effort to repel the invading citizenry with severely restricted admission. What was worse, from time to time, the authorities considered it more important to close the Castle for private functions than to abide by the terms of their own notice of admission times — meaning that a trip to darkest Drimnagh could be a frustrating occasion, necessitating a diversion to a more forthcoming venue such as Phoenix Park. But the Drimnagh restoration is such a fine achievement that the risk of facing a barred door is still worth taking. And perhaps it is comforting to reflect that, in these enlightened days, a polite but firm refusal of admission has taken the place of boiling oil or a shower of arrows from the battlements. Open: winter, 2.00 p.m. to 5.00 p.m., summer, 12.00 noon to 5.00 p.m. — but confirm by phoning 01-4502530. Fee charged, wheelchair access to ground level only, teas served.

Parks

Parks began their lives as exclusive domains for kings and nobles. As time went by, some members of these classes engaged in altruistic enterprises to welcome the populace to their property — with or without charging a fee for the privilege. The first, and still the greatest, of these acts was the opening of Phoenix Park in 1747. Powerscourt came later and retains the status of a private estate.

The eighteenth and nineteenth centuries saw the establishment of the Botanic Gardens and the Zoo, respectively. Both were essentially educational establishments, conceived to reveal to the people the wonders of nature. The Botanic Gardens had a practical side as well, in the days when virtually all medical practice was based on herbal remedies.

The twentieth century witnessed the erosion of the properties of the great landlords. Many were simply divided amongst the former tenants. But some were either presented to the State or acquired by government or local authorities. The National Stud and Japanese Gardens were a gift from their owner to the Crown — in due course made over to the Free State.

The practice of the Land Commission, when one of its acquisitions included an area of woodland, was to allow state forestry to manage the parcel. Three of the parks, Avondale, Knocksink and Massy's Wood, belong to this category and their primary use has changed from experimental or production forestry to providing space for quiet enjoyment.

Ardgillan Castle is an example of the vision of the 1970s, when local authorities were encouraged to buy great demesnes that came on the market, restore them where necessary, and make them fit for a discerning public. The results have been entirely delightful and a credit to the designers, craftsmen and gardeners.

Ardgillan Demesne

An avenue of ancient ash trees opens suddenly to reveal one of the most stunning views in Ireland. A great expanse of green lawn rolls down the hillside to end in a line of Irish yew; beyond this is a herbaceous border and a long, low castle with a garden and conservatory to its left. The Castle is flanked by trees and backed by the sea, with the Mountains of Mourne away to the north.

The name Ardgillan — *Árd choill* — means the High Wood, and it commemorates the forest that once covered these steep slopes above the sea, a little to the north of Skerries. Today, there is more lawn than woodland, but trees are in evidence everywhere — lining the old field boundaries or forming delightful shady copses. Beside the Castle are beautiful gardens, more rolling lawns and more views of the Irish Sea, with the picture-postcard islets of Rockabill and their lighthouse — the sort of scene that is so often created by popular painters that it comes as a surprise to see it in reality.

Ardgillan has a long history of landscaping and a remarkable family archive. This material has been skilfully presented, in a well-illustrated booklet, by members of a FÁS team which operated there in the 1990s. The story begins in Cromwellian times when Thomas Taylor, a wealthy English surveyor, came to Ireland to work as a deputy to William Petty on the Down Survey. Taylor had not served as a soldier of the Commonwealth and received no tracts of Irish land. However, he had clearly been so attracted by the country that he sold his estate in England. With the proceeds he bought some 21,000 acres in Ireland from supporters of Cromwell, who had been granted Irish estates and wanted to capitalise on them.

In 1738, his grandson, Robert, a wealthy minister of the Established Church, built a modest family home in the townland of Ardgillan. With a certain lack of originality, he named it Prospect House. Nearly a century later, in 1815, another cleric, Reverend Edward Taylor, had the house enlarged to its present size. He followed the fashion of the time by adding the military-style decoration and changing the name of his dwelling to Ardgillan Castle. The Taylor family continued to live there until 1962 and, over the generations, many of them distinguished themselves in public life and some married talented writers and artists.

The Taylors sold the house and grounds to Heinrich Pott, a German industrialist to whom it was a second home. Following his death, in 1966, his family used it as a holiday home, and maintenance lapsed seriously. In 1981, Dublin County Council, engaged in creating a number of public parks, bought the demesne and set to work on its restoration. The grounds, with no less than 5 miles of footpaths that have been either renovated or created anew, were opened to the people in 1986. The Castle was opened in 1992 and work on the gardens is still in progress.

The first of two car parks is at Blackhills, to the right of the ash avenue at the entrance. It gives a fine view over Skerries and allows a delightful walk down to the Castle — the scene changing at every step as the Castle looms higher and the details of its terraces and borders become apparent. The second car park is in woodland at the bottom of the hill, level with the Castle, and gives access to picnic tables and the view of Rockabill.

A fork in the path at the second car park gives a choice of either proceeding to the Castle or to the gardens. Both ways ultimately lead to the gardens and neither should be missed, as each has a character of its own. The upper path goes between the yew walk on the left and a superb herbaceous border on the right. It begins by concealing a blank wall and continues along terraced lawns that lead to the garden in front of the Castle itself. The yew walk was created by Mrs Marianne Taylor in the first decade of the nineteenth century. Nearly 200 years old, the trees remain strong and healthy and are probably the oldest living plants on the demesne. Common yew grows in the woodland nearby; the distinctive feature of 'Irish yew' is its upright, pillar-like habit. It can be propagated only from cuttings and all of those at Ardgillan are descended from two specimens discovered and nurtured by George Willis, in Florencecourt, County Fermanagh, in the 1740s.

The rose garden and greenhouse at Ardgillan

Beyond the Castle lie the marvellous gardens. Created in the nineteenth century, they were carefully tended by generations of the family until the 1960s, after which they became overgrown. In 1983, the County Council began the long task of restoration. The rose garden is laid out in two parts, separated by a pergola with climbers. The west section is centred on a fountain and lily pond with the roses arranged in curved beds around it. The scheme is a large number of separate beds, each planted with one variety of rose. At close quarters, they appear as masses of single colours while the impression from a little distance is of a multi-coloured carpet.

The white conservatory, that stands at the bottom of the rose garden, was built in the 1880s for a garden in Malahide and was presented to the Parks Department of the County Council by its owners.

Next to the rose garden is the walled garden, two acres in extent. Its purpose was to provide fruit and vegetables for the house and also for sale. It is subdivided by brick walls and a beech hedge and the restorers have created five compartments. In one of these various green vegetables grow, each in a small plot of its own fenced in by a box hedge — the crops themselves are made to look ornamental. In another, there is an Irish garden, containing both plant varieties native to Ireland and plants which were named in honour of Irish collectors. Two free-standing brick walls were built to support fruit trees. The walls provide both warmth and shelter, and delicate sub-tropical fruits such as peaches could be grown there.

Between the two gardens, the head steward's house now serves as a tea room that specialises in scones and good food, all baked on the spot. A side gate from the walled garden offers a way back to the house, overlooking another rolling lawn and a long-established patch of woodland called the Dell. It is marked on George Conroy's 1844 map of the demesne, as, indeed, are most of the fringes of trees that still are still growing there.

One of the demesne's pathways leads down to the Lady's Stairs — a footbridge over the railway to the sea shore. When the Dublin to Drogheda railway was built in 1844, it ran for some way through the Ardgillan property and cut off the access to the sea shore. Reverend Edward Taylor imposed conditions on the railway company requiring them to build a bridge so that he and the family would continue to have safe and easy access to their bathing place. They also won the right to have the trains stop at their lower entrance gate. The seaside part of the demesne today is partly left as 'wilderness', so that wild flowers are able to grow, and partly kept as a picnic place. A little cliff of glacial till stands above a stony shore, which strips out at low tide to reveal outcrops of limestone and patches of firm sand.

The Castle interior has been painted and polished and supplied with a collection of eighteenth- and nineteenth-century furniture and paintings. These are the subject of a guided tour which takes half an hour. Some of the bedrooms are used for temporary exhibitions from time to time.

Grid O2260, Sheet 43. Clearly signposted off N1, 3 miles north of Swords. Bus 33 stops at the Lady's Stairs where there is a pedestrian entrance. Buggy-friendly, wheelchair access to gardens and ground floor. A delight for children and dogs on leads. Very good tearooms. Open: Castle — winter, 11.00 a.m. to 4.30 p.m.; summer, 11.00 a.m. to 6.00 p.m. Park — winter, 10.00 a.m. to 5.00 p.m.; summer 10.00 a.m. to 9.00 p.m. Admission charge to Castle.

Avondale

The Mecca of Irish forestry, Avondale is perhaps the slough of
despond for extreme greens. It was here that the dreaded sitka
spruce proved its ability to outgrow any native tree, an achievement
which led to the blue-greening of many an Irish mountainside. To
ordinary mortals Avondale is an exquisite woodland park on a
hillside, with history in the shape of the home of Charles Stewart
Parnell at the top, and untamed nature in the Avonmore river at the
bottom.

The solid geology of Avondale is something of a nightmare.
Criss-crossed with fault lines, the rocks are of Ordovician age —
younger than the ancient shales and quartzites of Bray and
Greystones which lie a little to the north. After the rock was
initially formed from silty deposits in shallow coastal waters, the
titanic upheavals which formed the Wicklow Mountains began.
Volcanoes were widespread and the rocks were shattered by
earthquakes. The resulting formations, diorite and dolerite, can be
seen exposed in the cliffs of the Avonmore valley — diorite
outcrops just to the north of where the railway line crosses the
forest path and dolerite to the east of the Avondale House. Parnell
established the quarry at Avonmore that is still in operation — a

grey gash in the green hillside across the valley from the entrance to the park.

The complexity of the underlying rock masses, with hard material side by side with soft, helps to explain the dramatic scenery of this area. Outcrops of tough rock forced the river to take sharp bends and to cut its way downwards steeply in places, sometimes forming sheer cliffs. In the ice age, a glacier flowed from the higher mountains to the north-west, carrying with it enormous granite boulders which it dumped in the valley. Some of these have been collected and built into a cairn in the forest garden. A bigger one stands by the footpath near the river, but the finest of all, the Mottee Stone, lies outside the demesne on a hillside of Cronebane about a mile to the south-east.

After the ice receded, oak forest grew on the slopes of Avondale and ancient farmers subsequently cleared much of it to make grazing pasture. In the seventeenth century, any worthwhile woodland that remained was felled and the hillsides remained bare until the demesne became the property of Samuel Hayes in the latter half of the eighteenth century. He was the pioneer of re-afforestation in Ireland. In 1788, as MP for Wicklow, he introduced a Bill to the Irish Parliament 'for encouraging the cultivation and better preservation of trees'. In 1788, the Dublin Society published his beautifully illustrated, *A Practical Treatise on Planting and the Management of Woods and Coppices*. Hayes developed his demesne as a productive forest and a few of the trees he planted are still alive and well. The single Spanish chestnut to the south of the House, the two huge silver firs near the river to the north of the railway bridge and some of the big beeches date to his time.

The big House was built by Hayes, in 1777, and he died there in 1795. The property then passed into the possession of the Parnell family. Charles Stewart was born there in the summer of 1846 and, in the course of time, became an enthusiastic owner and developer of the forest. A double tragedy for Avondale occurred with the death of the leader, in 1891, and the subsequent sale of the property to a butcher. Having felled most of the trees, this man sold out to the Government in 1904 when the resurrection of Avondale began.

A.C. Forbes, the Director of Forestry, together with Augustine Henry, a medical man who became a tree collector and was finally appointed Professor of Forestry at Cambridge, conceived the plan for an experimental forest garden. They also had the artistic spirit which allowed them to design a beautiful arboretum at the same time. In 1907, one-acre strips of the hillside were planted, each with a single species of a timber-producing tree. The strips lie parallel in two ranks facing each other across the Great Ride, a magnificent sward of mown grass which is the central feature of the park. A little way out from the end of each strip, a single tree of the species was planted on its own. The main mass of the planting was to show how the trees would develop in forest conditions, and the lone trees were given space so that landscape architects could judge their appearance as single plantings.

Avondale House

Nearly a hundred years after the creation of the forest garden, many of the trees still stand and have developed into magnificent specimens. Others perished — wind-blown or damaged by disease or simply proving to be so slow-growing that the more successful species seeded themselves and took over the plots. The first 30 years or so of cultivation showed that the sitka spruce would out-strip any of the others and this led to its establishment as the darling of State forestry — and anathema to those who want to see more of broadleaf planting, particularly of native oak and ash.

Avondale suffered a period of neglect for some decades when the State was less than enthusiastic about long-term research projects. Fortunately, more enlightened views developed in the 1960s, and both House and grounds were taken in hand again. The best rooms in the House were restored to the style of Parnell's time and display a collection of memorabilia. The remainder was refurbished to serve as a training centre and a wooden residence (imported cedar, not native timber, alas) was built. The garden was restored and, close to the House, deer pens and a pond to cater for wild duck were added.

The forest plots still provide information for research workers but, more and more, Avondale has become a delightful place for relaxation. From spring to autumn the House is open to visitors who can also avail of the snack bar. The park remains open throughout the year and is usually busy in summer. As it is visited by relatively few people in winter, those who want to can enjoy solitary walks among the trees. The Pine Trail and the Exotic Tree trail are relatively short but the River Walk is about 4 miles long. It includes part of the Great Ride and then goes downhill to the railway line. The ruined buildings that can be seen there are the remains of a water-powered sawmill and these are followed by a particularly pleasing stretch between forest and river. Samuel Hayes's two silver firs grow here — one on either side.

The trees to the left of the path include the two species of redwood from California which live for thousands of years. Popular since the mid-nineteenth century in Ireland as single-specimen trees, they are seldom seen in their forest form. These giants of Avondale are mere infants and it remains to be seen whether the future of Ireland will be stable enough to allow them to grow for the next three millennia.

Close to the trail, the clear water of the Avonmore is a favoured haunt of the dipper, an extraordinary black bird with a white bib. Usually seen perched on stones in the stream, and often singing a quiet song, it disappears beneath the surface now and then to hunt for insects on the river bed. By holding its wings at a particular angle, the dipper uses the current to stay submerged as it walks over the stones. Sometimes a pair of goosander visit Avondale. The goosander is a fish-eating species of duck — the drake easily recognised by its mainly white plumage. An extremely rare resident in Ireland, it seems to enjoy life in south County Wicklow.

After the river, the main footpath branches, allowing short or long walks, up the side of the valley amongst a splendid variety of exotic trees, to the House and car park.

Grid T1986, Sheet 62, Clearly signposted at the crossroads to the south of Rathdrum. Miles and miles of buggy-friendly paths, though the River Trail does descend steeply over rough ground in places. A good deal of level ground manageable by wheelchairs. Safe for dogs and children, but restraint of dogs is requested. House (with restaurant) open: 11.00 a.m. to 5.00 p.m. from St Patrick's Day to end October, except Good Friday. Admission charge. Large car park open all the time, endless picnic spots.

The Botanic Gardens

According to the eminent botanist Phyllis Clinch, Glasnevin is derived from the Irish *Glaisín aoibhinn* meaning 'pleasant little field'. *Glas* means 'green' but it is an adjective rather than a noun. Patrick Weston Joyce thought differently, saying that *glaise, glais* or *glas* means 'a small stream'. That sounds better and is accepted by Ó Dónaill's modern dictionary. But Joyce unwisely conjures 'an old pagan chief' by the name of Naeidhe to help with the 'nevin' bit. The matter is further complicated by the view of the Irish Placenames Commission, cited in their beautiful and scholarly book on the Gardens by Charles Nelson and Eileen McCracken. The Placenames people assert Glas Naoin, 'the stream of the infants'. Not knowing who the infants were and taking the topography into account, 'pleasant little stream' might be a better rendition — and a fitting title for the valley, occupied for just over two hundred years by the most delightful National Botanic Gardens.

The Gardens need to be seen and experienced rather than described. Within their bounds are various entities. The most botanical is the 'order beds' in which the flowers are arranged according to their scientific classification for the benefit of students and academics. They bring to life the dry world of the taxonomical textbook with its attention to the disposition and numbers of stamens, petals, leaves and branches, to say nothing of whether the pistil be syncarpous or apocarpous, the ovary inferior or superior and sundry similar attributes. The foundation of the Glasnevin gardens, in 1796, took place 18 years after the death of Carl von Linné, the Swedish naturalist who had developed the modern system of classification of flora and fauna. The order beds at the Botanic Gardens still adhere to his basic principles.

Classification of plants and animals, to this day, is an essential factor in the study and treatment of disease. Every species has its own particular chemical make-up and precise identification is essential to the extraction of drugs — medicinal and otherwise. This aspect of botany had been the main impetus behind the establishment of botanic gardens throughout Europe and was a significant factor in the foundation of the site at Glasnevin.

But it was far from the only one. The Gardens were founded and maintained by the Dublin Society. The members responsible included: John Foster, Speaker of the Irish House of Commons, Samuel Hayes of Avondale, and leading botanists such as Walter Wade. Foster's interest was that of a public figure concerned with creating things of beauty for the benefit and education of the citizens. Both Foster and Hayes were pioneers in the afforestation of their estates. Wade's interest was primarily in plants for their own sake. All were inveterate collectors with boundless enthusiasm for bringing together as many exotic species as could be obtained. Before the purchase, in 1795, of the land for the Botanic Gardens, the valley was already distinguished for its private gardens, established by Thomas Tickell on the right bank and Dr Delany on the left.

So, from the start, the Gardens encompassed a great deal more than a simple demonstration of the classification and variety of the species of plants. Specimen trees already growing on the estate were treasured and a large area of the Gardens was set aside as an arboretum. Well-regimented flower beds, with convenient paths between them, were set out and herbaceous borders developed. A dwelling house on the old estate was retained and remains to this day as the Director's home. The first glasshouse was built at Glasnevin just three years after the Gardens began.

From the very start, the Gardens were conceived as an amenity for the public and no admission charge has ever been made. They were also a teaching institution, with Wade delivering very popular lectures. A yew walk and the great cedar of Lebanon survive from those early days.

A cycad in the Curvilinear Glasshouse

The dominant feature of the Gardens is the palm house, standing taller than many of the trees. Built in 1884, it is a lovely, warm and steamy place on a cold day and gives a hint of the atmosphere of a tropical forest. But the Gardens' great pride is the long, low range of conservatory to the north. This, the Curvilinear

Glasshouse is a triumph both of nineteenth-century engineering and of late twentieth-century restoration. Designed and constructed by the Dublin iron master, Richard Turner, a few years before the Great Famine, it presents everything that a Victorian public garden could want. The proof of that lies in the fact that Turner was also commissioned to undertake major works in Kew Gardens and the Botanic Gardens in Belfast.

His masterpiece in Glasnevin suffered for some time from a lack of adequate maintenance but was rescued in the 1980s by a decision of its managers, the Office of Public Works, to fund a complete restoration. No expense was spared and no short-cuts taken. The gracefully curved panes of glass, prepared to order for Turner, were replaced with identical work. The multitudinous layers of paint, which had almost obliterated the ornaments in the original cast iron, were sand-blasted away to reveal the delicacy of the castings. Within this fine building, pride of place is given to the cycads, plants of a type now scarce, reduced from their ancient domination of the forests where the dinosaurs roamed.

The layout of the Gardens today does not follow the original plan but has held, with very little variation, to the design of Ninian Niven. Appointed Curator in 1834 and serving for just four years, Niven was a landscape architect and gardener of genius. His artistry made brilliant use of the natural hills and flood plain of the Tolka valley in which the Gardens lie. Niven's work can be seen in many gardens throughout Ireland but remarkably little is known of the man other than his Scottish birth.

At the time that Turner was building his glasshouses, the potato famine raged in Ireland and the Botanic Gardens played its part in attempts to eradicate the blight. In 1845, the Curator, David Moore, embarked on a series of experiments to find out how the disease was transmitted. Although his discoveries failed to save the crops in the famine years, they made a very significant contribution to understanding the cause, and laid the foundation for its successful treatment.

The glasshouses make the Gardens a perfect place to visit on a wet or wintry Sunday. Besides cycads and palms and tree ferns, they contain glorious orchids, cacti and succulents, as well as alpines, to say nothing of citrus fruits and bananas. In spring, the colours are those of magnolias and sheets of daffodils, together with blue and white anemones. As the year goes on, the herbaceous borders and the rose garden are the places where the finest colours lie. The formal beds and borders and glasshouses are near the centre of things and that is where most of the visitors congregate. A little way off are the trees of the arboretum and paths where you can wander almost in solitude.

Besides the restoration work, the 1990s saw major developments in new and very attractive buildings. The first was the herbarium and library, conceived for the nurturing of students and scholars. The herbarium contains many thousands of specimens of pressed flowers and other plants, that have been accumulating there since the eighteenth century. The beauty of the generally straw-coloured specimens is appreciated by few people outside the realms of the specialist but they have been the very basis of understanding the nature of the world of plants.

The second new building has infinitely greater appeal to the uninitiated. It contains a public restaurant — the only entity that was lacking from the Gardens throughout the twentieth century. Having regaled mind and soul with the beauties of trees and flowers, the National Botanic Gardens now offer solace for the body of the citizen — deliciously and in delightful surroundings.

Grid 12F OS Dublin City Map (16th ed.) Bus 19. Buggy- and wheelchair-friendly but definitely no dogs. Open: winter, 11.00 a.m. to 4.30 p.m.; summer, 11.00 a.m. to 6.00 p.m. Admission free, excellent restaurant. Good car parking to the left of the old entrance gate.

Knocksink Wood

A secluded valley, with a stream and an abundance of woodland birds and flowers, accessible by faintly adventurous paths. Suitable at any time of year, occupies half a day.

Knocksink Bridge is marked in very small print on the map, and Knocksink Wood lies in one of the most securely hidden river valleys of County Wicklow. The Glencullen River runs through the broad, open valley which separates Two Rock from Prince William's Seat. The hidden part lies in a deep cleft upstream of the bridge which carries the main road from the Scalp to Enniskerry. On the right bank of the valley is Patrick Byrne's splendid church which was one of the earliest Gothic Revival buildings in Ireland and was built in the early 1840s. The main valley, running north-west to south-east follows a geological fault line which goes right across the Wicklow Mountains. A parallel fault to the south has created the upper part of Glenasmole.

The entrance to the wood is not only discreet, but situated on one of the worst of the very bad bends on the road. It is best approached uphill from the church, where Knocksink Wood National Nature Reserve is announced on a sign board and the path climbs high above the river to gain access to the valley. At this point, the river runs along the foot of a cliff which, in places, had to be excavated to provide enough level ground for the road. Where the bank is vertical, it shows bare earth —a yellowish brown clay with many stones embedded. This is glacial till, deposited by the lowland ice which flowed down the Irish Sea basin and covered the lower slopes of the mountains. Farther up the valley, the till was derived from a local mountain glacier which fed in to the great ice field below.

From its highest point, the road descends into a lovely woodland of ash, hazel and birch, covering the sides of the hidden valley. Within the wood, there is a parking place close to the river. The large, but unobtrusive, building on the right is the National Environmental Education Centre. Built by the Office of Public Works in 1993, it is an interesting construction: a big bright central courtyard with a glass roof, bordered on both sides by offices, classrooms, laboratories and exhibition space. The present Centre was set up in 1998 as a joint initiative of Dúchas, the Heritage Service, and the Dublin Institute of Technology. The staff provide talks, demonstrations and guided walks for education at every level — from mixed infants to post-graduates and adult education groups. Essentially a normal working hours service, the Centre frequently opens on Saturdays and Sundays to cater for specially arranged visits.

John Taylor's 1816 map of the *Environs of Dublin* shows nothing of this area besides the steep-sided valley — apparently devoid of trees. A house on the hillside at Killegar is completely isolated. The 6-inch map of 1912 draws a very different picture. The valley is shown as Knocksink Wood and woodland extends along its flanks, with much the same distribution of trees as exists today. Three footpaths are shown, two following the river as closely as possible, the third higher up the hill to the east. Most significant is a path leading away to Killegar House. Evidently, its owners had followed the lead of many of their nineteenth-century contemporaries and created a woodland retreat on a steep and soggy part of their estate. The better land above the valley provided valuable grazing for cattle and horses and was not to be sacrificed for recreation.

Some of the trees of the demesne days survive: the splendid Scots pines which stand like sentinels above the river on the access road, two oaks down at the car park and a goodly scattering of fine trees more or less hidden amongst the younger ones. The oak beside the training centre was inadvertently assaulted and nearly killed by the builders. They had treated the tree with the respect it deserved, but JCBs and other things compacted the soil round about and nearly suffocated it. Remedial efforts were successful, and the oak, a sprightly centenarian, seems set to outlive even the youngest of its present-day admirers.

From the centre onward, cars are forbidden, and there are many footpaths. Up to the 1980s, there were two bridges so that you could make a convenient round trip up and down the valley. However, a flood carried them away leaving nothing but some rough masonry on either side. Concrete stepping stones now allow a dry-shod crossing to be effected where the bridges once stood — at least these facilitate such steps when the river is at its normal lowish level. At times of flood, stepping stones and practically everything else are obliterated by a brown torrent which has been known even to pick up and carry away the large concrete slabs.

The Glencullen River in Knocksink Wood

The riverside footpath heading downstream leads to the narrowest part of the valley where mature oak trees abound. An outcrop of rock — the Ordovician greywacke which borders the Wicklow granite — forces the river to take a sharp bend to the right. Just upstream of the outcrop, where the river loses strength and speed, huge granite boulders have piled up and created a small waterfall which is quite impressive when the river is in spate. Beyond this point, the rock confines the stream to a narrow gorge and the footpaths have to climb higher. Farther downstream, close to the bridge, the bedrock changes — according to the geological map — to a pleasantly-named 'buff coloured tuff'. Formed from volcanic ash about the time the Wicklow Mountains arose, this very unusual rock extends over the floor of the Enniskerry valley.

The oak wood is old, practically untouched and, besides being home to ferns, wild garlic, holly and other woodland plants, is a place to look for two very rare flowers: bird's nest orchid and yellow archangel. The orchid is a drab plant, brown stem and brown flowers, but very interesting because it lives on dead leaves rather than depending on sunlight. Gorse can be found in abundance as can frochans.

Upstream of the car park, there are several paths leading along the river bank and up the sides of the valley. Birch, ash and hazel predominate, all of them native species. Together with oak, elder, alder, holly and rowan they constitute one of most exciting features of the glen. After the almost total destruction of the Irish woodlands in the seventeenth century, much of the re-generation was of imported species — beech, Scots pine and sycamore having done particularly well. Then the twentieth century saw the arrival of the even more successful North American conifers: sitka spruce, Douglas fir and western hemlock among others. Beech and Douglas fir have been planted farther up the valley — the beech in the days of private ownership and the firs when Knocksink Wood was Forest Service property.

A woodland in which most of the trees are native gives some idea of how the Irish forests used to look; although, in Knocksink, most of the stems have grown up from coppicing and are relatively young. Such woods provide a habitat for birds and for many of the wild flowers and insects associated with the native trees of Ireland. From early spring to autumn, Knocksink Wood is rich with bird song and, even in winter, thrushes, robin and wren continue to sing. Blackcap, willow warbler, chiffchaff and blackbird all add to the chorus from March or April onwards.

Finally there are the stones. The two rival glaciers that met in the valley each carried their share of till; this was dumped when they finally melted away and it filled the original valley. Ever since then, the Glencullen River has been carrying the glacial till away, trying to find its own valley once again. The silt and sandy particles from the till have, for the most part, been carried away to sea; but the stones remain in a marvellous variety: mountain glacier-carried granite, quartz and mica schist. The granite is in the form of large boulders because it came from nearby and could not be easily broken up in the time that the ice had to work on it. The Irish Sea ice brought flints from Antrim, pebbles of purple sandstone from Portraine and, from Lambay, a blue-grey porphyry speckled with cream-coloured crystals. These need to be searched for. The more plentiful stones are limestone from north Dublin and greywacke from closer to hand.

Grid O2117, Sheet 56. Bus 44. Knocksink is a treasure-house, open to all. Some buggy-friendly paths and a board-walk specially to allow wheelchair users to enjoy the 'nature garden' at the car park. Most of the paths upstream of the car park are safe and easy going. Paths downstream in the narrow valley need care. Free from sheep and ideal for dogs. Delightful picnic spot. Open: October to March, 8.30 a.m. to 5.30 p.m.; summer, 8.30 a.m. to 9.00 p.m.

Massy's Wood

Massy's Wood is a slightly unknown but altogether entrancing valley on the lower slopes of Killakee Mountain, in the townlands of Jamestown and Killakee. Numerous footpaths are well maintained by its owners, Coillte. These lead up and down, and round about the two streams in the valley and are shaded by fine trees except in the mid-regions where a deserted garden still shows traces of its nineteenth-century days of glory.

There are so many paths that a step-by-step guide would be tedious in the extreme. The only way to approach Massy's Wood is to visit it again and again, wandering in a different direction each time. Some paths are shown on the 6-inch map of 1937, but not all of them have survived. Others are marked on the 1:50,000 sheet of 1995, but it is far from complete; perhaps the trees defeated the best efforts of the aerial survey to detect them. Most of the paths, though some are steep, can take buggies. It is easy to lose your way but the wood is small enough — a mile and a half long by a quarter of a mile wide — to make it relatively easy to find it again.

Valley and wood lie in a north–south direction and the car park is about half way along their western edge. The paths from it lead down into the valley, through a beautiful and very unusual plantation. Most of the trees are broad-leaved, planted in the 1930s: Spanish chestnut, beech and oak. They provide exquisite autumn colours as well as, in winter, bare branches and ground covered with crunchy drifts of fallen leaves. Celandine and wood sorrel brighten the valley in spring, before the trees come into leaf. From an earlier generation of landscaping there are many splendid beeches, some surviving amongst the younger trees, others tracing the lines of old field boundaries or roadways.

An ancient oak on the Military Road in Massy's Wood

The stream, which rises near the summit of Killakee Mountain and joins the Owendoher at Rockbrook, has carved itself a beautiful valley with gorges and waterfalls — on a very small scale but bright with sparkling peat-stained water and luxuriant green ferns. It is cutting its way down through a mantle of glacial till, material deposited by a complex system of glaciers during the last phase of the ice age.

The rock in the upper part of the valley, above the 240-metre contour, is granite. This is the bedrock of the hillside and it extends down to Rockbrook. The ice of a mountain glacier flowed towards the north, breaking up the rock and filling the valley with the glacial till — material ranging from large boulders to finely ground clay. As well as the granite there are some pebbles of diorite, a pale bluish-green rock. Its presence shows that the mountain ice sheet must also have passed over the volcanic hills overlooking Glenasmole.

At the same time as the mountain ice was carrying granite downhill, a colossal ice field was moving southwards over the northern half of Ireland. This eventually collided with the mountain ice in the region of the 240-metre contour. The deposits from this encounter are mainly limestone and its grey pebbles are mixed in with the granite where the two glaciers met and mingled. Stones from both sources lie together in the stream bed.

The first known humans in the valley were the Bronze Age community who lived — or at least buried their dead — on the hill slopes of the Dublin Mountains. One of their tombs was discovered in Massy's Wood in the 1960s and was described by Paddy Ó hÉailidhe. Marked on the 1:50,000 map, it stands beneath a group of great beech trees overlooking the main stream. It is a 'wedge tomb', a low, almost rectangular structure of large granite slabs set on edge and surrounded by a cairn. Many of its stones have been removed and may have been used in the nearby wall.

Downstream of the tomb, a double row of old beech trees marks an abandoned roadway. This is now replaced by a path which leads down into the valley to the great enclosed gardens and the arboretum which was planted outside them. There is a series of orchard and vegetable plots to the south, which have been planted with ash and other trees. Below them lies the tragically abandoned pleasure garden, overgrown with trees and shrubs but with just enough stonework to give an impression of its former beauty. The circular stone pavement to the left of the entrance arch was the foundation of an iron-framed conservatory that was designed by the master, James Turner. In front of it were two fountains and they look up the hill over three terraces whose granite steps are now nearly overgrown. On the top level, a row of evergreens represents the last living survivors of the old days.

A number of superb trees from the nineteenth-century arboretum still stand, however. Some, such as the giant sequoia and the coast redwood were very popular. Others, including the Afghan spruce, with its dangling fronds, are relative rarities. Sadly, a particularly fine Scots pine fell in the storms of 1998.

Something of a ravine lies to the south of the garden, and beyond it a well-built road winds its way up the hill towards the car park. It is paved with carefully-selected pebbles and has a gutter on its outer side. For some of its length, a retaining wall has been set in to the hillside and there is one stone drinking trough. This was the Military Road, built after 1798 and leading in to the depths of the mountains. Most of it is still in use as the main road to Glendalough, but this lower part, which avoids the steep hill on the present road, was abandoned.

A section of the forestry plantation beside the Military Road was clear-felled in the 1990s and replaced with oak trees surrounded by a high fence — protection from the fallow deer which visit the woods from time to time. Up the hill from this are the remnants of an avenue of monkey-puzzles which led from the big house (demolished in 1941) to the pleasure garden.

Early maps show most of the hillside as pasture. At the beginning of the nineteenth century, Luke White, a successful bookseller and financier, purchased an estate of 2,900 acres in the region. He built an elaborate two-storey mansion with a bow front facing out from the hills towards Dublin Bay. His second son, Samuel, inherited the estate in 1824 and is credited with the superb landscaping. The house, together with its parterrre garden at the front to the east, and a straight avenue leading down to the great pleasure garden, are all marked on the 1837 Ordnance Survey map. On Samuel White's death the estate passed to his sister who was married to Baron Massy. The Massy family enjoyed the property for some generations, but the high life proved too expensive for the seventh Baron who was evicted in 1924.

The old woodland was made over to the State forest service and this is where one of the most significant events in the history of the valley took place. From 1936 to 1939, the forest service was directed by a German *Oberforestmeister*, Otto Reinhardt. According to Jack Durand, Reinhardt made no substantial contribution to Irish forestry as a whole — but he most certainly exerted a benign influence on Massy's Woods. He believed that a forest such as this, on the edge of the city of Dublin, should be a place for public enjoyment. So, the woods were blessed with the stands of hard-woods, and provided with level places, free from trees, for camping and picnics. Reinhardt, a reserve officer in the German army had to cut short his work in Ireland, in 1939. He survived the War, but died not long afterwards. Some 60 years after his visit, Massy's Woods stand as a delightful memorial to his influence.

Grid O1223 Sheet 50. Entrance on the Glencree Road at a small unmarked car park on the left, a quarter of a mile up the hill from the Hellfire Club car park. Bus to Rockbrook, south for 400 paces then keep to the right. Dog- and buggy-friendly, heavy going for wheelchairs: paths well-surfaced but steep in places. Perfect for picnics.

Phoenix Park

Parks

Unending space at the end of a short city bus ride, scarcely credible that it is entirely enclosed by city and suburbs. Many visits, occupies half a day

One of the biggest city parks in the world, Phoenix Park has been a public playground for the people of Ireland for more than 250 years. Its area is just over 7 square kilometres and the size alone makes it an exciting place — big enough to fit the entire population of Ireland in comfort. To that may be added some of the finest views of Dublin and its mountains, together with the Zoo, the President's palace, innumerable playing fields and a visitor's centre where they supply lunch and tea as well as information.

Neolithic people buried their dead in the Park and two tombs were discovered during the 1830s at Knockmaree, near the Chapelizod gate. Dated to between 3300 and 3500 BC, some centuries before Newgrange, they were chambers built of large upright stones, each roofed with a massive capstone. About a thousand years later, Bronze Age people used the same site to bury the cremated remains of their dead. Then there is a long gap in knowledge, until the early Christians and, later, the Vikings left traces of their use of the Park in the form of Christian farmsteads and Viking burials.

Written history of the district begins in 1174 when Strongbow granted a huge parcel of land, on both sides of the Liffey, to the

Knights Templar who held it until their suppression by King Edward II, in 1312. Their property was transferred to the Knights of St John of Jerusalem (Knights Hospitallers), a charitable order who provided for the sick and the poor. King Henry VIII seized their property in 1542, and the land continued to be a royal possession for the greater part of the two following centuries.

Early in the seventeenth century, a house was built where the Magazine Fort now stands and, in 1618, this became the official residence of the King's representative in Ireland. In 1662, James Butler, the great Duke of Ormonde, extended the Park and put into effect plans that had been in existence for some time, to create an enclosure for deer. The following year, the building of a wall began. The original was badly built and was subsequently realigned, providing the space which still exists between the Liffey and the Park. Fallow deer were imported from England and a Ranger and two keepers appointed to take care of them.

The Park remained an exclusive royal property until the Earl of Chesterfield was appointed Lord Lieutenant. He was an enthusiast for undertaking public works to provide employment for the poor and one of his schemes was the landscaping of the Park. This included the planting of many stands of trees and the construction of the magnificent avenue that runs through the demesne, in a straight line, from end to end. Its official name is Chesterfield Avenue and it commemorates not only the landscaping, but the fact that, in 1747, the admirable Earl presented the Park to the people of Ireland.

The post of Park Ranger was a high office suitable only for a wealthy noble. On his appointment to the post, in 1751, Nathaniel Clements, a talented architect and one of the developers of eighteenth-century Dublin, built himself a two-storey house with a magnificent garden. His son later sold these to the Government for use as a residence for the Viceroy. Some of the best architects of the time were employed to expand and embellish the Clements dwelling. Its present appearance is largely the work of Francis Johnston who completed his alterations in 1815. In 1937, it became the official residence of the President, changing its name from

Viceregal Lodge to *Áras an Uachtaráin*. Every Saturday, except over Christmas, tours of the Áras are provided free of charge, starting from the nearby Visitors' Centre. Unfortunately, at the time of writing, the tours were not available on Sunday.

While this part of the Park increased in importance in the eighteenth century, maintenance of the public areas left much to be desired. Trees were decaying, the ground was badly drained and boggy, and the roads were in poor order. Remedial work was put in hand early in the nineteenth century and, by 1828, visitors were once again writing of its beauty.

But that was only the beginning. In the 1830s, Decimus Burton was commissioned to undertake a survey of the amenity and recommend improvements. His association with the Park extended over 20 years and much of its present-day appearance reflects his planning. Among other major achievements, he ordered the removal of the high stone walls, which hid the important buildings, and designed the existing entrance gates with their picturesque gate lodges. Since Burton's time, with contributions by a succession of advisers, Park Superintendents, officials in the Office of Public Works and, most recently, Dúchas the Heritage Service, the Park has maintained its splendid appearance.

There are 20 miles of roads within the boundary wall. Cars are second-class citizens, required to observe a speed limit, even on the enticingly straight and broad Chesterfield Avenue. In recent years, a number of the lesser roads have been closed to traffic, providing even more space in which dogs, children, joggers and other mortals are safe to disport themselves. The entire park is a thing of beauty, a pleasure to stop anywhere in, to rest or to wander.

Since 1734, the Magazine Fort occupied the site of the original residence of the King's representative. It was possibly never a great success. Not long after it was built, Swift wrote these lines:

Behold a proof of Irish sense,
Here Irish wit is seen,
When nothing's left that's worth defence,
We build a magazine.

Worse was to come. On 23 December 1939, the IRA successfully raided the Magazine and seized over a million rounds of ammunition. The arms were recovered, but removed to a safer place, and the Fort was left to rest in peace.

James Malton included in his collection a view of the city from the Fort in the 1770s. His print shows a wide expanse of open fields through which the Liffey meanders gently. His was an almost treeless landscape; trees nowadays hide much of the river and block the view to the north. While the Guinness Brewery now occupies centre stage, the Royal Hospital and the spires of St Patrick's and Christ Church Cathedrals are still in view; Lutyens's War Memorial has been added to the scene also. The Fort continues to be one of the finest viewing points in the Park.

From the Magazine Fort, a path called Khyber Road leads through a valley and one of the many woods to the Fifteen Acres. A little stream of crystal clear water debouches from a neatly-built stone channel to run down the valley. Fed by two large drainpipes, it is part of the major nineteenth-century undertaking which replaced open ditches with an underground system.

Reflections of poplars in the Furry Glen pond

165

Construction of the Wellington Testimonial nearby began in 1817, but, although most of the work was completed within three years, it was not finished until 1861. The letters that appear on it, giving the names of the general's famous victories, were melted down from two cannons captured in the Peninsula Wars. The stepped base of the obelisk discourages those who wish to climb, the steps being set at an angle rather than horizontal.

The main entrance gate on Parkgate Street was, at one stage, completely removed but eventually its pillars were restored. The People's Garden, close to the gate, was laid out in 1864, and the charming Gardener's Lodge added in 1867. Popular from their first beginnings, the Gardens with their superb borders and fine specimen trees remain, although slightly hidden, one of the great features of the Park.

The Fifteen Acres is the name of an area of 200 acres of level ground with trees on its margins, maintained as a heavenly stretch of uninterrupted greenery for the pleasure of citizens and their dogs. In September 1979, more than a million people gathered there to greet Pope John Paul II. The tall cross and an inscribed stone at the top of the green mound commemorate the event. The car park beside it is a good spot to begin a walk around the Fifteen Acres.

Phoenix Park, from its first days as a royal deer enclosure, has been an artificial landscape. Nearly every tree was planted by hand — the deer remove any that manage to sprout as seedlings. The lovely shape of the trees, with their branches spreading horizontally at a convenient height, results from the same deer browsing as high as they are able. Old trees are few: the occasional hurricane fells them by the thousand — 2,948 in February 1903, and many more in subsequent storms. Re-planting is in evidence everywhere, every young tree encaged in mesh to protect it from the deer.

The least artificial region of the Park is the Furry Glen — a term probably corrupted from the furze which abounds there. A nineteenth-century causeway has formed a kidney-shaped pond which is now home to moorhen, mallard and sometimes coot and dabchick. The upper part of the valley makes a wooded swamp with hints of a Tolkien landscape.

The most recent development for the public has been the transformation of the grounds of the Under Secretary's Demesne — latterly the residence of the Papal Nuncio — into an outstanding Visitor Centre. The nineteenth-century house had decayed and was demolished, revealing the sixteenth-century castle which had been incorporated within it. The stable yard, in very much better condition, has been converted to an exhibition centre and includes a restaurant. Some of the finest specimen trees grow in the demesne, pride of place going to the wellingtonia: a green memorial to the man, to complement the stone one at the other end of the Park.

If you want to know more about Phoenix Park, two excellent books are on sale at the Centre: *Wild Plants of Phoenix Park* and *Nature in the Phoenix Park*. If you are not a naturalist, do not be deterred by the titles — both provide a wealth of information on the history of the park in addition to details on its wildlife.

Grid 9H, OS Dublin City Map (16th ed.) Buses 9 and 10 to North Circular Road gate, car parking by roadsides nearly everywhere. A haven for dogs, toddlers, picnics — miles and miles of buggy-friendly paths and wheelchair access to all the important parts. Good food at the Visitor Centre.

Powerscourt

One of the most beautiful gardens in the world with a
romantic deer park added in, to say nothing of an
exclusive shopping centre and a stately home to visit.
Allow half a day for gardens and a meal, longer for a
riverside walk.

The gardens and deer park of Powerscourt, the private home of
a wealthy family, have been open to the people for generations and
are a dearly loved place for a picnic. More recently, substantial
parts of the House have been transformed to exclusive shops and a
restaurant which enjoys one of the finest views in Ireland. They
demand at least two Sundays, because the House and garden are
manicured and acceptable to polite persons, while the deer park is
rugged and suitable for dogs and clambering.

The House was built in 1731, to a design by Richard Cassels, the
German architect who conceived a number of the best Irish
houses. From the start it was planned on a grand scale, commissioned by Richard Wingfield, a member of the Irish Parliament
who was later ennobled as the first Viscount Powerscourt of the
third creation.

An accidental fire in 1974 destroyed the roof and most of the
interior. However, the House — completed more than 250 years
before — had been built to last and, after the fire, the walls still
stood in all their magnificence. The rebuilding, in 1996, was a
tremendous achievement and an inspiring reversal of the usual
dismal effects of the twentieth century on the great houses of

Ireland. Furthermore, much of the interior was rebuilt, not as a house, but as an up-market shopping centre with an excellent, and not unduly expensive, restaurant. The latter overlooks the magnificent terraced gardens, designed to incorporate the Great Sugarloaf mountain across the valley. A Mecca to horticulturists, Powerscourt Gardens are, even to the uninitiated, a place of joy. The serenity of the green lawns with their stately trees, fine sculpture and magnificent fountain, combined with the mystery of the deep valley, all conspire to give an almost spiritual experience.

A delightful little book by Alan Mitchell, with illustrations by Jeremy Williams, describes no fewer than 87 species that can be found on a tree trail around the Gardens. In addition, it gives a complete catalogue of the trees on the estate — 229 varieties in all.

Beyond the main car park, presentation of an admission ticket to an electronic scanner opens a gate to the magic Riverside Walk — a slightly unkempt woodland contrasting with the formality of the garden. A steep corkscrew roadway leads through laurels down into the valley of the Dargle. A turn in either direction gives access to picnic tables widely scattered amongst green lawns along a mile of river bank.

The original landscaping is by courtesy of the last glaciation, aided and abetted by the River Dargle. Glacial material filled an older valley and the Dargle has been carrying it away ever since. Man, in the form of the sixth and seventh Viscounts Powerscourt and their estate workers, took a hand a century and a half ago. Between 1867 and 1869, they planted hundreds of trees and, in places, shored up the river bank with retaining walls of large granite boulders. These are placed at the outer curves of the meanders where the current is fastest and is continually trying to cut away the bank.

The finest of the trees are the sequoias or wellingtonias lining the boundary of a field to the south of the entrance (right turn at the bottom of the hill). These giants rightly enjoyed huge popularity amongst landscapers after their introduction to England, in 1853. Virtually every demesne, large or small, had its wellingtonia, and a small number of the great estates planted avenues of them. The Powerscourt collection is one of the best. In February, the fronds are bright with the yellow dots of the male cones. Many other fine trees, together with laurels and rhododendrons, grow by the river banks. Ivy and wild garlic cover the ground beneath them and male fern abounds on the damper, darker banks.

The river gravel is a bewildering conglomeration of stones from the glacial till. Some of them — granite, greywacke and mica schist — have come from nearby, but others, among them limestone and a purple sandstone, have travelled for many miles. In the Powerscourt valley, smallish mountain glaciers met with the colossal ice sheet which travelled down the Irish Sea basin. Between them, they brought to Powerscourt local stones from the mountains, and limestone and sandstone from the coast.

The upstream path leads south, and then west, and ends in an ornamental gate where a lattice-girder bridge crosses the Dargle. Huge laurels grow on either side of the bridge on the right bank, and a fine Monterey cypress is the principal specimen tree on the left. Downstream from the entrance, the path goes through an arboretum, planted in the sandy soil of the flood plain. It ends at the magnificent Golden Gate, the work of the Frenchman, J. Roy. This was put in place, in 1869, at the order of Lord Powerscourt who had seen Roy's work at the Great Exhibition in Paris two years earlier. The pillars were hewn in Glencree by a gentleman named Noble, and the Gate Lodge was built in 1854.

The above facts were set down by the seventh Viscount in a book about the estate — a magnificent and delightful volume, its style a combination of sensitivity with the touch of arrogance that might reasonably be expected of a great Victorian landlord. Justly proud of his record of never evicting a tenant, he makes a less than politically correct comment on one of the landscape contractors, Tom Parnell:

> *He used to say that he could make a road up or down any of the hills which a horse could trot up or down hill on. How much more useful a work than that of his nephew the agitator !*

The entrance to the deer park, and one of Ireland's noblest waterfalls, is 3 miles from the entrance to the House and Gardens, and is approached by the public road rather than through the demesne. It's a lovely hillside drive in its own right.

Wellingtonias by the Dargle in Powerscourt Demesne

The deer in the park are an almost unique variety. By the nineteenth century, the native Irish red deer had long been extinct in Wicklow so the Powerscourt family purchased European red deer and Japanese sika from a park in Germany. Red deer live on heather moors while sika like woodland and, in the wild, they keep away from each other. But in the German park, their close association led to cross-breeding. So, while there are large and small deer in Powerscourt, and elsewhere in the Wicklow Mountains, it seems that none of them nowadays are undoubtedly red or sika, all having some traces of both species in their genetic make-up. But that is of little enough consequence: the big ones are still magnificent and the small ones more delicate and graceful.

Much of the deer park has been planted with forestry over the past two centuries and many fine trees remain from earlier plantings, particularly wellingtonia and oak near the waterfall. Stands of beech, larch and other species grow within the safety of deer fences. But the crowning glory of the deer park is the waterfall, a thin white streak of water cascading down an almost vertical cliff at the head of the valley.

The valley itself was shaped by fire and ice. Hundreds of millions of years ago, continental plates collided, crumpled the ancient rock strata and generated enough heat to melt the deep-seated rock and force it in amongst the greater folds to crystallise slowly and form granite. At the edge of the granite, the older shales were baked and changed to a flaky, shiny schist. This is tougher than the granite and weathers to form the cliff scenery on the east side of the Wicklow Mountains. Much more recently, less than a million years ago, glaciers re-designed the former valley of the Dargle and produced not only the amphitheatre and its cascade, but the lovely patch of level ground at the bottom of the cliff as well. The ice was also responsible for the presence of the great boulders which give a special character to the river before it finds its bed lower down the valley.

The whole concept of Powerscourt House was that of a palace and, all in good time, a king came to stay. He was George IV, and the fact that he survived his visit in 1821 stems from his over-indulgence at luncheon. To put on a special display for the King, the Dargle above the waterfall was dammed so that a tremendous rush of water could be released. A special road was built to convey the royal party in comfort from the House. However, his Majesty enjoyed such a splendid meal that he fell fast asleep and never saw the waterfall. So nobody knows how history might have been affected, had he been graciously pleased to view the spectacle — the liberated waterfall, in its enthusiasm, had carried the entire royal viewing platform away with it.

Amongst restored farm buildings, a shop and shelter were added to the deer park, in the 1990s. Besides ice-cream and crisps, they sell Roger Goodwillie's excellent little guide to the nature trail.

Grid 2216 (house and garden), 2013 (deer park entrance) sheet 56. Bus 44 from City and 185 from Bray to Enniskerry, also shuttle-service from Bray and Enniskerry to gardens and waterfall. Good car-parking facilities. Buggy-, wheelchair- and dog-friendly. Open: house and gardens, 9.30 a.m. to 5.30 p.m.; waterfall, winter, 10.30 a.m. to dusk; summer, 9.30 a.m. to 7.00 p.m. Admission free to shops and restaurant, charge for gardens and deer park. Excellent restaurant. Many picnic places.

Islandbridge

Islandbridge is a very special part of Dublin. The bridge over the Liffey is one of the most beautiful — a graceful, single arched span. Just upstream is the island, created when a milldam was built in the twelfth century, stemming the tide and, a little more recently, making a perfect spot for boat-racing. The lands on either bank, being portions of Phoenix Park (see p. 162) — though beyond its modern boundary wall — are the property of the people and remain free of dwellings, other than the acceptable pavilions of the rowing clubs. Many of the houses that line the left bank downstream are tolerable, or even attractive — but their presence does prevent access to the river bank. The right bank was the spot chosen for the memorial to Irish soldiers who died in the First World War; to their names were added those of the dead of the Second. Today it speaks of peace.

In the nineteenth century, Viking graves were found in a cemetery on the right bank and more were discovered in the course of the construction of the war memorial in the 1930s. The burials dated to the ninth century, and two skeletons of warriors which were discovered, complete with their armaments, may now be seen in the Museum in Kildare Street. These pre-date the time of the Viking settlement of Dubh Linn, further downstream.

Written records of Islandbridge go back to the twelfth century when the weir and the salmon fishery came under the control of the Knights of St John of Jerusalem, at Kilmainham. Salmon are particularly easy to catch in narrow estuaries, of the kind that existed at Islandbridge before the weir was built. In the Middle Ages, when food became seriously scarce in winter and early spring, the value of the salmon which appear in the Liffey around Christmas was beyond any modern reckoning. Consequently, those who owned fishing rights guarded them jealously.

John de Courcy, in his excellent book, *The Liffey in Dublin*, quotes a letter from King Henry III, in 1220, which showed how the pious brethren of Kilmainham had incurred the wrath of the citizenry:

> *The prior and friars of the Hospital of Kilmainham have however lately made a pool (stagnum) there, whereby the city and citizens are much damnified; their fishery is totally destroyed because the pool prevents the fish from ascending, and the boats can no longer pass up and down as they used to do.*

The King's Justiciar, Geoffrey de Marisco, evidently took some action, otherwise salmon might have disappeared from the Liffey. Nevertheless, the milldam and the pool upstream remained, making a boundary to the navigable portion of the river, but providing an important source of drinking water, valuable power, and the calm millpond which is very much more attractive than tidal mud. The monks enjoyed the fishery and operated a corn mill and were still in possession some centuries later, in 1541, as recorded in an inquisition of that date. The suppression of the monasteries under Henry VIII marked the end of their ownership.

John Rocque's map of 1762 shows a crossing of the river and calls it Island Bridge. Built in 1577, this bridge was destroyed by a flood in 1784. It was replaced by the present structure and named Sarah Bridge in honour of the Countess of Westmoreland who laid the foundation stone in 1791.

In 1741, Dublin Corporation bought the mills. They harnessed the water wheels to drive a pumping system which raised water for domestic use to higher levels to supply the city. This served its purpose for 70 years until 1811, when the Manders family re-established flour milling and also used the power for a calico printing works. Traces of their establishment remain, with an old millrace running downstream of the Dublin University Boat Club. Mallard, heron, moorhen and, occasionally, coot dwell in its calm water.

The weir is the lowermost on the river and forms a boundary for mullet and occasional seals which rarely venture above the tidal portion. Across the river, on the left bank, a salmon ladder allows the migrating fish to pass in comfort and safety. Upstream of the weir, the Liffey has been cutting its way down through a great mass of glacial deposits which filled its original valley. This geologically recent behaviour explains why the banks are relatively steep on either side. Subsequently, the river's

The Temple at Islandbridge War Memorial Gardens

meandering created the flood plain which provides the level ground for boat clubs and the road on the left bank, and the pleasant lawn on the right. At some stage, the river found a lower level so that the former water meadows are now firm and dry. The public path along by the riverside continues all the way to Chapelizod. To the north, the Magazine Fort (see pp 164–165) in Phoenix Park sits on the high ground, while the war memorial lies on the slope of the right bank, a site chosen by Sir Edwin Lutyens.

The location was selected in 1933 and, in the interests of providing the greatest possible level of employment, excavation and construction were largely done manually. The workforce comprised ex-soldiers, half from the British Army and half from the Irish forces. The granite pavilions and steps with rose gardens and pond were completed in 1940. The temple below the garden was built very much later, while a bridge over the Liffey, part of the original grand design, has yet to be constructed. The trees planted in the 1930s are well-grown now and form delightful shaded avenues.

Lutyens's design makes brilliant use of the sloping bank and the level plain beneath. Pathways lead through the trees to the higher ground, giving an inward view down to the formal garden and outwards across the Liffey to Phoenix Park. The names of the war dead are inscribed in books preserved in the pavilions. The gardens are beautifully kept — visit them any time, but particularly in summer when the roses are at their best.

Grid 10L, OS Dublin City Map (16th ed.) Bus 23. Approached by South Circular Road or Conyngham Road and indicated by a rather discreet signpost at Clancy Barracks. A place for a gentle, contemplative walk, admiring the youthful energy of the boat-racing enthusiasts. Buggy- and wheelchair-friendly and safe from traffic for dogs and small children, but the river is relatively deep. Dogs need leads within the Memorial Park but may be let slip beyond its western gate where the footpath continues for a pleasant riverside mile to Chapelizod. Rather distant from restaurants and perhaps a little too manicured to enjoy a picnic. The car park closes at 4.00 p.m. in winter, with much longer opening hours — up to 9.00 p.m. — in summer

The National Stud and Japanese Gardens

Parks

A place of pilgrimage for devotees of two of Ireland's foremost recreations, gardening and the Turf. Allow a full day to enjoy all of the features and to include the journey.

In 1900, Colonel William Hall-Walker, an amiable, faintly eccentric and immensely talented Scot, bought an estate at Tully close to the Curragh and the cathedral town of Kildare. The practice of horse-racing on the Curragh can be traced back to the Iron Age and may well have an even longer descent. The rich limestone soil of the region is credited with providing grazing of exceptional quality for the nurture of bloodstock, and that is one of the reasons why the colonel decided to settle there.

Like many of his neighbours, he established a stud farm and, in common with rather fewer of them, developed it as a highly profitable enterprise. He was a perfectionist and everything about the farm was designed to the highest standards. The horses were given — and still enjoy — spacious accommodation, the stable yards were planned to give a pleasing appearance, and flower beds were planted wherever possible.

One of the most remarkable features of the stables is that they all have skylights. The Colonel had a strong belief in the importance of the heavenly bodies in the production of winning horses. So, besides making good use of their horoscopes, he made sure that the brood mares would be fully exposed to the influence of the moon and planets. Few scientists, and not many horse breeders, took his ideas seriously. Nonetheless, he enjoyed a great deal more success than did most of his more rational competitors.

Perhaps it was the same preoccupation with the spiritual world and with temporal excellence that led Hall-Walker to engage Eida and Minoru, the legendary Japanese father-and-son team of garden designers. They created an exquisite garden, using mainly Japanese trees, shrubs and flowers, combining these with pools and cascades formed from the crystal-clear water which flows from springs in many parts of the demesne. The same limestone substrate that produces the splendid horses, gives the water its special clarity and provides superb garden soil.

A Japanese garden, however small, is a place of pilgrimage and symbolism. The trees, shrubs, bonsais and flowers are a delight at any time of year. Even in winter, pines and other evergreens give patches of green, blue-green and yellow foliage together with brown and orange bark, while the bare branches of their deciduous companions make exquisite patterns of tracery. From spring onwards to autumn, flowers add to the variety of colour in the Gardens. It is delightful and a pleasure to walk along the paths simply to admire the beauty of the plants — large and small.

But that alone would be to miss half the offering. A Japanese Garden is more than a beautiful landscape; it tells a story. The paths lead uphill and down, cross the river and enter a tunnel as you follow the pilgrimage of the human soul from birth to the hereafter. The idea is that visitors should meditate on life as they go. A guide leaflet outlines the story. The entrance is the Gate of Oblivion where the soul departs from eternity and, forgetting the joys of the other world, embarks on its period of mortality. Twenty such symbolical stopping places include an Island of Joy and Wonder, a Marriage Bridge, a Hill of Ambition, a Well of Wisdom and, finally, the Gateway to Eternity.

In 1915, when Ireland was still part of the United Kingdom, Hall-Walker presented his farm to the Crown and it was managed by the British National Stud Company. In 1943, the whole complex was made over to the Free State Government. Two years later, the

Irish National Stud Company was formed and has carried on the good work ever since, making a notable contribution to the Irish bloodstock industry. Maintenance of the stud, as of the Gardens, continues to observe the highest standards.

The complex takes its status as the property of the people of Ireland very seriously, and visitors, once they have paid for admission, are free to wander at will. The admission charge also covers a half-hour guided tour which illuminates the many mysteries of the world of horse-breeding. A particular attraction of the tour is that the guides are hands-on experts, spending most of their working time tending the horses in the stud and then going home to look after their own. They speak with a deep love and knowledge of the noble animal.

After the tour, visitors are free to walk for miles amongst the enormous paddocks where, from mid-February to July, mares and foals feed and relax. All are beautiful, some a bit stand-offish but lovely to watch as they amble or gallop about. Others are friendly and come to the fence to nuzzle. The atmosphere is so delightful that it scarcely matters that these are some of the finest horses that have ever existed.

A health warning at the National Stud

In the fourteenth century, the Knights Hospitallers instituted a 'preceptory', long known as the Black Abbey. The tower of the abbey church is all that remains, standing on a hillside surrounded by tombstones near the stables. The twenty-first century has been greeted by the creation of a new garden on the estate. It is dedicated to St Fiachra, in honour of the sixth-century hermit and missionary who became patron saint of gardeners. Like the Japanese Gardens, it is centred on water but, in contrast, depends mainly on wild plants. It includes a complex of beehive huts, reminiscent of the cells of the monks of Skellig Michael, but modernised within by an amazing array of glass sculpture.

The entrance to the complex is through the car park, shaded by pine trees and a pleasant spot for a picnic. The entrance building has a souvenir shop, an excellent restaurant and a Lego playroom. Nearby, is the fascinating museum of the horse, with artefacts and posters tracing its importance to the people of Ireland since prehistoric times.

Grid N7311, Sheet 55. About a mile's walk from Kildare town. Direct approach from Dublin is by main road to Cork (N7), but an indirect way through Blessington and Kilcullen and through the Curragh is very pleasant. Buggy- and wheelchair-friendly. Admission charge, picnic tables in tree-shaded car park in which dogs can be exercised. All sorts of food available inside.

The Zoo

Sixty years after my first exposure to its charms, a visit to the Zoo still remains a thrilling experience. Over the decades, I have visited a great many zoos, lived for some years in Africa and enjoyed satisfactorily close encounters with wild elephants and other beasts. I have debated with myself, and with other people, the morality of keeping animals in captivity and have come to the conclusion held by the majority of citizens: zoos are fun, good and here to stay. And the Dublin Zoo, managed by marvellously dedicated people, is one of the best in the world.

The Royal Zoological Society of Ireland commissioned Decimus Burton, the English landscape architect who had already made a major impact on Phoenix Park, to plan a zoological garden for Dublin. Burton, shortly before, had distinguished himself as the designer of the London Zoo in Regent's Park. The Lord Lieutenant, in 1830, made over the Phoenix Park site to the Society, and Dublin Zoo was born. The lake was there already as the centre of the gardens, having been created by damming the valley at its north-east end.

Together, the lake, the steep sides of the valley and a covering of woodland provided everything a landscape gardener could desire. Burton was well pleased with his commission and the Zoo has never looked back from its foundation when the gardens as well as the animals were given equal care and attention. One of the most distinguished twentieth-century gardeners was the botanist Robert Lloyd Praeger who, during his tenure in the office of President of the Royal Zoological Society of Ireland, spent much of his time in gardening clothes, engaged in practical horticulture.

Skills in collecting and keeping preferably large and fierce animals for exhibition have been developing for at least 2,000 years. Sacred crocodiles in ancient Egypt and wild-beast shows in Imperial Rome had their unpleasing side but, whatever the captives were used for, it was essential for custodians to keep the animals alive and in good health. As civilisation progressed, the animals came to be accepted as interesting in their own right, without the need for bloody spectacles. The nineteenth-century developments took place in parallel, first with the excitement of new understanding of classification and anatomy, and then with the dramatic times of Darwin's theory of evolution.

A carefully preserved exhibit, the original 1830s entrance to the Zoo

Although there were honourable exceptions, such as Hagenbeck's beautiful animal park in Hamburg, Victorian zoos vied with each other to put on show as many varieties of animals as possible, with a minimal regard for the creatures' comfort. Well into the second half of the twentieth century, Dublin Zoo presented the public with rows of cages, strongly resembling prison cells and inhabited by solitary creatures. It has to be said that the animals enjoyed good health, excellent food and, for the most part, lived to great ages. Some species, the lions more than any, produced large and happy families.

Changes began in the 1940s, the first major step being the construction of an outdoor arena for a family of lions. Over the years, the barred cages have almost disappeared, replaced by very much larger enclosures, in which compatible species are housed together and breeding pairs with their families are the rule rather than the exception. In common with all good zoos nowadays, animal welfare rather than mere survival is a first requirement. Apart from the little thatched entrance gate – the only original 1830s building to survive — and the red-brick exterior of the Roberts House, little remains of the Victorian menagerie. The modern zoo celebrated the beginning of the twenty-first century by extending its land into the grounds of Áras an Úachtaráin to create spacious paddocks for the larger and more active animals.

The other great change has been the evolution of zoos from collections, which sometimes threatened the survival of rare species, to sanctuaries for animals whose continued existence in the wild is far from certain. Dublin Zoo is making an impressive contribution to the worldwide programme for breeding endangered animals. Families of gorilla, orangutan and the exquisite little South American monkey, the golden lion tamarin, are notable success stories.

Since its foundation, the Zoo has had a serious undercurrent of education, enhanced more recently by its rôle in conservation and its provision of facilities for research projects on animal behaviour. But, for the greater public, it remains an extremely popular place of entertainment. This, of course, helps with the

---

The Zoo

fund-raising, but the Zoo, at the same time, stands in the front rank of institutions painlessly contributing to popular culture. Founded much earlier than still photography, let alone movies, before the railways, to say nothing of aircraft, it was the only way in which most Irish people could gain an appreciation of the greater part of the world of animals.

What is most interesting in the twenty-first century is the Zoo's continued charm. Wildlife films of scarcely credible excellence are commonplace on television. For less than €1,000, and in under 24 hours, Dubliners can reach Victoria Falls and walk amongst monkey and baboon troupes in the rain forest. The same day they can take a morning safari trip to meet with elephant and hippo. Most people have access to television, and large numbers can afford a game-park holiday.

And still the Zoo has something special — perhaps partly the thrill of close encounters, such as a tiger separated only by an inch of glass. There is also the satisfaction of watching animals, albeit captive, going about their business, either indifferent to the human presence or maybe even taking an interest in human behaviour. Zoo animals, unlike many in the wild, are neither afraid of humans, nor, being well fed, do they particularly want to eat us.

Grid 1035, Sheet 50. Buses 9 and 10 to North Circular Road gate to Phoenix Park, then half a mile walk. Roadside car parking. Totally child-friendly, no dogs, wheelchair access, good fast food, wonderful assortment of soft toys in shop. Open: 10.30 a.m. to 5.00 p.m. winter; 10.30 a.m. to 6.30 p.m. summer, admission charge.

The Seaside

Above all places on earth, the seaside is the one that presents its devotees with ceaseless change. Although nothing in nature is constant, there are differences in time-scale. It will take some millions of years for erosion or earth movements to obliterate Howth and Bray Head and it takes weeks to transform woods and parks from brown to green in springtime. By the sea, visible movement and change of colour never cease. On the calmest day, the surface of the water ripples and the tide rises and falls. Meanwhile, the horizon seems to be fixed and gives an impression of stability. Above all, the seaside allows the inhabitant of built-up areas to enjoy the respite given by unlimited space.

With the exception of coral reefs, mangrove swamps and pack ice, the coasts of Dublin and Wicklow contain just about every kind of seashore that exists. Howth and Bray Head offer steep cliffs inhabited, in spring and summer, by myriads of breeding birds. The opposite extreme lies in the North and South Bulls and Sandymount strand, where miles of almost level sand flats give safe paddling in summer and, in winter, a home for an even bigger, but different, population of birds from many distant lands. There are many miles of golden sand, beloved by the plain people but considered by learned persons to be less interesting than rocky or muddy shores.

Finally, there are the creations of generations of harbour engineers: docks, breakwaters and various structures which attempt to keep the sea within bounds. Ancient legal principles preserve by far the greater part of the coast for the enjoyment of the people, since private individuals are not free to exclude their less affluent fellow citizens from the foreshore. Within our chosen area, the sea is free.

Bray Head

A cliff path with unrivalled views of the coast and a
generous sprinkling of nesting sea birds and wild flowers.
Suitable all year round, occupies half a day — more for a
longer walk.

The bastion which protects the southern end of Killiney Bay
shares with Howth the distinction of exhibiting the most ancient
rock strata in County Dublin. Another common factor with its
northern counterpart is the Head's endowment with a cliff walk,
enabling citizens to appreciate in great comfort primeval forces
and contemporary beauty of wild flowers and seabirds. For good
measure, feats and failures of railway engineering are added in,
together with traditions of smugglers and brandy.

A fan-like pattern in the green and purple siltstones, each unit
about the size of a two-euro piece, was named *Oldhamia antiqua*,
in honour of Thomas Oldham, a nineteenth-century director of
the Geological Survey of Ireland. Its presence reveals that the
strata can be dated to the Cambrian era, more than 500 million
years ago, when the sediments were laid down in a shallow sea.
Geologists can trace in the rock the patterns of marine currents
which reflect the conditions in which the sediments were first
deposited. The siltstones have a large mud content, indicating that
they were laid down in the calm water of lagoons or sheltered
bays. Other parts of the primeval coast were more exposed so that
the mud was carried away to leave clean sandy beaches. These

solidified to form quartzite, an extremely tough rock. Its resistance to weathering led to its standing out above the softer siltstones and slates, forming the many peaks of Bray Head — and the neighbouring cones of the Sugarloaves (see p. 42).

Before the sediments had solidified as rock, earth movements caused them to slip and curl up in places and these slump structures are also visible. But these are on a small scale compared to the folding and faulting which took place tens of millions of years later when they were crumpled by the collision of continental plates that built the Wicklow Mountains.

The lower slopes of the Head, at the end of the esplanade and at the feet of the delightful Victorian hotels, are covered by glacial till. This material was scooped out of the bed of the Irish Sea by the ice field which filled it on its journey towards the south-west. This material is a more or less muddy matrix containing stones large and small. For centuries before the County Council built groynes and made other efforts to protect the coast, the sea had been tearing this material away to the best of its ability.

The fine grains of the muddy material were carried away offshore. But the stones from the glacial till were too big to be removed so they lay at the foot of the cliff. They are never allowed to lie still: heavy seas have been rolling them about for centuries, knocking off all the rough edges and producing the polished shingle that makes a walk on this strand mildly uncomfortable. The pebbles include red sandstone from Portraine, limestone from farther south and granite from the region of Killiney. Some of the limestone pebbles are honeycombed with the burrows that small shellfish make for themselves by digesting the stone with an acid secretion.

The till is still being eroded and on the right, a little way uphill from the last of the houses, old field drainage pipes protrude from the cliff face. Exposure to the salt air, combined with grazing by goats and occasional burning of the gorse, discourages the growth of trees on Bray Head. Consequently, the greater part of the hill is a dry heath land with gorse and heather as its main vegetation. But there are pockets of woodland, one of them in a deep damp valley to the right of the footbridge over the railway. Pine and spruce were planted there — some of the pines early in the twentieth century, and receiving honourable mention in Joyce's *Neighbourhood of Dublin*, published in 1912.

The lower slopes, above the cliff path on the northern side of the Head, are covered by bracken, a particularly vigorous fern which invades poor, acid pasture land when given the chance. In autumn, the fronds die back, with a beautiful golden brown colour and in spring, before they grow up again, bluebells appear amongst the young shoots. They complete their flowering cycle before the bracken fronds grow up again to cast a dark shade and prevent any other green plants from growing. The southern slopes of the head have gorse, rather than bracken, as the dominant plant cover.

Other components of the vegetation are smaller but delightful. The rock faces that have been exposed for a long time are coated with a variety of lichens. Many of these are grey or grey-green and inconspicuous. But one species is outstanding and forms spots of yellow-green which look like splatters of paint. Lichens are good news, indicating a satisfactory level of freshness of air. Although very sensitive to air pollution, they grow where no other plants can survive. Rock surfaces are about the most inhospitable substrates in creation but the lichen evolved a means of living on it. It is a dual organism, the greater part being fungus, the lesser an alga. Algae have chlorophyll which allows them to subsist on carbon dioxide and water. Fungi can live only by digesting food which has been derived from living plants or animals. But no green plants can live on a bare rock surface and the lichen algae live in a bed of fungi. The fungi provide shelter and support and reap their reward by consuming the algae when they die.

The flowering plants are at their best in the month of May. Many of them are confined to the seaside, giving a pleasing element of rarity.

Sea pink, with its unmistakable colour, grows in tufts on peaty soil. Sea campion, with white flowers and pale bluish-green leaves, is plentiful beside the footpaths. Little stonecrops, with fleshy leaves and tiny white or pinkish star-shaped flowers creep over the rocks or on burnt soil. Towards the south of the cliff path, bloody cranesbill, a low-lying plant with big, reddish-purple flowers, grows in places. It also grows in Howth but is much better known as one of the outstanding wild flowers of the Burren.

As with the wild flowers, the bird life of Bray Head is at its best in spring and early in the summer. That is when the seabirds gather to nest on the ledges of the cliffs or on the steep banks. The most abundant species is the kittiwake, a delightful small and delicate seagull, its name a good rendering of its trisyllabic squawk. It has probably lived there for centuries, in contrast to the fulmar which is a blow-in, almost unknown on the Irish coast until the twentieth century. Guillemot and razorbill breed on the less accessible slopes, and the most remarkable nesting place of all is that occupied by the black guillemot. They occupy drainage openings in the masonry that supports the railway on the cliff edge.

Besides being host to the seabirds, which leave the coast after the breeding season and stay away until the following spring, Bray Head is one of the places where two relatively rare terrestrial species are sure to be seen, one large and one small. The large one is the raven, a splendid black bird with a deep-throated croak which obviously enjoys sailing around in the air. The small bird is the stonechat, a little smaller than a robin, coloured in shades of chestnut, but with a dark brown cap and white collar.

Before the days of steam, Bray Head, rugged and remote, was a haven for smugglers. Joyce fondly recounts traditions of how contraband would be landed. The tradition is supported by the fact that one of the bays is still marked on the Ordnance Survey map as the Brandy Hole. It is said to have been a labyrinthine cave which could comfortably accommodate a smuggler's skiff. The cavern was used as a store for contraband which had been liberated at night from vessels anchored off the Head. These ships would then proceed to one or other of the harbours of Dublin Bay to discharge what was left of their cargo in the presence of the customs officials. The cave had a natural chimney which gave access to the land-based contingent of the smugglers' team.

Killiney Bay and Bray Head

Then came the railway, making the remote cliffs accessible to the authorities and, in the course of construction, unroofing and partly filling in the Brandy Hole. Another tradition tells that the engineer in charge laid the track on the outside of the head because a friend wagered that he couldn't. Whatever the facts, the railway remains a noble achievement, though not without its problems or share of disaster.

From the cliff path, traces of the first line, abandoned because it lay too dangerously close to the edge, may still be seen. The disaster occurred at the Brandy Hole, on 8 August 1867, when, following derailment caused by the 'wretched manner in which the line was being re-laid', an engine and tender fell into the chasm, bringing parts of the bridge and a third-class carriage with them. The higher-class carriages stayed above in comparative safety. Two passengers were killed but, remarkably, driver and fireman survived, although seriously injured.

From Bray it is possible to walk for four miles, by the cliff path and along the railway, to Greystones. An alternative is to make a round trip by taking the cliff path, crossing the railway boundary wall two miles out and taking a steep climb to the summit of the Head. Footpaths lead all the way back to Bray.

 Grid 281, Sheet 56. Bus 45, 84, or DART to Bray and walk southwards along the Esplanade. Car parking near the esplanade, but rather congested on a fine summer's day — anyway, the best time for birds and flowers is early summer when there are fewer people. Safe for well-disciplined dogs and children but the safety barriers are easily scaled and the cliffs are very dangerous in places. Buggy- and wheelchair-unfriendly except for the first half mile from the esplanade. Picnics possible off the cliff path.

Killiney Bay

Killiney Bay is where a great many Dubliners have their first close encounter with the sea. That meeting is a major event in anyone's life, but the Killiney Experience is particularly exciting. The approach is made through a dark, dank tunnel beneath the railway line that frames the beach and the sea beyond. This presents all the mystery of walking into a picture which suddenly transforms into reality. The beach itself offers smooth, rounded pebbles to collect, and sand of just the right consistency for the construction of the finest castles. Sand is to dig in, though few young children — and not many adults — cogitate on why there should be shingle and where the stones come from.

Such matters did, however, concern many nineteenth-century naturalists, and a week before Christmas 1893, W.J. Sollas accompanied Robert Lloyd Praeger on a walk from Bray to Killiney. Sollas was Professor of Geology at Trinity at the time and Praeger was a leading founder member of the Dublin Naturalists' Field Club. Sollas published an account of their walk in the *Irish Naturalist*, describing three different kinds of glacial deposits: boulder clay, 'a stiff, resistant reddish clay on which walking is sure and easy', contorted drift, 'a marvellously irregular patchy series of sand and gravel', and gravelly boulder bed, 'more horizontal, more regular, full of great blocks of stone'. Praeger contributed an appendix listing 22 species of sea shell identified from fragments which they found in the boulder clay. His list includes *Astarte compressa*, a sub-arctic clam now extinct in Irish waters.

More recently, William Warrren made a distinction between a lower glacial till, with abundant limestone pebbles and fragments of marine shells, and an upper till, with few shells and plentiful granite. The lower material was deposited by the ice which flowed through the Irish Sea basin, and the upper till arrived, at a later stage, from the midlands. Coming from inland it had to pass over the Wicklow and Dublin Mountains where it collected the granite.

Most of the glacial till is composed mainly of a brown, clayey material in which angular stones, large and small, are embedded. The large ones can be spectacular — a metre and more in length and fully justifying the warning notices advising citizens to keep clear of the cliffs. The cliff section also displays beds of gravel with hardly any clay — some are horizontal, some almost vertical. These outwash gravels show where torrential streams that followed summer thaws carried away the clay and sorted the gravel and stones into masses of sand grains, or pebbles of more or less uniform size.

In the course of the past ten thousand years since the ice finally disappeared, the waves took over from the melt water, removed the clay matrix and left the gravel and stones. The clay lies offshore, forming the mud inhabited by marine worms and shells. These provide food for cod and other fish which, in turn, are a source of recreation for the hardy men who can be seen on the beach armed with enormous casting rods. Along the shore itself, the stones, released from the cliff, are constantly thrown against each other by the breakers. This knocks their corners off and leaves the beautifully smoothed and rounded material of the shingle.

The variety of stones to be found at Killiney shows how far the ice travelled. Limestone from the Dublin coast is the most plentiful. Antrim flint is common, though purple sandstone, from

Portraine, and porphyry, from Lambay, less so. The prize find for specialists is riebeckite microgranite from Ailsa Craig in the Firth of Clyde. It is of particular geological interest, being unique and establishing the direction of the ice flow beyond any doubt. The more local stones include granite, quartz, greywacke and schist. The granite boulders are the biggest, because they have travelled the shortest distance and were not so broken up by the grinding action of the ice and the other stones within the mass.

The attempts of the sea to continue to eat away the cliffs have been thwarted to a great extent by the counter-attack of the local authorities. They go to considerable lengths to preserve the land, mainly by planting stout wooden poles at intervals near the base of the cliffs in the most threatened parts. Elsewhere, they have built a wall of boulders, contained by a plastic coated steel mesh, which has remarkable powers of resisting corrosion.

The car park in front of the Court Hotel and the railway station a little way to the south of it are the most popular approaches to the bay. Loos, lifeguards and a lawn greet the visitor who attains the strand, after passing through the tunnel beneath the railway

Granite and Gila at White Rock

line. The beach runs northwards as far as White Rock where the cliffs of granite meet the sea. Between the lawn and the fishermen's colony, the beach is being built up rather than eroded. Marram grass grows in the fine sand at the base of the retaining wall. Whatever it might do if left alone, this pioneering sand-dune system has little hope of developing in the presence of people who, innocently, dislodge the sand as they walk and leave it at the mercy of the wind.

Sorrento Point and Dalkey Island mark the eastern extremity of the great granite mass which forms the backbone of the Wicklow Mountains and extends to the Blackstairs range in County Wexford. At White Rock, the granite meets the older 'country rock' into which it forced its way in a molten state some 400 million years ago. Above the granite, the contorted silvery-grey rock is mica schist, baked, twisted and recrystallised where the granite made contact.

The little conglomeration of houses, shelters and a tea-room on stilts has a respectable degree of antiquity. Peter Pearson points out that a bath house is marked in the vicinity on Rocque's map of 1757. Lobster creels are stored there in winter and are put to use in the bay during the summer.

At low tide — the best time to visit Killiney — it is relatively easy to clamber over the boulders at the base of the cliff to gain the next bay which lies between two tongues of granite and schist. This little bay cuts into the hillside interrupting the route taken by the nineteenth-century railway engineers who had to build the imposing stone viaduct to carry the line across the chasm. The drainage holes high up in the structure proved to be just what was needed by fulmar petrels to make their nests in. Fulmars are very wonderful birds which came south to Ireland from the Scottish islands only during the twentieth century — it took them until the 1950s to discover the attractions of Killiney. They spend half the year at sea, returning to the coast to breed in January or February.

The schist at the base of the viaduct is patterned with big crystals of andalusite, a mineral which is formed in the high temperatures of molten granite. Beryl and garnet occur, too — but as such small crystals that none but geologists can get excited about them.

In 1875, Sir Francis Brady, of Sorrento Cottage, planted in his garden some seeds of a Mediterranean ragwort with silver-grey leaves and bright yellow flowers. Their seeds drifted away on the wind and germinated in the little bay and over the hillside nearby. And there they stay — abundant over half a mile or so of coastline, and virtually unknown as an established plant elsewhere, except in small patches on Howth Head.

South of Killiney Station the cliffs rise and the railway goes through a cutting instead of running on the cliff top. Then the cliffs fall away again, breached by two rivers flowing from the west which form the Vale of Shanganagh. One is a local stream, coming from Ballybrack. The other, the Loughlinstown River, has two branches which rise on Three Rock and Two Rock. They form beautiful clear pools at the top of the strand and support a small reed bed. A little way inland, the river flows under willow and alder and forms a pleasant oasis in the midst of growing suburbia.

Grid 2624, Sheet 50, also Dublin street map. DART to Killiney Station. Maps are coy about car parking; the simplest one to find is below the Court Hotel, just north of the railway station. Ideal for dogs, children and picnics, approachable by buggy and wheelchair — but sand and shingle are uneven or soft, or both. It is possible to walk all the way to Bray along the strand — though uncomfortable in places where large boulders extend from the cliff base to the sea. Several of the roads shown on the Dublin street map — Station Road, Seafield Road and Corbawn Lane — have car parks and access to the strand.

Dalkey and Killiney Hills

The Seaside

A pair of hilltops, combining rocky wilderness with respectable suburban park and breath-taking views of the coast. Suitable all year, occupies half a day.

The hills that stand above the southern border of Dublin Bay have been enclosed to form a gently rugged park — a place of contrasts with tree plantations and footpaths at one extreme, and a gorse-covered granite wilderness at the other. The scale is small, a place for a polite walk with all generations of the family on a Sunday afternoon. But the view is unrivalled because the hills, although low, stand out above the coastal plain that, interrupted by a few bumps, extends from the Mountains of Mourne to Carnsore Point. Wicklow Head, one of the said bumps, marks the southern boundary of the panorama. The Mournes, 60 miles to the north, can usually be seen — and also, on exceptionally clear days, the Welsh mountains. Closer at hand are Lambay, Howth and Ireland's Eye, together with Dalkey Island and, to the south, the incomparable Killiney Bay (guarded by the geologically ancient bastion of Bray Head.

The high ground is part of the eastern extremity of the granite of the Dublin and Wicklow Mountains, a narrow tongue which extends from White Rock northwards to Blackrock. The white rock is the granite while the black is limestone which was deposited on top of it. Towards the south, the boundary of mica schist, formed where the hot granite met the older shales, explains the steep sides of the hills. The gentler northern slopes are typical of the inner — rather than the outer — edge of the granite mass. Most important of all in shaping the hills was the Midlandian ice sheet which completely covered the slopes and sculpted the summit of Killiney Hill in a particular way. The ice flowed over granite tors and ground them down. On the northern, upstream, side its passage simply smoothed the tor. But, to the south, it plucked away blocks of stone, giving a steeper angle. The abraded rock outcrops are oblong, with the long axis parallel to the flow of the ice. They are called *roches moutonnées* because their shape resembled a nineteenth-century *moutonnée* wig made of sheepskin.

Much of Dalkey Hill has been quarried away, to the satisfaction of the rock-climbing fraternity who may be seen, equipped with brightly coloured abseiling ropes, perilously disporting themselves. Quarrying probably began here in medieval times, to provide building material for the numerous castles down below. In the eighteenth century, Dalkey was the source of the rocks and paving stones for the great South Wall in Dublin Bay (see p. 233). The rocks were transported across the bay by boat. The last major operation, which left the quarry with its spectacular present-day cliffs and ledges, was to provide stone for the 'harbour of refuge' down the hill, at Dún Laoghaire. An ingenious railway system was developed, with a slope descending gradually all the way to the harbour works. The weight of the loaded trucks rolling down the hill was used to haul the empty ones up to the quarry again. It is still possible to follow its path to the sea.

The slopes above the car park at Dalkey Quarry are covered in a plantation of Scots pine with some beech and oak — the pine needles providing a pleasant carpet, soft and springy to walk on. Spruce and larch grow at the edge of the wood and give way to gorse. But a pathway offers a less prickly walk and is provided with a granite wall to protect the visitor from the perils of the quarry.

The highest point of the hill is crowned with a castle — sadly now a building sufficiently dangerous to have induced the authorities to block the doors and windows to prevent access. It was built in Napoleonic times as a signal tower, from which invading ships could be observed and their presence communicated by semaphore to the garrisons. It was repaired — and probably embellished — by the landlord, Robert Warren, in 1851, as he recorded on a marble tablet embedded in the wall. Small ferns, polypody and maidenhair spleenwort grow in the mortar. Whereas the signal tower certainly never had to serve the purpose for which it was created, the height and location of Dalkey Hill are used today as a location point in air navigation, and a fenced enclosure contains an elaborate system of aerials.

Wild flowers and shrubs abound in the quarry. The most interesting of them is Swedish whitebeam, considered 'very rare' in the Dublin Naturalists' *Flora of County Dublin*. It is abundant in the quarry, and some quite large bushes, with many smaller ones, spring from crevices in the rock. It can also be found on some of the nearby hills. Whitebeams bear bright red berries, avidly eaten by thrushes who carry the seeds far and wide.

The signal tower on Dalkey Hill

The central point of Killiney Hill is the obelisk at the summit, flanked by the *roches moutonnées*. The obelisk bears a touching account of its building in these words:

Last year being hard with the Poor the walls around these HILLS and THIS etc. erected by JOHN MAPAS June 1742.

Details of the history of the landscaping of Killiney Hill and of the buildings around it are given by Peter Pearson in his excellent book, *Between the Mountains and the Sea*. A second, smaller obelisk was built at a date unknown, but may also be an eighteenth-century structure. It bears the inscription, *Mount Mapas*, the name modestly given by the owner to his home nearby, later to be enlarged and called Killiney Castle. A second plaque on the obelisk tells that a later owner of the estate, Robert Warren, repaired the building in 1840. He was probably also the builder of the stepped pyramid.

Erecting monuments to themselves was something of a habit of the local landlords. The final one on the hill is the broken cross, dated 16 July 1906, which is decorated with heraldic animals and dedicated to the memory of Thomas Higgin Chippindall. Higgin had been another owner and embellisher of the Castle, which he bought in 1872.

The most recent construction near the summit, in contrast to its companions, is functional. Surrounded by a dense hedge, a large concrete reservoir contains pumped Vartry water, which descends therefrom to the homes of the people of Killiney.

The hilltop is covered with a lawn and patches of gorse within the wall. Beyond the wall, gorse and wild flowers abound amongst the granite outcrops. The assemblage of wild flowers is a curious one. The bright yellow bird's foot trefoil is abundant. It needs plenty of lime in the soil and this is provided by the thin layer of yellow-brown glacial till which covers the rocks in places. This material was scooped up from the bed of the Irish Sea by the same glacier that formed the *roches moutonnées*. Another of the oddities is climbing corydalis, a creeper with long reddish stems and tiny yellow and white flowers. This is a rare plant, almost confined to the south-eastern counties, for which Killiney Hill is a major stronghold and has been for at least 200 hundred years. Walter Wade noted the presence of corydalis in 1804 and, a century later, Nathaniel Colgan put it on record in his *Flora of County Dublin*. It thrives in places where gorse is burned from time to time.

The eastern slopes of Killiney Hill are steep and faintly unwelcoming, being covered in gorse and scrub of a less than penetrable kind, though there is a path down to the Vico Road; the western side of the hill is more inviting. The covering of glacial till is thicker here so the soil has a greater depth, there is also a degree of shelter from the salt-laden easterly winds. It has been parkland since the time of John Mapas, and is planted with many fine specimen trees. Open to the public, even in the days of the landlords, the park was purchased from Robert Warren Junior by the Queen Victoria Memorial Association, and was opened by Prince Albert, in 1887. Dún Laoghaire County Council greatly enlarged the park by acquiring Dalkey Quarry and the surrounding land, in the 1930s. Peter Pearson's book includes details of a plan by Robert Warren, in 1840, to divide the hill into lots for the construction of elegant dwellings. Fortunately, the scheme was abandoned and citizens have been free to enjoy the combined glories of polite park and rugged wilderness within the remarkably small area of 200 acres. Somehow, it feels infinitely bigger.

Grid 2626, Sheet 50. Car park on Burton Road, off junction between Dalkey Avenue and Saval Park Road. Bus 59 from Dún Laoghaire to entrance on west side, on Killiney Hill Road. Paradise for dogs, buggy- and wheelchair-friendly with good — but sometimes steep — paths. Plenty of open space for picnics. Dangerous cliffs safely walled off.

Dún Laoghaire East Pier and Scotsman's Bay

The Seaside

A genteel walk with healthy sea air, a good deal of history, distant horizons and a wonderful view of the Dublin mountains. Suitable all year, occupies a couple of hours.

Thirteen thousand years ago, according to that brilliant geologist and exceptionally talented teacher Frank Mitchell, the surface of the Irish Sea lay some 90 metres below its present level. The climate was improving after the worst of the ice age and many of the now familiar plants and animals had moved northwards to replace the arctic creatures that had survived in the cold times. The low sea level left a broad corridor of dry land between Holyhead and Dún Laoghaire, and grasses, trees, flowers and insects, together with a handful of mammals, including the great Irish deer, gradually moved westward beneath the ferry route of today.

Then the sea rose and rose until, 5,000 years ago, it stood a few metres above its present level. It fell once more, but only a little way, and has been fairly stable for the past 2,000 years or more. Why this matters in Scotsman's Bay, the inlet between the East Pier and the Forty-Foot, is that the sea abandoned the higher beach and cut away a low cliff at its edge. This 'raised beach' is buried now beneath the railway, the coast road and the gracious nineteenth-century houses that sprang up along their route. Although the old beach is hidden by concrete and car parks, the position of the little cliff is easy to see from the vantage point of the East Pier.

In contrast to the situation in the inner part of Dublin Bay, where sand is constantly being deposited and creates broad strands, the sea is attempting to carry away the land of Scotsman's Bay. Consequently, any sand exists only in little sheltered corners, such as Sandycove, while the granite rocks are exposed and kept washed by the breakers. It was an extremely dangerous section of coast, the scene of many shipwrecks, and that is why the 'harbour of refuge' (see p.209) was made close by.

To thwart the tide, low sea walls have been built, some of concrete, some of limestone, along the margin of Scotsman's Bay. The rocks behind them have been covered in, over a period of a hundred years or so, and transformed to lawns, promenades and car parks. Surprising safety notices warn of the very real danger of the swell induced by the manoeuvres of the high-speed car ferry, which can cause a sudden wall of water to arise and sweep the unwary away.

Near the base of the East Pier, the abandoned Kingstown Baths display a tragic hint of former grandeur, with their Doric pillars and classical front — and peeling paint and neglect to the rear. The pier itself, however, is a delightful place, its air of gentility maintained in its smooth, concrete paving which makes possible effective sweeping and litter collection. Beyond the toilets, which cater for 'ladies' and 'gentlemen', are, first, a ship's cannon and then a plan in bronze relief to indicate the surrounding sights and give their distances. It shows its age in a pointer to the Kish lightship — replaced by a lighthouse in the 1960s.

The breakwater is arranged in two promenade levels protected by a wall of enormous blocks of granite nearly 6 feet high. This requires smaller people to climb over or go through one of the many openings in order to view the scene to the east. It's a dramatic view on a day with an easterly gale, and a delightfully placid one on a fine, sunny day — winter or summer. At the far end of the bay, the coast defences stand proudly: the Martello tower, pacified and immortalised by James Joyce and stately, plump Buck Mulligan, and the walls of a shore battery at the point.

The truly Victorian/Edwardian amenities of the pier are the band stand on the lower level, with its wrought-iron roof brackets in the form of lyres, and the shelter for the audience above it.

The obelisk farther along the pier gives the name of Captain Neill Boyd and some of his colleagues, of HMS *Ajax*, who perished in 1861 in an attempt to save the crew of a wrecked sloop. It was the tragic end of an heroic seaman who had led many previous rescue missions.

To celebrate the Millennium, a little notice was attached to the wall beside the anemometer, originally an instrument to measure the speed of the wind, but given additional duties of recording the same and also measuring the purity of the salt air. The notice tells that it was built in 1852 to house the instrument, one of the first in the world, made to a design perfected by the Reverend Thomas Romney Robinson. A Director of Dunsink Observatory, Robinson was a very distinguished scientist and inventor. The restored equipment includes a unit displaying wind direction and speed, and a record of what they have been doing over the preceding 24 hours. The classical design of the granite housing is topped off by the word Anemos in boldly-carved Greek lettering.

A rope of granite surrounds the base of the spire of the Boyd memorial

The pier ends with its lighthouse, cut off by the formidable granite wall of a shore battery which complements that at the Forty-Foot. The mounting of a gun, which was actually functional during the Second World War, stands on the parapet. Patrick Campbell wrote of his personal contribution to our defence in a book entitled *A Short Trot with a Cultured Mind*.

The view back towards the land from the end of the pier extends from Dalkey Island (see p 238–242), over the Dublin Mountains to

Lambay Island. The winter sun sets over the hilltops, making them glow with delicate colours.

The eastern end of Scotsman's Bay contains the tiny harbour of Sandycove, one of many such built in sheltered coves to provide important refuges and landing points for small sailing ships. Silting has long since made it almost useless as a harbour — but it caters well for canoeists and wind-surfers. Nearby, the literary pilgrim — and the plain Dubliner on a rainy day — may find shelter and stimulation of an afternoon in the Joyce Museum, from May to September.

Beyond it, the Forty-Foot bathing place offers deep clear water, beloved by sub-aqua people as well as the 'Gentlemen' for whose use it was once reserved. The granite formation provides some of the best rock-pools anywhere in reach of Dublin — ponds where the sea water is trapped as the tide recedes, gardens of green, brown and red seaweeds, inhabited by shrimps and sea anemones.

Scotsman's Bay and the East Pier cannot be conceived as 'out of this world'. With their dogs and citizens, often-crammed car parks, container ships, like blank walls, and a host of other human creations, they are vibrant with twenty-first century life. And yet the atmosphere is utterly remote from that of any land-based park. The difference lies in the horizon. Not too far away, the mystery it may have had for our Celtic ancestors who usually kept their feet on the ground, has long since gone. We know that Holyhead is somewhere out there. Even so, it gives a reality of limitless open space and a sensation of freedom from an enclosed world.

Grid 23R, OS Dublin City Map (16th ed.) Bus 7, 7A, 46A to Dún Laoghaire, DART to Glasthule Station. Car parks can be full, but roadside parking available close by. Buggy- and wheelchair-friendly, if slightly bumpy. For dogs, leads and poop-scoops *de rigueur*. Not especially inviting for picnics; all sorts of food and drink within walking distance.

West Pier, Dún Laoghaire

The Seaside

The less populous of the two piers, inhabited by serious dog-walkers, ornithologists and anglers. Suitable all year, occupies a couple of hours.

Construction of the 'harbour of refuge' at Dún Laoghaire began in 1817, and work was well in hand when the West Pier began to grow seawards, in 1820. Not surprisingly, it took more than 20 years to build as it extends for more than a mile. The South Wall of Dublin Port, ending in the Poolbeg Lighthouse, had been completed in the eighteenth century, and Bull Wall had just begun. Dublin Port could be difficult for sailing craft to enter and the rocks around Seapoint, and elsewhere, had been the scene of a horrifying number of disasters. Dún Laoghaire Harbour, colossal by the standards of its time, would provide a safe anchorage.

The West Pier provides shelter for shipping from the west wind, shelter for seabirds in easterly weather, and a most delightful walk for citizens and their dogs, unless it's raining. A map of 1821, reproduced by Peter Pearson in his delightful book, *Between the Mountains and the Sea*, shows the West Pier ending at a little distance from the land, giving an entrance to the Coal Harbour from the west, in addition to an outlet into the main harbour. The Coal Harbour pier was built some years before the great breakwaters.

In the good old days before the European Commission imposed
draconian regulations on sewage disposal, the turn of the tide was
announced by the release of unsavoury material off the second
bend of the pier. This attracted a joyous gathering of seagulls of
several species, including, now and again, the rare Iceland gull.

While diversion of the sewage impaired the enjoyment of
ornithologists, the act was mitigated by the construction, at the
base of the pier, of one of the most attractive of the many fine
buildings of Dún Laoghaire. A stone plaque on its walls announces
that this is the West Pier Pumping Station of the Corporation of
Dún Laoghaire. In the form of a cluster of five pagodas, clad in
polished granite, it contains the pumps which propel the sewage
through a pipeline, beneath the waters of the bay, to the treatment
works at Ringsend.

The pumping station, together
with a car dismantler's yard and
other unsightly undertakings,
occupies a landfill site, contained
by a concrete barrier behind the
breakwater. A car park and a
lawn provide space for sailors,
and the seaward edge of the lawn
is frequented by canoeists and
windsurfers.

A few buildings of the
twentieth century, including the
Dún Laoghaire Motor Yacht Club
and a Navigation School, are the
only substantial additions to the
pier itself since its completion in
the 1840s. A notice-board, beside
the school, displays a dis-
concerting poster telling how
healthy will be the walk to the
lighthouse and how quickly it
should be accomplished. Its

The West Pier lighthouse, a peak of
perfection of the stone-mason's art

brighter and more artistic companion depicts the birds that those who concentrate on an athletic walk will probably fail to see.

In common with the great South Wall (see p. 233) across the bay, the breakwaters of Dún Laoghaire are made from granite hewn from Dalkey Hill (see p. 200). A railway line, constructed to bring the stone to the harbour, ran downhill all the way. The descending laden trucks provided the energy to haul the empties back to the quarry.

The most remarkable feature of the Pier is that, in spite of its conception as a purely functional harbour wall, it has become something of a haven for wildlife in the form of birds, butterflies and flowers.

While the sea bed within the harbour is submerged at all levels of tide, an area of mud flat is exposed at low water outside the harbour at the base of the pier. Lying in a sheltered position, the mud is stable and makes a fairly secure home for a variety of burrowing shellfish, small shrimps and marine worms. Free from strong currents, the worms and shellfish relax in their burrows and filter digestible organisms from the sea when the tide covers them. The shrimps are more active and go hunting on the surface of the mud. Insecurity for these invertebrates stems from the birds which spend the winter in Dublin Bay and have developed bills, legs and habits to hunt for them. Known generally as 'waders', they have relatively long legs and narrow, pointed bills. Their long legs and splayed toes enable them to stalk or run across the mud without sinking. Those with long bills probe for shellfish and worms. Others run hither and thither in pursuit of the shrimps or anything else that is unwise enough to stay exposed.

The birds are much of a muchness in shape, but they come in many sizes, from the curlew, to the bar-tailed godwit and down to the dunlin and to the little stint — something of a rarity. They are the species which hunt by probing and they all have similar colour patterns, of speckled brown — dark on the upper parts, pale below. Some, such as the curlew with its curved bill and the redshank with red legs, are easy to distinguish. Others give to ornithologists that special feeling of satisfaction that rewards all holders of arcane knowledge. The active hunters include the sanderling with its silver back and the ringed plover with a black collar. The outstanding species, which anyone can recognise, is the oyster-catcher — black and white with red legs and a powerful pink bill. It is able to crunch the shells of hapless molluscs. Other places within the Bay, Bull Island (see p. 228) above all, have far more birds and a greater variety, but the West Pier allows close-up views from a wall of just the right height for comfortable support.

Granite weathers to form an inhospitable acid soil in which few plant species can thrive. However, the blocks of the pier are fixed with mortar, made from lime, which counteracts the acidity. This is enough to allow a variety of flowers and shrubs to colonise the pier, and even for a grass sward to develop in places. Sycamores root in the crevices, and there is an abundance of red and white valerian, which grows on the walls nearly all the way along.

Away from the pier, swimming birds take over from the waders. Most of them are species which distribute themselves very widely in coastal waters so that they are seldom plentiful. Some, such as the great crested grebe and the merganser, nest in inland waters. Others, the great northern diver, the red-throated diver and the long-tailed duck breed in the far north.

The end of the pier is inhabited by fisherfolk and, sometimes in winter, by one of the most specialised of the birds of the Bay. The purple sandpiper, a not-particularly purple bird with dumpy form and orange legs, lives only by the edge of the rocky shore, where it hunts for small creatures amongst the wrack at low tide.

At the end of the pier, the lighthouse, together with the long disused store and keeper's quarters, show the stone-mason's art at its peak of perfection. The granite blocks are cut and shaped to fit together and create a marvellously elegant finish. Any good mason can achieve this with Portland stone — but to work to such a high degree in granite takes more than ordinary skill. The lighthouse is surrounded by a concentric pattern of paving stones, and the whole complex bears a silent testimony to designers and craftsmen who put their souls into the work.

Grid 21R, OS Dublin City Map (16th ed.) Bus 7, 7A, 46A to Dún Laoghaire, DART to Dún Laoghaire Station. Notices demand that dogs be leashed — but their owners often pay no attention. A delightfully gentle, level walk but with absolutely no shelter. Manageable by well-sprung buggies and wheelchairs with large wheels. Pleasant picnic spots on the outer side of the breakwater and near the lighthouse. Food and drink in Old Dunleary. Car parking at the Coal Harbour.

Sandymount, Booterstown and Blackrock

A decidedly suburban wilderness, abounding with birds, sea shells and wide open spaces. Suitable all year, occupies a couple of hours each visit.

Dublin Bay is disappearing. It has been doing so for some thousands of years and, all things being equal, will continue to into the unforeseeable future. There are always possibilities for its salvation. If global warming lives up to the worst predictions, sea level will rise, Dublin Bay will grow again, and all those lovely houses on Strand Road will be lost beneath the waves. Every so often, the port authorities reclaim more land — in the face of fierce opposition from some conservationists. But the land would emerge anyway, not only because the Liffey and the smaller rivers deposit silt, but because the marine currents have been bringing in material from the bed of the Irish Sea since the end of the ice age.

Luckily for living Dubliners, the changes are gradual and the pleasurable experiences of exercising dogs, watching birds, digging lugworms, or just walking over the sand flats, will not vanish overnight or even within a lifetime. At low tide, wellie-clad citizens can walk all the way from Ringsend to Blackrock. The wellies are necessary because, although the sand dries up, a number of permanent streams run out from surface drainage pipes which penetrate the sea wall. These streams can be a little too broad to jump, but are shallow enough to paddle across.

The construction of breakwaters of large boulders, and of the railway embankment of neatly-fitted granite paving, prevents the development of a natural succession of sand dunes. But, at the corner formed between Strand Road and the playing fields of Seán Moore Park, blown sand makes a little effort to assert itself, and marram grass grows on tiny sand hills. From this point, all the way to Blackrock, the limestone bed-rock is covered over with the sand flats. The rising tide covers the sand completely, though with relatively shallow water. Notices warn of the dangers of the in-coming tide and the risk of a severe wetting is real because the water moves at a remarkable speed. Getting cut off on a sand-bank is a distinct possibility, though the danger is more of discomfort than of drowning.

At high water, enjoyment of the coast is confined to the narrow strip of footpath and lawn that runs between the breakwaters and the busy road. Such a walk does give the pleasure of admiring the neat houses and encountering the occasional Martello tower. From a military point of view, the south side of Dublin Bay was vulnerable, a convenient spot for invading forces to be landed from vessels lying just offshore. The shore battery at the Half Moon, on the South Wall (see p. 233) commanded the main approach to the port, but fear of Napoleon led to the building of the chain of towers along the exposed flank, each within gunshot of the next.

Sea shells are plentiful close to the tide-line. They belong to a number of species of bivalve mollusc, creatures whose shells grow in pairs and are hinged at one point. All of them burrow in the sand so that the shell is completely hidden. When covered by the tide, each individual extends a pair of tubes to the surface of the sand — one to suck in, the other to expel the water. The mollusc filters out and digests the small organisms from the water, rejecting the sand grains and other indigestible objects.

The most abundant species is the razor shell, very much the shape and size of the old-fashioned barber's razor. It lives at the outer margin of the sand flats. The other familiar species is the cockle, which has a wider habitat and can be found in the shallows. Cockles abound but mussels are rare because they need rocks or some other fixed support to attach themselves to, and these are scarce at Sandymount. All of these creatures are very good to eat — except that in Dublin Bay they are highly dangerous because their filtering habits lead to their accumulating quantities of what are politely known as 'faecal coliforms' — bacteria released from inadequately treated sewage. Greatly improved treatment works have made the Bay a very much safer place than it has been, but the risk remains.

Amongst the shells at the tide-line lie heaps of pencil-shaped tubes of sand. These are the discarded coats of *Lanice*, the sand-mason worm which constructs the tube by cementing sand grains

The pond in Blackrock park, its level controlled by pumping within the Doric temple

together with a secretion. When covered with water, *Lanice* extends a fan of tentacles, which form a net, to capture planktonic creatures. A little way out towards the sea, the sand flats, in places, are decorated with small conical heaps of grey material. These are the castings of the lugworms, which live in U-shaped burrows and pass the sand through their guts, digesting any edible portions and making neat heaps with the rest.

More numerous than the human bait-diggers, are the many species of birds that come to hunt for the worms and molluscs. Gulls remain there year-round but the majority of fowl are waders with long legs and sensitive bills. The black-and-white oyster-catcher is strong enough to prize open the cockles. The curlew has a long, down-curved bill which can dig successfully for the lugworms. The knot — short, stubby and generally nondescript — was named in honour of King Canute who shared its predilection for the edge of the tide. Bigger than any of these is the brent-goose which feeds on green algae and sometimes on the grass of the playing fields and lawns. All of these retire to arctic regions for the summer, returning with their families in autumn, while their nesting places freeze.

Nineteenth-century photographs of the Dublin to Kingstown Railway show an engine with a tall smoke-stack puffing its way across the strand. A long section of the track was laid on an embankment, a considerable distance from the shore. At the time, there were few protests about the risks of ecological damage — indeed the phrase had not yet been invented. Without doubt, the embankment reduced the area of cockle habitat. But its construction added greatly to the biodiversity of the area, forming as it did the remarkable entity of Booterstown Slob. Although man-made, the Slob has many of the features of a coastal lagoon and is a favoured haunt of teal, heron and lapwing, among other birds, which find little to attract them on the sand flats.

Eastwards from Booterstown, a pleasant stretch of lawn, sheltered by the railway embankment, runs behind the houses as far as Blackrock Park. For part of the way there is a drainage channel, sometimes visited by kingfishers. Like Booterstown Slob, this region is politically incorrect, being the final stage of a landfill operation. The lawn ends at the boundary of the beautifully landscaped Blackrock Park. The swimming baths, followed by road, rail and seaside properties, effectively terminate the easily accessible and traffic-free open spaces.

Grid 17M to 19Q, OS Dublin City Map (16th ed.) Many buses, including 3, 5, 7 and 45, give access to various points along Strand Road and Rock Road. There are car parks along Strand Road and at Booterstown and Blackrock. The sand flats at low tide are safe havens for dogs and for people of all ages, free from traffic — a rare quality in these days of off-road vehicles and mountain bikes. The footpaths and lawns are buggy- and wheelchair-friendly; the sand flats are not. Not an especially inviting region for a picnic, but food and drink abound in the nearby townships of Sandymount, Merrion, Booterstown and Blackrock.

Malahide

The Seaside

As good a seaside as any — with the special added attraction of a fine display of fossils from the days when Malahide was a coral sea. Suitable all year, occupies a couple of hours.

Malahide grows and grows, with more people and many more houses. But the seaside remains with few alterations — besides greatly improved car parking — and the fossils which can be found there are very much the same as they have been for the past few hundred-million years. The coast road runs along a raised beach so that the foreshore lies three or four metres below it, effectively screened from the traffic above.

To the north of the car park, a row of sand dunes with marram grass lies at the edge of the broad beach. Beyond them, a narrow strip of water, bordered by the marvellous strand which extends to Donabate, defines Malahide Island, a peninsula firmly attached to the shore farther to the north. From Malahide, it looks very much like a real island, and golfers used to travel to their club there by ferry. A notice warns of perilous currents which arise from the fact that the 'island' is a large sand spit extending southwards across the estuary of the Broad Meadow Water, the river flowing from the east. Twice a day, the enclosed lagoon fills and empties with the tide. As it is more than a mile wide at its mouth, all the water contained must rush through the channel which is not much more than a hundred metres in breadth. In the nineteenth century, the Great Northern Railway Company built the embankment and bridge across the river to carry their Dublin to Belfast line.

At low tide, there is a seaside walk of 4 miles along the shore to Portmarnock Point, at the tip of the Velvet Strand. High tide interrupts this for a while between Robswalls Castle and the southernmost of the two domesticated Martello towers. The Castle was built in the fifteenth century by the Anglo-Norman Birmingham family. The Martello towers were sea defences to keep the French at bay in Napoleonic times.

The clean sand, scattered with the shells of razor shell, oysters and others, is deposited by marine currents. Liable to be shifted by the wind, it is stabilised by the growth of the marram. Over the years, dunes build up and, later on, other grasses grow to form spits — such as the Island and Portmarnock golf links — or simply add to the coastal land as has happened around the car park. In the absence of lawn mowers or grazing beasts, woodland would ultimately take over.

Seashore birds abound here, though not in such enormous numbers as on the sand flats of Dublin Bay (see p. 228). In winter, brent geese feed on the green algae that cover the rocks near the top of the tide line. Oystercatchers abound and turnstones work over the seaweeds on the lower rocky places. In summer, terns are plentiful.

The concrete walls at the top of the strand have been built in the places where the sea, instead of building up the dry land, is attempting to carry it away. In places, stones from the till lie at the base of the walls, and these are angular, rather than rounded. This shows that they have only recently been released from the glacial deposits and have not been rolled around by the waves for long enough to have been ground to smooth shingle. The limestone bedrock is exposed in places and it forms the most interesting feature of the seashore at Malahide.

Southwards from the car park, the walk along the strand is interrupted before long by the first ridge of limestone. The ridges become more and more frequent and, eventually, the scene changes from one of beach with rock outcrops to one of rock with small beaches. A little to the north of Robswalls Castle, the beach is covered by the high tide which laps about the base of a retaining wall. Here the rocks have a number of brachiopod fossils, traces of creatures which bear a slight resemblance to cockle shells. There are also crinoids or sea-lilies, animals — not flowers — which grow on long stalks. Like the other fossils at Malahide, they are so firmly embedded in the rock that they can seldom be chipped out: visitors must be content with looking at them.

Fossil sea lily exposed on the shore at Robswalls Castle

Immediately after the gents' shelter lies a high ridge of rock followed by a low one. The low ridge abounds in fossil corals which faintly resemble cushions. Some show a pattern of small white circles; others are fan-like. These corals lived in colonies, each individual animal having a tube of its own, a little smaller than a cigarette. The pattern of white circles is made where the waves have eroded the fossil colony across the tubes. The fans result where the tubes have been cut at a slant. On the same shelf of rock there is one much bigger coral, about 5 cm wide by 15 cm long with a ladder-like structure. This is *Caninia*, which you may find also on the banks of the Shannon and on the Sligo coast at Streedagh. Its presence shows that all these strata were laid down at the same time.

After the rock comes a small beach and then another bed of limestone — pale grey, much purer and, therefore, more easily dissolved by the sea than the blackish stone. It has been worn into curious shapes with ridges and deep round hollows. Towards the south, the angle at which the rocks dip becomes more pronounced. The dip is to the north, giving a smooth, gentle ascent from the south, which ends abruptly in a sharp drop of a metre or so. This dip angle steepens quite suddenly and changes abruptly so that the downward slope runs towards the south. There is a geological fault at this point where the strata were broken and forced out of alignment. However, it is so difficult to see that the nineteenth-century workers of the Geological Survey failed to record it.

The slope of the rock reverses once more to take a northerly dip below the next retaining wall. Beyond the bathing place, the concrete pier follows the line of a bed of black shale. The shale is derived from silt, carried down by a river, rather than from the skeletons of marine organisms in clear salt water.

Then there is a little bay with cliffs at the back, marking the position of the next fault. The strata leading up to it become more and more broken and are suddenly replaced by completely different rock after the fault line. This is the best place for brachiopods which abound in the pale brown broken stones on the shore.

Corals, by and large, are associated with glorious warm water and coastal conditions far removed from those at Malahide. The creatures whose traces remain in these rocks lived and died in the Carboniferous era, some 300 million years ago. At that time, Malahide did indeed enjoy a tropical climate, being located some-where close to the Equator. But the continental plate on which it lay meanly moved northwards to our present, cooler regions.

Grid 02445, Sheet 50. Bus 42, 43, DART or train to Malahide Station and follow the road eastwards to the sea shore. Lovely beach, safe for dogs and children but best at low tide. Busy with possible traffic problems in summer; peaceful in winter. Car park on the seafront. Seaside footpaths for buggies and wheelchairs, endless picnic spots and good food and drink in the town.

Loughshinny

The Seaside

A secluded seaside place with exceptionally impressive geology and an Iron Age rampart. Suitable all year, occupies half a day.

Fortunately, the dreaded developers seem to have forgotten Loughshinny. Tucked in between the busy dormitory resorts of Rush and Skerries, it remains a haven, a remote cove — scarcely a lough — with a cluster of houses, a pleasant beach and a busy little fishing harbour. This alone would make it well worth a visit, but Loughshinny can lay a fair claim to having some of the most dramatic rock formations in the country. It also comes with an archaeological site which is impressive in its own way and may be one of the most important yet un-dug in Ireland. While rejoicing in these superlatives, it must be said that everything is on a modest scale and waiting to be enjoyed in the course of an afternoon walk.

Large signposts on the Belfast road show the way to the well-known seaside places: first to Portraine and Donabate and next to Rush, Lusk and Skerries. The latter is the turn for Loughshinny and leads past the wonderful fifteenth- or sixteenth-century church tower of Lusk. A square structure, it has a turret at each of three of its corners to complement the ancient round tower which forms the fourth. From the village of Lusk, signposts show the way to Loughshinny. The road runs between fields of wheat and market vegetables, passing an occasional thatched cottage as well as some of the last remaining houses in Ireland that have mud walls.

A car park at the end of the road gives a view, to the east, of a breakwater and fishing boats, and, to the west, of the astounding cliff section. Across the cove, to the south, is the long, level promontory of Drumanagh with its Martello tower beyond which, and visible as an unprepossessing hump on the skyline, lies a cross-section of the earthen rampart that protected the headland from the neighbours in the Iron Age.

The breakwater, built originally of the abundant local limestone but repaired with concrete, gives the best view of the most spectacular of the rocks. They were deposited in the Carboniferous era at the bottom of a tropical sea. The oldest strata are the Loughshinny black shales, formed from muddy deposits, similar to those forming at present in the Bull Island lagoon. In these, the decay of dead plants and animals released carbon particles amongst the silt grains. Subsequently, for a long period, the sediments were laid down in deep, clear water. This succession of

Folded rock strata at Loughshinny

alternating clear and muddy water was repeated a number of times and helps to explain the appearance of the rocks. In the course of some millions of years, the sediments solidified — the clear-water deposits forming grey limestone and the carbonaceous mud becoming black shale.

These rocks originally bedded down in horizontal layers. Then came the drama. An African continental plate collided with its European neighbour and crumpled the rock strata. The crumplings were very irregular. They formed the Hartz Mountains in Germany which gave their name to the event, the Hercynian. They also built the parallel mountain ranges of Cork and Kerry. However, these formations are so big, only a geologist with the aid of surveying equipment can make out what was happening. The beauty of the Loughshinny folding is that, as it is on such a small scale, it can be appreciated by anyone. What is more, the alternating dark and pale rock makes the structure even clearer. The folds opposite to the pier are extremely sharp, giving the impression of a series of capital 'M's. One more piece of geological drama can be seen in the cliff section. This is the much more recent deposit of glacial till from the great ice sheet which travelled southwards in the Irish Sea basin and over the midlands. This mass of rock fragments of all sizes — from large blocks to gravel and clay — lies on top of the folded rocks and is the base material of the fertile soil of Fingal.

At low tide, there is a pleasant, sheltered strand bounded by a footpath which leads from the car park to the cliffs. The path is bordered by lyme grass, a tall blue-green plant which is one of the few able to grow on blown sand. Sea beet, with shiny, green, spinachy leaves, grows amongst it. The wild ancestor of spinach and sugar beet, it is good to eat although better collected from the cliffs where there is no risk of contamination by dogs. Tree mallow, a tall plant on cabbage-like stalks with big purple flowers, is plentiful and is sometimes planted in cottage gardens.

The path runs along the base of the cliffs of black shale at the head of the bay and then rises where a small gulley gives access to the cliff path and a wonderful walk around the Drumanagh promontory.

The walk is good any time of year, but possibly at its best in August when the greatest variety of wild flowers is in bloom and the fulmar petrels are still on their nests and flying close to the cliff top. The petrels look rather like seagulls, but they hold their wings stiffly and glide on the thermals. It is more interesting to visit at low tide, when the rocks at the base of the cliffs are exposed and oystercatchers, together with the big, handsome black-and-white shelduck and other shoreline birds, are more active.

The rocks at the edge of the tide have been worn down so that only the inner parts of the folds remain — a series of whale-like humps. There are caves in the cliffs, excavated by the waves where they have removed the softer rock from the inner sides of the folds. The coastline is unstable, in witness whereof stand the remains of the ruins of a house which was built a little too close to the edge.

The entire promontory is cut off from the mainland by a great earthen ditch and rampart which runs from north to south for 400 paces. The enclosed area of 15 hectares is a great expanse of almost level ground, bordered by the low cliffs, the highest point being 14 metres. The Martello tower near its eastern extremity is a useful reminder of the fact that the headland and cove made an ideal landing place in the days of sailing ships.

Excavations within the area revealed, not surprisingly, traces of a settlement of huts. In the 1970s, Professor Barry Raftery picked up one shard of Gallo-Roman Samian pottery from this region. Subsequently a number of metal artefacts were removed illicitly by a metal-detector enthusiast. These have not been fully described but they include both Roman and native goods which had no military connection. On the basis of these finds Drumanagh attained prominence in the pages of *The Sunday Times*, in 1996, as evidence of Roman invasion and occupation of Ireland — views which had been kept under wraps by some conspiracy of traditionalist scholars and were courageously revealed by the writer of the article. It made entertaining but singularly unconvincing reading. Roman or Roman-derived objects had long been known from many places in Ireland, including burials on nearby Lambay — but even the Roman writers who mentioned Ireland had nothing to say about invasions.

More excavation may very well reveal further Roman remains on the promontory, and a great deal more besides. Meanwhile, it's a lovely quiet place for a Sunday walk and a dream of Celtic and Roman peoples enjoying the peace of the seaside and the view of the mountains two thousand years ago.

Grid O2756, Sheet 50. Number 33 bus for Rush passes within a mile of the cove. A safe seaside and good for dogs; the path to the seashore is good for buggies and wheelchairs, difficult thereafter. Car parking at the harbour; an endless variety of picnic places.

Bull Island

One of Europe's best places to see sea birds in winter, and a garden of wild flowers in summer — to say nothing of a marvellous strand, and all within Dublin's fair city. Suitable all year, occupies half a day.

The great sand spit which extends from Clontarf to Sutton makes a fair claim to being Nature's most generous gift to the people of Dublin. On the seaward side, Dollymount strand, 3 miles of safe bathing beach, provides a perfect playground for the enjoyment of a variety of activities. Towards the shore lies an equal length of incredibly interesting salt marsh and lagoon — the delight of ornithologists and earnest ecologists. Between these, golfers disport themselves on a green sward — edged with an abundance of rare and beautiful wild flowers. The shallow lagoon, which gives the island a measure of isolation and makes it a secure roosting place for myriads of birds, is also a haven for small boats and those who love them.

Many of the scientists who have made special studies of the Bull collaborated to produce a beautiful and scholarly book about it. Edited by David Jeffrey, it was published by the Royal Dublin Society, in 1977. Jeffrey subsequently produced an introductory guide to the island. In 1953, the Three Candles Press published a charming book on the birds of the Bull and on its importance as a sanctuary for wildlife. The author was a Jesuit, P.G. Kennedy, who was one of the best ornithologists of his time and a founding father of nature conservation in Ireland.

Bull Island may properly be considered a gift to the people, because it is very much younger than the city of Dublin. Sand flats, appearing at low tide, had long been present to north and south of the Liffey, but they were always covered at high water and, therefore, devoid of any land plants. The South Wall, built in the course of the eighteenth century, helped to keep the main channel free from unpredictably shifting shoals (see p. 233). But the sand had to go somewhere and began to accumulate in the region of the North Bull sandbank, ultimately appearing as dry land. Captain William Bligh's map of Dublin Bay, drawn in 1800, marks as 'dry' a tiny oblong island due north of the Poolbeg Lighthouse, roughly where the causeway now crosses Bull Island.

In 1801, to keep the North Bull in its place and prevent it from encroaching into the port, Richard Broughton revived an earlier scheme for the construction of a north wall. The timber bridge at Clontarf was built in 1819, and the great North Wall itself was completed in 1825. Silt from the Liffey and seabed sediments, carried northwards by the rising tide, were deposited in increasing quantities between the North Wall and Sutton. Bull Island has been growing rapidly ever since — inwards towards the shore, until thwarted by the two streams Nanikin and Santry, and outwards into the Bay where tidal and Liffey currents may eventually halt its advance.

Dublin Corporation's Parks Department, custodian of the Bull, has deposited a row of boulders over the whole length of the strand, close to high-tide mark. This is to keep cars away from the outer edge of the dunes. In the absence of cars and people, sand-dune formation follows a fairly orderly sequence, though it may be disrupted from time to time by particularly fierce storms. Blown sand forms a ridge above the line of the highest spring tides. Marram grass, a rush-like plant with sharp spikes at the leaf tips, establishes itself. Below the ground, its long, branching roots form a mesh which prevents the sand from being blow any further. Above ground, the tufts of leaves capture the errant sand grains and build the dunes higher and higher. The older grasses die away and newer plants grow on top of them. The height attained by the ridge, at any particular place, is dictated by a combination of wind, marine currents and weather. From time to time, a new ridge begins to develop, parallel to the existing one and further out to sea; at least four may be made out on Bull Island.

Marram grass on the sand dunes of Dollymount Strand

Although the marram grass thrives under the extremely harsh conditions of salt air and a shortage of fresh water, it is not equal to the effects of car parking or of too many people climbing the slopes. This is the reason for the car barrier; pedestrian incursions have not been too serious yet. Damage to dunes can have catastrophic results, bringing about sudden changes whereby the sand moves to invade fields, houses and even golf links.

The Visitor Centre, at the outer end of the causeway, offers a variety of information leaflets and books, together with a good video and exhibition, all under the control of knowledgeable and helpful officials. A gentle walk for three-quarters of an hour along the strand takes you from the Centre to the tip of the island. Although the least adventurous route, it is a wonderful walk between a wall of high sand dunes to the north-west, and the seascapes and sky of Dublin Bay to the south-east. The dunes isolate the beach completely from the traffic and suburbs less than a mile away, and give a wonderful feeling of remoteness from the pressures of the modern world. The sea, depending on the weather, offers a choice of calm, sparkling blue, or of angry breakers beneath a dramatic ceiling of storm clouds.

The dunes, with their waving marram grass, are never quite uniform and there is a stretch near the tip where they are being eroded rather than building up. At the tip itself, one or more new islands grow or disappear over the years and there is a fence to discourage people from straying there and walking on the well-camouflaged nests of the little tern. On the main island, at the tip, the dune system becomes much more complicated, and the sand banks reach their greatest elevation of more than 10 metres. These heights provide a fine view back over the salt marsh — the side of the island where the greatest numbers and variety of birds congregate in winter.

The most adventurous walk is back along the edge of the salt marsh — which edge depends on the state of the tide. High-water spring tide covers the marsh completely and that is what gives it its special character. Only a very small number of plant species can survive this twice-monthly inundation. Some, such as the sea pink, in May, and the sea aster, in September, are beautiful by any standards. Others appeal mainly to ecologists on account of their unusual life styles. The outer edge of the marsh marks the point to which all tides flow and where hardly any species of flowering plants can survive. Among the exceptions are sea grass and the slightly edible glasswort. Beyond the edge lies a great expanse of mud — soft in places, firm in others. Beneath its surface dwell, in astronomical numbers, shellfish, worms and shrimps. Each species of wildfowl that visits the Bull has evolved to prey on one or more of these creatures.

About a dozen different species of birds arrive on Bull Island in autumn and stay till spring. They have travelled south from the enormous areas of Arctic land and lakes which provide them with endless food and space in summer, but are barren, cold deserts in winter. The brent geese go to Canada to breed, the knot to Siberia, while the others live somewhere between these two extremes. Some are easy to identify, particularly the shelduck which is white with a harness of black and chestnut. The oystercatcher is black and white with a red bill, the curlew is grey-brown with a long, downcurving bill. Thereafter, identification becomes complicated. It is better simply to enjoy the spectacle of thousands of birds feeding contentedly or taking to the wing and giving wonderful displays of precision flying — dark as they turn their backs and suddenly turning to dazzling white as the whole flock changes direction in the sunlight.

In spring, most of the visiting birds depart. A few pairs of shelduck and oystercatcher stay to breed, and large numbers of gulls feed or rest in the lagoon. On dry land, amongst the dunes, skylarks sing all day long. Spring also brings the wild flowers and brilliant colours to last throughout the summer and late into autumn. More than 300 species have been recorded here, amongst them perhaps the greatest profusion of wild orchids to be seen anywhere in Ireland. None of these are quite in the bracket required by florists for their more affluent customers, but the abundant spikes of little pink and purple flowers more than make up for what they lack in size and shape. The best wild-flower patches lie on the low, sometimes damp, ground between the high dunes and the salt marsh.

The wildlife of Bull Island is so rich that it is bewildering to a casual visitor. The Dublin Naturalists' Field Club and Birdwatch Ireland both organise conducted tours.

Grid O2135, Sheet 50. Bus 30 to Dollymount. Firm sand for buggies and wheelchairs and very safe shallow water. Dogs should be kept away from the salt marsh and lagoon to leave the birds in peace — too much disturbance damages their health. Dog-on-lead orders meet you at every point of entry. Endless picnic spots on the strand. Car parking on the approach roadside and on the shore.

South Wall

If the Great South Wall were merely a world-class feat of engineering, it would merit a visit. But, snaking its way out to the Poolbeg Light far out in Dublin Bay, the breakwater has an atmosphere of pure magic — perhaps coming from the sense of isolation it creates as you walk along it.

The wall is wide enough to be safe, but so narrow that there is simply nowhere else to walk. The view on the outward journey is, beyond the sea, of Howth and the Dublin and Wicklow Mountains. On the return, the chimneys, cranes and ships of the port provide an opposite, but equally pleasing, scene — the contrast between wilderness and the country's lifeline to the goods of the outside world.

With just one gap, where the River Dodder flows, the South Wall runs all the way from Heuston Station to the lighthouse, a distance of nearly 6 miles. But, in the docklands area, much of its length is inaccessible, being the property of ESB, Dublin Corporation and other honourable public bodies. The usual Sunday walk begins at the eastern extremity of the ESB premises, where there is a lovely little triangle of beach with silver sand and marram grass. This is an accumulation of blown sand, whipped up by the wind from the South Bull at low tide. The two great sand banks of Dublin Bay have born the surname 'Bull' for centuries, perhaps derived from the ancient settlement of Clontarf, *the meadow of the bull.*

The South Bull gets covered by all tides except at its northern end in the region of Irishtown where, with a little help from the authorities, it is slowly adding to the dry land of Dublin and encroaching into Dublin Bay. If there were no sea walls in the region, the blown sand from the Bull would have formed sand dunes; indeed, Ringsend was built on an ancient sand spit. The angular sea wall and the road by the shore prevent the development of dunes. However, they do allow the growth of the marram, which anchors the sand so it forms firm, dry land. This in turn will eventually be invaded by clovers and a variety of other plants.

A westerly breeze wafts an interesting, though unsavoury, aroma towards the sea at this point. This is no new phenomenon to the residents of Ringsend, since, towards the end of the nineteenth century, the village was given the honour of purifying the sewage of Dublin's fair city. Previously, this material had passed without any such ceremony into the river within the confines of the inner city. For the greater part of a century, the treatment at Ringsend was simply one of maceration and release on the flowing tide, so that the waste would not return back up the river from whence it came. Releasing sewage to the sea in this way is one of the most effective ways of rendering it innocuous — up to a point. The point comes when the human population becomes too great for natural purification to take place. This happened some years ago, and the treatment plant is being modernised to meet the extra load. Therefore, appreciate the odour, an element of old Dublin about to vanish for ever.

The dam which controls the release of the sewage lies within the fence to the west of the beach, which is where the South Wall proper begins. A little way to the east the site of an abandoned treatment plant has been tidied up to form a little park. Hedge *Veronica*, a shrub with dark, leathery leaves and a blue flower, was planted there long ago and still survives. It is one of few species which can thrive in the salt-laden atmosphere. Sea spurge, a plant with pale green fleshy leaves, is one of the more conspicuous wild flowers there.

The last building at the landward end of the wall is a one-storey house, neatly constructed of limestone with granite door and window frames. It was once a pumping station to deal with drainage water from the low-lying township of Pembroke. Here, the great breakwater begins, welcoming visitors with a warning notice of the inherent dangers of uneven stone paving. Though uneven, the surface is unusual and interesting. The paving stones are hewn from granite, each one measuring about 3 feet 6 inches long by 1 foot wide. They came from Dalkey (see p. 200), ferried across the bay in sailing barges known as gabbards.

Details of the building of the wall are given in H.A. Gilligan's masterly volume, *A History of the Port of Dublin*. The problem confronting the authorities was that the great sandbanks shifted continuously and ships regularly ran aground when attempting to locate and sail up the main channel of the Liffey. Moreover, the estuary was extremely difficult and dangerous to navigate in strong winds. The solution was devised early in the eighteenth century, and the City Assembly agreed to fund the building of a sea

Rock defences of the South Wall

wall along the south bank of the Liffey, seawards from Ringsend. In 1715, work on the first structure, of wattle and stones supported by piles, began. Completed in 15 years, it made a great improvement but was frequently damaged. The present wall, clad on both sides with neatly-cut and fitted granite blocks, and filled in with sand and rubble, was begun in 1759 — at the seaward end — but not completed until 1788. In the meantime, the existing lighthouse had been built and its candles first lit on 29 September 1767. One reason for beginning the wall at the outer end was to provide foundations and security for the lighthouse as quickly as possible.

The sand flats of the South Bull, as long as they are uncovered by the tide, teem with bird life. Black-headed gull and herring gull are there throughout the year. In winter, it is a favourite haunt for oystercatchers, which dig for cockles. A smaller bird with a beautiful silver-grey back, the sanderling, runs hither and thither at the edge of the tide, hunting for shrimps. The rocky shore, created by the stones and boulders which form the outer protection of the sea wall, is the haunt of the turnstone, a handsome bird with mottled chestnut plumage. Also found here is the rarer, but less striking, purple sandpiper with purplish grey colouring.

The perilous bathing place of the Half Moon Swimming Club makes a break in the line of the breakwater. This also marks the spot where the wall's surface is built at a higher level, providing shelter from the stronger waves of the deeper water. In the early 1990s, a notice told of the perils of submerged rocks, moved in by Hurricane Kay, in 1988. The latest edition of the notice warns of water quality which is below the standards demanded by the regulations of the European Union. Nonetheless, people swim there and survive. The Club's nameplate reads, 'Half Moon Swimming and Water Polo Club founded 1898'. It occupies the buildings of a shore battery, whose guns were supported on 'half-moon' mountings. The inner walls are plastered and whitewashed, but the outer wall, to the south, displays its original granite with a curious insertion of red sandstone.

The power of the sea, even of a shallow sea within the limited confines of Dublin Bay, becomes ever more evident as you progress towards the end of the breakwater. After a storm, the wall is littered with stones and boulders that have been carried by the waves from its outer defences. Beyond the lighthouse, great chunks of masonry rest amongst the breakers which have torn them away from the wall.

The original lighthouse, designed by the architect John Smyth, was altered to its present shape in 1813, and the last lighthouse-keeper left the post in 1964. Poolbeg is a 100 volt, 1.5 kilowatt occulting light showing two red flashes every 20 seconds. It is painted red because you must keep red to your port side as you sail upstream. Its companion across the way is green.

Major repairs and refurbishment to the South Wall, undertaken at the beginning of the twenty-first century, improved the surface and provided a footpath around the tower. There is a park bench in front of the lighthouse on which citizens can relax for a few minutes before beginning the homeward trek. Attaining the Poolbeg Light gives all the satisfaction of the conquest of a mountain peak — with a satisfactorily small fraction of the effort.

Grid O2133, Sheet 50. Bus route 1, for Pigeon House Road, stops about a mile from the beginning of the South Wall. A faintly dangerous seaside place, since there is a drop down to the sea and no fences. Uncomfortable for buggies and wheelchairs, fine for dogs once they don't frighten small children. Car parking on the breakwater. Best at lowish tides which happen between full and new moon.

Dalkey Island

Dalkey Island is a tautologous translation from a confusion of Irish and Danish. Its ancient name in Irish was *Deilg inis*, meaning 'thorn island'. The Norsemen tacked their word *oe*, meaning 'island' on to the *Deilg*, so that 'Dalkey', without the inis still means 'Thorn Island'. So the name *Deilgoe* does not refer in the first instance to the township on the mainland nearby. Thorns are scarce or absent from the island nowadays, but would have been plentiful in times gone by. The Four Masters called it Deilginis-Cualann, the thorny island of the holly.

Excavating in the 1950s, Gordon Liversage discovered that people had lived on Dalkey Island from the mesolithic period right up to the nineteenth century. It may have been an unbroken succession as there is solid evidence of habitation there from every one of the major periods of Irish history and pre-history. This is hardly surprising. Dalkey Sound is narrow enough to have allowed easy access by boat over the whole period of nine or ten thousand years.

The gently-sloping rocky shores around all the islets of the Dalkey archipelago provide a huge area of habitat for limpet, periwinkle and shore crab, and other food for the ancient hunter–gatherers. Remarkably, the bones of a goshawk were found amongst the mesolithic remains, suggesting that the people practised falconry. The neolithic farmers had brought cattle, pigs and sheep to the island, which is covered with a good depth of glacial till and supports rich pasture to this day. The remnants of these animals have been carbon-dated to 5,300 years ago.

A notable cow lived there in 727, according to the Four Masters:

There was a cow seen at Deilginis-Cualann, having one head and one body as far as her shoulders, two bodies from her shoulders hindwards, and two tails; she had six legs, was milked three times each day, and her milk was greater each time. Her milk, and some of the butter made from it, were tasted by many persons.

The same Annals have two more references to Dalkey. In 938, an abbot was drowned nearby 'while fleeing from the foreigners'. Four years later, some citizens survived the sacking of *Ath-cliath* by an army of Leinstermen. They 'fled in a few ships, and reached Deilginis'. These two records are interesting in coming so close together and implying that it was considered to be a place of refuge.

The stone church of the singularly obscure St Begnet is also dated to the tenth century. Its presence suggests that a monastic settlement had been in existence on the island for some time, perhaps several centuries before. The structure of the church is very interesting. The lower courses of the walls are made from large, rounded pieces of granite, collected from the glacial till or from the foreshore. Smaller stones are used on the higher courses. The doorway — and the windows — are supported by lintels rather than arches, and these are the principal evidence for the early date. The most intriguing features are the projections of the walls flanking each of the gable ends. Known as 'antae' they are thought to be copies in stone of the heavy timber beams used in the construction of wooden churches. The theory is that the stonemasons used wooden buildings as their models and copied their shape without realising that such projections were no longer needed. The fireplace in the east wall was added in the nineteenth century by the workers who camped in the church while engaged in building the Napoleonic fortifications.

Whitewashed rocks, a little way above the shoreline on the western side of the island, mark the position of a well in a small cavern. Even in the long, hot summer of the year 2000, it was full of clear water. Once known as the Scurvy Well and credited with curative powers, such a supply of water was a key factor in the 9,000-year occupation of Dalkey Island. Rain water, which might otherwise have seeped through the glacial till to go directly into the sea, was trapped there as a ready supply for people and cattle. Many animals, including sheep and goats, can get their water from the grass that they eat — but humans and cattle both need to drink.

The granite foundation of the island is the ultimate outcrop of the massive pluton that forms the mountain chain that extends from Dublin to the Blackstairs Mountains, in County Wexford. Plutonic rock belongs to the underworld. Crystallised at great depths in the course of mountain building, it remains there until its exposure by the erosion of the overlying rock in the course of many millions of years. The blanket of glacially-derived soil that covers the granite has been carried away by the sea in its lower courses and by over-grazing in the upper, so that bastions of solid rock stand out.

Where the soil is deep enough, grasses, nettles, thistles and bracken thrive. The grass makes a delightful close-cropped sward, maintained by the nibbling of a large population of rabbits and a small herd of feral goats, some of them patriarchal billies with magnificent horns. The low rocks along the east side of the island are a nursery for herring gull and great black-backs. A few other species nest there, but there is nothing like the numbers and variety to be found on Ireland's Eye (see p. 250). In contrast to the slates of Ireland's Eye, granite does not lend itself to the formation of steep cliffs so there are few secure ledges for guillemot, razorbill and kittiwake to congregate on. The accessibility of all parts of the island to picnickers is also a likely factor in controlling the nesting birds.

Thanks to the shelter provided by the islands and the natural harbours formed by creeks and crevices on the granite headland, Dalkey became a place of the greatest strategic and commercial importance. Although narrow, Dalkey Sound is very deep and ships as large as the old mail steamers could pass safely through it or stand at anchor. Its prominence began to decline following the eighteenth-century building of the North and South Walls (see p. 233) at Dublin port, and the later construction of Dún Laoghaire Harbour (see pp 205, 209). In Napoleonic times, the island's potential as a landing place was fully recognised, and formidable coastal defences were built early in the nineteenth century.

The ancient gable of St Begnet's Church on Dalkey Island

The Martello tower, on the highest point of the island, remains the dominant feature. The circular plan and massive walls were likely to have been able to withstand any ship's cannon. The tower is built from granite — with a few internal details in red brick. Granite is an intractable stone and the size of the subtly-curved blocks and regularity of the courses of hand-cut stone testify to remarkable skill of the army of stone-cutters employed in the construction of Dublin's Martello towers. Below the tower, at the south end of the island, there are further gun emplacements, with a little of the original metalwork left — a central pivot and a semi-circular rail so that each gun could command a wide arc.

The walls of the fort are bright with wild flowers — the yellow lady's bedstraw and birds-foot trefoil among others. Both are lime-loving species which would normally reject the acidic granite habitat. But the stones are joined by lime-mortar, and that makes the critical difference.

Dalkey Island, on a bright summer's day, has all the atmosphere of a Mediterranean resort — though perhaps less of a crowd. Blue sea, the mainland cliffs, crowded with the homes and gardens of the affluent, and a great congregation of worshippers of sea and sun, in sailing, rowing and motor boats of endless variety make an idyllic scene — and one long appreciated by the people of Dublin.

In the eighteenth century, thousands of citizens gathered regularly to celebrate the coronation of

His facetious majesty, King of Dalkey, Emperor of the Muglins, Prince of the Holy Island of Magee, Elector of Lambay and Ireland's Eye, Defender of his own Faith and Respecter of All Others, Sovereign of the Illustrious Order of the Lobster and Periwinkle.

Sadly, the celebration was suppressed in 1797 — although it was scarcely a republican occasion, the authorities were not well disposed towards large gatherings. Revived now and again in the ensuing centuries, the sovereignty has sadly been in abeyance for some time.

Grid O2726, Sheet 50. DART or bus 59 or 7D to Dalkey. Very tough going for wheelchairs, robust buggies only, fun for dogs. Good casual ferry service on fine summer days from Coliemore Harbour (amazingly not marked on the map, but north of Sorrento Point) — ask anybody standing near a boat — rowing boats with or without outboards for hire. Excellent for picnics, good food and drink in the hotel by the harbour.

Howth

The cliff walk of Howth is the most remote and wonderful part of the mainland of Dublin. This is all the more remarkable, because in no place is it more than ten minutes' walk from the suburban bus route which encircles the Hill. The magic lies in the fact that the narrow footpath runs between the sea on one hand, and steep hills on the other. Hills and cliffs are too steep for motorbikes and domestic animals and therefore make a paradise of bracken, wild flowers and sea birds.

To a southsider, Howth and the Bailey give the impression of being a long, narrow headland, because the distant profile across Dublin Bay appears to compress the land mass, which is actually square in outline. Cloud often hangs above the headland or descends to cover the top of it, or sometimes hovers round the middle so that the summit appears to float in the air. It is a textbook example of an orographic cloud, forming because the air just above the sea is suddenly forced upwards and the water vapour condenses to form droplets. There is a plausible theory that the disembodied, floating summit gave Swift the idea of the Island of Laputa.

Ireland's Eye and Howth form the northern boundary in Ireland of the Bray Series of rocks. The Series is assigned to the middle of the Cambrian era, between 700 and 800 million years ago, making it far and away the most ancient rock in County Dublin. As on Bray Head, there are two principal rock types: quartzite and shale. What is very wonderful about them is that the same processes that led to their original deposition can be seen at work in present-day Dublin Bay. Clayey material, such as forms the bed of the Bull Island lagoon, is destined to become shale, while the clean beach sand will form quartzite. Both types of sediment exist side by side — as they did when Howth was an assortment of soft submarine sediments.

The important fact about this geology is that quartzite is extremely tough and resists weathering, while the slate is more easily worn away. So, all the high points of Howth are of quartzite, and the lower ground is slatey. The low-lying northern part of the peninsula is underlain by limestone of the Carboniferous era, deposited some 300 million years ago when Ireland enjoyed a tropical climate. Between the Cambrian and Carboniferous periods, the Wicklow Mountains were built and the earth movements which raised them crumpled the Howth strata like a concertina. The lines of folding stand out clearly at several points along the cliff walk. The variations in the nature of the rock strata helped to define the shape of present-day Howth with its steep cliffs to north and east, and not-so-steep crags to south and west.

There is a gap in the geological story from the Carboniferous period until the very much more recent ice age. The ice sheet, which covered the greater part of Ireland, flowed southwards and deposited material rich in limestone on the lower slopes of the peninsula. This has had a profound effect on the inhabitants of Howth. Originally, the lower slopes made excellent pasture land, encouraging the neolithic farmers to establish themselves some 5,000 years ago. They were eventually succeeded by the Anglo-Normans, with their feudal demesnes, and much later by Dubliners using railway and tram to get to and from the desirable seaside properties. What all these people needed was ground that was not too steep and that had soil suitable for farms or gardens. In the course of the twentieth century, people colonised most of these lowlands. However, the steep slopes and the boggy uplands, with their unproductive acid soil, kept potential householders away for long enough for their value as wilderness to be appreciated. The uplands of Howth fortunately remain as open ground, criss-crossed with footpaths.

A satisfactory exploration of Howth will require many trips, during all seasons. The village, made particularly charming by its steep hills and narrow roads, is packed with old and living architecture, to say nothing of excellent restaurants — and a most delightful harbour.

Howth Castle demesne, a little way to the west of the harbour, is inhabited by an ancient castle and its even older family. This remains a private house, but the road past it, leading to the Deerpark Hotel, is open. The oldest part of the Castle dates to the 1500s, while the most modern was designed by Lutyens in the nineteenth century. Granuaile, it is said, paid a surprise visit there and was none too well received.

Up the hill, beyond the hotel, signposts show the way to the rhododendrons. This grove was begun in the 1850s by Lady Emily St Lawrence, who made skilful use of the magnificent cliffs. A problem arose from an insufficiency of soil, and this was solved by transporting it from other parts of the demesne. More than 2,000 varieties of rhododendron now grow there, some on the level ground, others cascading down the cliffs, a kaleidoscope of brilliant colours. Himalayan plants for the most part, they look very much at home in Howth. May and June are the best months to see them in flower.

Long before the gardens were created, neolithic nobles left their mark in the form of one of the biggest dolmens in Ireland. The capstone of this has been calculated to weigh 90 tonnes. It was evidently designed to stand on two great upright stones — and may have done so — only to collapse in the course of the ensuing four thousand years. Whatever its history, the achievement of moving a rock of that size, with nothing more than wooden levers and bare hands, testifies to a remarkable degree of teamwork and suggests the involvement of a person with an exceptional gift of leadership.

A pleasant little guide book, *The Howth Peninsula*, was published locally and gives a description of many of the features of Howth: buildings, wildlife and topography. It includes a picture map which shows the footpaths and gives the names of some thirty features around the coast. Some have the air of long-established Gaelic or English names. Others are fanciful: *Gaskin's Leap*, *Piper's Gut*, *Hippy Hole* and *Fox Hole*, to name a few.

Motorists seeking the cliff walk can drive past the harbour and up the hill to the car park at the end of Balscadden Road. Public transport demands a walk past the harbour, then up the steep hill which climbs the west side of Balscadden Bay, and so to the car park. The old harbour walls, built early in the nineteenth century, now serve to protect a substantial fishing fleet and a host of pleasure craft — the latter accommodated by the marina built in the 1980s. Both of the original breakwaters are a pleasure to walk along: the west pier, a busy fishing quay; the east, a promenade for leisured strolling. A recent new resident below the lighthouse on the east pier is the black guillemot, an uncommon species which nests in summer in gaps between the stones. It is a black bird with a big white patch on each wing.

Howth stone and Howth Harbour

Tower Hill, overlooking the east pier and dominated by its Martello tower, is made of sand and pebbles, not of solid rock. This is the glacial till, deposited by the ice sheet. Most of the pebbles are of limestone, but there are a few purplish ones, scooped up from Portraine where Old Red Sandstone strata reach the surface.

At the base of the pier, the sea breaks over the low-lying limestone rocks of Carboniferous age. Immediately to the south, the character of the Cambrian rock is completely different, with steep cliffs in place of level strata. A dark-green roadside herb can be seen here with its shiny leaves and yellowish flowers. This is called Alexanders and established itself as a wild plant on the coasts of Dublin and Wicklow during the eighteenth century. It was originally a garden herb, used in salads, but fell from favour when celery was introduced.

At the top of the hill, the road runs between wind-shaped sycamores on the left and cliffs of flaking slatey rock on the right. The first steep and tall hill that rises above the upper car park is composed of quartzite, the extremely tough 'Howth stone' which is stained with the iron oxides that provide the lovely golden colour.

The car park at the end of the road is dominated by a latter-day round tower, built of Howth stone, in the 1950s. It serves as defence not against any militaristic invader but from the more insidious noxious effluent of Dublin's populace. It houses part of the controlling system for the sewer which, in the carefree days when public authorities were permitted to dump everything in the sea, released its burden a little way offshore.

There is always plenty to look at on the cliff walk, but the best time for a visit is between April and the middle of July when the wild flowers are in bloom and the cliff ledges are tenanted by thousands of seabirds. Early in summer, the fresh crop of bracken has yet to grow up and sheets of bluebell flower amongst the brown stems of the previous year's growth. The bluebells develop quickly in spring and complete their annual cycle before the bracken shades them out. Where the grass is short, the beautiful and rather rare little pale-blue lily, called squill, grows.

The cliff path leads eastwards from the car park, passing above the flat-topped islets called Puck's Rocks. The birds on them are mostly herring gull. Their chicks like to walk away from the nest within a few hours of hatching, and therefore the parents prefer to nest on level spaces. Also present around Puck's Rocks is the great black-backed gull, a magnificent bird with a 6-foot wingspan.

On the cliffs to the east, fulmar and kittiwake nest on small ledges; but they can be seen in much larger numbers, and in greater comfort, at Casana Rock, half a mile farther on. The path from here goes quite steeply uphill and takes a sharp bend before flattening out at the 60-metre contour, which it follows from the next mile.

The slope to the east is the Nose of Howth and the sea close by is discoloured by the aforementioned effluent. The sewer at this point runs in a tunnel below the all-too-aptly named Nose. The outfall is attended by a gathering of herring gulls, consuming unspeakable morsels. This sight should become a thing of the past when the EU Directive concerning discharge to the sea takes effect.

For the next mile, the sole permanent artificial creations visible are the Kish Lighthouse and occasional granite posts and concrete seats by the path. Bracken is the dominant plant, growing luxuriantly in spite of periodical bush fires. In early summer, there are gardens of pink and white stonecrop and, in places, clusters of white burnet rose and purple bloody cranesbill.

The best bird cliffs are on the north-facing slope of the bay at Casana Rock. The massive, grey-green rock there is an igneous dyke, forced into the older rock in a molten state, perhaps at the same time as the volcanic eruption which formed Lambay Island. The steep, rocky cliff has many narrow ledges and nooks, and these are just right to provide safe nesting places for the birds which spend the greater part of their lives far out at sea. The gulls are nearly all kittiwake, small and delicate and quite easy to distinguish from the herring gulls because their wingtips are black with no white 'mirrors'.

Birds which resemble gulls, but have rather blotchy-coloured wings, enormous noses and big black eyes, are fulmar petrels.

Newcomers to Howth, having first nested there in 1955, they sail on the air currents, wings stiffly stretched out and scarcely moving. Finally, there are two species of penguin-like birds: razorbill which are black and white; guillemot, dark brown and white.

The next little bay gives a closer view of the kittiwake, after which there is a relatively long walk where the slopes are too gentle to be safe for seabirds. The outward route ends at the wall of the lighthouse property on the Little Baily. From there, the view is northwards along the cliffs of Howth and south to Wicklow Head and Bray Head, and takes in the great sweep of hills along Dublin Bay. The bird cliffs around the Baily are less accessible and more dangerous than those on the cliff walk.

The cliff walk within Dublin Bay is less dramatic and less of a wilderness — but it offers the great panorama of coast and mountains as well as the activity of sailing boats and shipping. A short walk up the hill leads to the 'Summit' — it was the summit of the tramway, not of the peninsula. There, pubs and refreshment and a bus back to Howth are available — or, alternatively, access to other footpaths.

Grid O2839, Sheet 50. Bus 31 to Sutton or Howth Harbour, 31A and 31B to the top of the hill or DART to Sutton or Howth. The Cliff Path is a public right of way, safe for well-controlled dogs and children. It is busy on a fine Sunday and not buggy-friendly but there are gentler footpaths which can take buggies and wheelchairs on the hill. The cliffs themselves are highly dangerous, but the path keeps a safe distance from them. Innumerable picnic places; excellent food and drink around Howth Harbour and elsewhere.

Ireland's Eye

I slands are magical. The fact that Ireland's Eye is small and less than a mile from Howth Harbour is of no significance. You must take a boat to reach it, so it remains aloof, beyond the unassisted reach of even the most redoubtable of pedestrians. It is also a singularly inhospitable spot — equalling mountain tops in the absence of shelter and scarcity of potable water.

But on a fine summer Sunday, the magic is palpable. All day from 11 o'clock each morning, from April to October, the stalwart ferries, *Angelus Bell* and *Little Flower*, await trippers at the East Pier of Howth. They have been in the business since 1921. On the west side, facing Howth, is one of Dublin's best bathing beaches. Behind it, the ground rises to the superb cliffs and rock stack to the east. Between them, in May and June, the sward is bright with bluebells and, later on, bracken grows up to colour the landscape green in summer and autumn.

The boat lands at the north-eastern corner of the island, either on the north or the east side according to the height of the tide. A short climb brings you to a small piece of level ground near the Martello Tower, across a patch of soft, peaty soil. Sea beet is the dominant plant here, its dark green, spinach-like leaves covering much of the ground. Several other wild-flower species, almost unknown inland, bloom in summer: sea pink, with tufts of slender stems with pink pom-poms; sea campion, with white bells; and the pink, star-shaped flowers of spurrey.

Until the 1990s, much of the level ground of the island which was free from bracken, was a home for thousands of herring gulls. This was the breeding place of the gull population that had expanded during the twentieth century, thanks to the new source of food which became available as rubbish tips increased in size and number. Then disease, mainly botulism, contracted from the same unwholesome food source, attacked. By the summer of 2000, the herring-gull numbers were greatly reduced, and hundreds rather than thousands were then nesting on the island. They had been replaced to some extent by the larger great black-backed gull — a magnificent bird with a wing span of 6 feet. This gull is more confined to the seashore and traditional seagull food than was the highly adaptable herring gull, and this will probably keep the numbers of black-backs within bounds. Neither species of gull, exquisite creatures though they might be, is quite *persona grata* to conservationists since they eat the eggs and chicks of their neighbours and severely threaten the stocks of other sea birds such as terns.

June is the best month to visit the island, when most of the eggs have hatched and big, woolly chicks with lovely pepper-colouring wander in the grass. Some young, non-breeding gulls are usually present, distinguished from the white and silver adults by mottled brown colouring. It takes four years for the big gulls to develop their full colouring. Where the gulls roost, the ground is bare, the grasses and sea-pink killed by the excessive nutrients in the droppings. Enrichment from the same source produces such a growth of microscopic algae in the little pools of fresh water that the water is bright green.

The cliffs to the north are steep, but furnished with innumerable ledges, providing nesting places for a myriad sea birds. When the young are fully grown, by about the middle of July, the cliff birds move out to sea, and few of them, except the big gulls, will be seen inshore until the following spring. They scatter over a huge range of sea and ocean, never coming in to land. Then, in spring, they return to the cliffs to lay their eggs and rear their young.

A small species of gull, the kittiwake, is the most abundant of the nesting birds. Two penguin-like species are razorbill and guillemot, and one of the most impressive of all is the fulmar. This grey bird, resembling a gull, is related to the albatross, and roams the ocean, gliding above the waves with wings held stiffly and seldom flapped. The fulmar is a newcomer to Ireland from more northerly haunts, and began to nest on Ireland's Eye in the 1950s. The most charming bird is the puffin, having the same black and white colouring as the razorbill, but a less elegant, dumpy shape, a clown-like white face and an incredible multi-coloured bill. The puffin disappeared from the island for 30 years, returning once more in 1986, but the numbers are always small.

There are nests and eggs on every available ledge, and it is easy to get very close views. Although completely out of reach, the cliff birds are only a few yards away and stay where they are as you watch them. In spite of their apparent tameness, they are never fully relaxed in the presence of spectators, and it is kinder to move away from them before too long.

The view from the summit is over the magnificent rock stacks to the east and down to the lowlands of the south of the island. The stacks are densely crowded with nesting birds — the same species as inhabit the other cliffs, with the addition of the gannet. One of the largest and most magnificent of all the birds of Europe, the gannet hunts for fish by flying as much as 20 metres above the surface, half-closing its wings and plummeting down to catch the prey. The first gannet nested on Ireland's Eye late in the twentieth century, and since then their numbers have been climbing steadily. Indeed, all the cliff-nesting birds on the island have been on the increase for many years and their numbers may well be greater than ever before.

The rock stack of Ireland's Eye, surrounded by gannets

One of the most interesting ecological features of Ireland's Eye is the fact that there are no grazing animals. In their absence, a jungle of bracken and tall grasses grows up every summer. Interesting though it is, the jungle abounds in thistles and nettles and is uncomfortable to penetrate. St Nessan's Church stands amongst the bracken, the sole monument to a community which flourished on the island for 500 years from the sixth century on. It is easier to walk all the way around the island than to beat a track across it. Many more of the cliff birds nest on the east side, including, sometimes, a pair of peregrine falcons. And on the west side, near the strand, there are shelduck, a white duck with black markings and an orange sash, which nests in burrows in the sand dunes.

The geology of Ireland's Eye is an entity of horrendous complexity. Piers Gardiner and K.W. Robinson of the Geological Survey published a description of it in 1970. The highest ground is at the north end of the island and its rock is quartzite, an extremely tough material which withstands weathering. In contrast, the shales and sandstones which underlie the greater part of the island have been worn away to give a lower land surface. A variety of red sandstones and shales, in various degrees of contortion, stand out at both ends of the strand. Vigorous earth movements left the island criss-crossed with geological faults which explain some of the deep gullies that mark the landscape.

It is worth going to the island just for the strand, a wonderful stretch of clean sand, with lots of sea shells and a bank to shelter you from the east wind. Ireland's Eye makes a fair bid for first place among the treasures of the wilderness, not just of Dublin but of Ireland — so much to see, so easy to get to, and incredibly close to the centre of the fair city.

Ireland's Eye

Grid O2841, Sheet 50. Bus 31 or DART to Howth, with a short walk along the sea-front from the station to the east pier — whence the boats depart. There is a car park at its base. The terrain (except for the strand) is utterly unfriendly to buggies and wheelchairs, and the cliffs are very dangerous — though the birds are easy to see without any climbing. Not a good place for dogs — unless you enjoy the spectacle of the munching of helpless young birds. Picnics are the sole source of food on the island, but everything from the simplest form of convenience meals to some of the finest cooking in the land is available in the village of Howth.

Inland Waters

Water is the mainstay of all life on earth. It also wets — and occasionally drowns — people and, except for sustaining swimmers for relatively short periods, is in some ways, an entity mildly hostile to humankind. This degree of hostility leads to the greatest contribution made by inland waters to the enjoyment of the environment. Rivers, canals and lakes keep buildings firmly at bay and seldom accommodate crowds of people. As a result, even a small river like the Dodder, or the narrow canals of Dublin, can create a significant measure of open space. With very few exceptions, the banks of these watercourses have room for footpaths and wild flowers, while the surface of the water is a haven for delightfully tame wildfowl. The canals are always peaceful, the river on occasion positively menacing. But they provide a welcome respite from crowded places.

County Dublin has no natural lakes, and County Wicklow but a few. For various utilitarian purposes, the authorities dammed two valleys to create some and these are suggested as places deserving a Sunday visit. The Blessington Lakes constitute the biggest water body in the entire south-east quarter of Ireland. The two lakes in Glenasmole are very much smaller. They are liberally endowed with access points and footpaths. As time goes by, they come to look more and more like the natural mountain lakes which occupied the same valleys some thousands of years before.

The Blessington Lakes

Blessington was — and still is — a charming village above the Liffey valley, and Pollaphuca was, at one time, a splendid waterfall, accessible to Dubliners by steam tram from Terenure. The last tram ran in 1932, and the waterfall is now nearly dry. But the valley has been transformed to a mountain lake which, although man-made, must be classed amongst the most beautiful in the land. Wildfowl abound beside the shallow water at Threecastles, especially in winter.

Having spent most of the Sundays of my childhood there, I admit to bias — but the endless variety of pleasures offered by the Blessington Lakes qualifies them as worthy of the attention of Dubliners for many a month of Sundays. And, if you want more detail than this chapter provides on their history — natural and human — consult the beautiful book edited by my friend, Elizabeth Healy.

The village of Blessington was created, on the edge of the Pale, by Michael Boyle, Archbishop of Dublin, in the seventeenth century. The church was founded in 1682 and, not long afterwards, was provided with a peal of six bells. The church clock claims to be the oldest public timepiece in Ireland. The Archbishop owned estates centred on Blessington that extended to near the Source of the Liffey (see p. 64). These later passed, by marriage, to the Hill family. Wills Hill crowned a highly successful career in politics by being created the first Marquis of Downshire, in 1789. Towards the end of the eighteenth century, his mansion was destroyed by an accidental fire, and the village itself was devastated in 1798, with most of the houses being burned down. The stately present-day appearance of Blessington, with its broad street, market square and courthouse, was decreed by the third Marquis, an outstanding landlord who worked ceaselessly to keep his colossal estates in order. The bizarre fountain opposite the church bears a suitably loyal inscription. In this case, it may indeed reflect the sentiments of the tenantry. The manor house, conveniently situated beside the church, is now a delightful family hotel.

The Blessington Lakes look as if they belong there, and the forests that surround them blend perfectly with the mountain scenery. It is hard to believe that they owe as much to engineers, foresters and landscape planners as they do to nature. The lakes were created in 1940, when a dam was completed at Pollaphuca. Strictly speaking, there is just one lake, but the hill of Baltyboys divides it into three. It is an enormous sheet of water that fills the valley of the King's River, along with two smaller lakes, on the main course of the Liffey. The forests, mostly sitka spruce and Japanese larch, were first planted in 1959. Curiously, the ancestral trees hail from opposite sides of the Pacific Ocean — from the State of Washington and from Japan, respectively.

Perhaps the most surprising fact is that the lakes are not as artificial as they seem. Some 10,000 years ago, the great ice sheet which covered the midlands retreated slowly towards the north. For a long period it formed a dam along the line of hills to the north and west of the present lake. This natural dam impounded a much bigger area of water, extending from Brittas to Hollywood Glen, some 12 miles overall.

Evidence for the former existence of the lake lies in the nature of the gravel and silt deposits in the valley. Details of its history and eventual fate are given in a paper by Anthony Farrington. The lake varied in extent in the course of many thousands of years, at one stage coming to occupy an area very much the same as the present-day reservoir. Then, together with the last remnants of the ice sheet, it finally disappeared and left the valley to the river until 1940, when the ESB built the dam.

It is possible to walk very nearly all the way around the lakeshore. However, it would be a trek rather longer than the 30-odd miles of beach. Several tributary streams inhibit an easy passage and, therefore, it is more satisfactory to make the circuit by road. Fortunately, the shore can be approached easily at the nine 'Amenity Sites' provided by the ESB, and at the bridges and other convenient spots. Each of the amenity sites has parking space, picnic tables and easy access to the shore.

An arm of the Blessington Lakes at Burgage

The roadway has the added attraction of leading through a number of charming and unusually interesting villages. Most of these grew up high above the floor of the valley, making use of the drier and more level ground. This proved to be an important social and economic benefit when the region was flooded, since only 76 homesteads stood below the planned level. The circuit of the lake entails a journey of more than 60 miles. This takes you around it, but leaves out some important bits, so a number of diversions need to be made in order to see everything.

When the valley was first flooded, the lake water lapped upon green pasture. But the intervening 60 years have been more than enough to transform the greater part of the shoreline from damp grass or mud, to clean white sand, which is almost as good as any on the best beaches of Dublin. The waves have carried away the clay portion of the underlying glacial till and left behind the heavier particles of sand. In places, the banks behind the sand are masses of grey or brown clay, sometimes marked with fine horizontal lines. This material is the compacted mud deposited on the floor of the original glacial lake. Each of the horizontal lines represents a winter, when the water was frozen and no mud was carried down by the in-flowing streams.

Blessington stands on the right bank of the Liffey where the soil is rich in lime and therefore good for raising stock. Consequently, this land was much fought over in days of old. History records a bloody skirmish in 1538, at Threecastles. Presumably, there were three towers once upon a time, but only one remains. A castle of the Pale, it overlooked a ford on the Liffey, beyond which the mountain clans of O'Toole and O'Byrne held sway. Life and death in the sixteenth century were not all that simple and the *Annals of the Four Masters* record a defeat of the Fitzgeralds, at the Castle, by an unholy alliance of the English and the O'Tooles.

The east side of the Liffey section of the lake has a fringe of fertile limestone ground, but it is backed by the granite mountains with their poor soil. The greater part of the ground surrounding the King's River lake is equally poor. However, the granite, which is generally so inhospitable, transformed the life of the community on a remote portion of the bleak mountainside.

At Ballyknockan, a fine-grained form of the rock provides an excellent building stone that has been quarried for generations. The quarrymen also built their houses and field fences of granite. Some of them were talented sculptors and have left to posterity a lion and a Virgin and Child which still receive occasional offerings of flowers.

Virgin and Child at Ballyknockan

The Pooka, a mean-minded sprite who usually adopted the form of a horse, dwelt in the middle pool of three in the cascade that bears his name. The waterfall, in a magnificent deep gorge, descends from a rock sill which effectively divided the Liffey in two, forcing it to behave like a lowland stream in its upper reaches. The tall and narrow dam at Pollaphuca diverts the water from the cascade — some to the taps of the citizens of Dublin, some to the hydro-power plants of Pollaphuca and Golden Falls.

Downstream of the dam, the road crosses the gorge on the great stone bridge, built in the 1820s to the design of Alexander Nimmo, who combined an artist's eye with an engineer's mind. His beautiful structure was refurbished in 1999 and successfully carries heavier traffic than anything he could have dreamed of.

Grid N9814, Sheet 56. Bus 65. The map marks many car parks, most of which give access to substantial stretches of sandy beach, though footpaths are few. Sheep are fenced out from the lake so dogs may be exercised freely. Excellent for picnics, mostly rough for buggies and wheelchairs outside the car parks. Bathing is forbidden, but boating can be arranged at the recreation centre south of Blessington. All kinds of food and drink in Blessington, mainly pubs elsewhere.

Glenasmole

A secluded and sheltered valley with a beautiful man-made lake and positively artistic engineering works. Suitable all year, occupies a couple of hours.

Fionn Mac Cumhaill, redoubtable reducer of biodiversity, slew the monster of Glenasmole. At another time there was a 'city that shone like gold' there. Fionn's grandson, Oisín, met his doom in Glenasmole, after he fell from his white steed on that fateful visit from Tír na nÓg — transformed in an instant from immortal warrior to blind old man.

St Patrick provided the hero with lodging and food, which included a daily allowance of seven cakes of bread and a large roll of butter. But Oisín demanded to be led to Glenasmole where rowan berries grew to twice the size of rolls of butter, and ivy leaves were larger than the saint's cakes of bread. An enormous ivy leaf, found in the glen by the nineteenth-century antiquarian, Eugene O'Curry, is preserved amongst the Ordnance Survey Letters, in the Royal Irish Academy.

Today, at the opening of the twenty-first century, Glenasmole remains an enchanted valley. Part of its magic stems from the unlikely source of the minds of nineteenth-century engineers. They created the beautiful lakes which add to its mystery. A steep-sided glen at the northern end of the Dublin Mountains, it has about a magic which lies in the sense of tranquillity brought about by the shelter of the hills, the pine and larch woodland, and the reflections of all of these in the water. A slightly inconvenient approach from the city admits it to the realm of places of rare beauty which attract a rather small number of visitors and, thus, have the added enticement of uncrowded ways.

Before the ice age, an ancestral River Dodder created the valley now known as Glenasmole, the thrush's glen. Ice, flowing from the north, filled the valley with limestone rubble, properly known as glacial till. For the past 10,000 years, the Dodder has been carrying this material away again in an effort to regain its buried valley. In the course of a notable phase of global warming, melting ice from local mountain glaciers transformed the Dodder and its tributaries to raging torrents, helping them to cut away the earth, and forming gorges on the flanks of Kippure.

At one stage of the recession of the great midland ice field, which extended into the valley to a height of about 300 metres, a lake existed in the glen. A grey sticky mud is exposed in places by the footpath on the right bank of the upper reservoir; this was deposited at the bottom of the ancient lake. Sometimes, horizontal, parallel lines can be seen on the face of the mud; each of the bands between them represents a spring flood. This means that the age of the lake can be calculated, and that it is even possible to tell something of the weather at the time when the mud was first laid down.

The fact that an ice dam created a natural lake in the valley may help to explain why the nineteenth-century, man-made Bohernabreena Lakes look as if they really belong there. Two dams were built in the 1870s — the upper impoundment was to provide a water supply for the Rathmines and Rathgar township, while the lower was a reservoir to extend the working season of the many watermills on the Dodder. Details of the undertaking are given in my own book, *Down the Dodder*.

Apart from the grey sediments, the most remarkable feature of the valley is the 'Artificial Watercourse' which runs by the footpath on the left shore of the upper lake. Its function is to take the brown, peat-stained water of the upper valley of the Dodder past the reservoir. Only the water which drains the lower slopes was suitable for the nineteenth-century supply, and it is led into the reservoir by pipes which run beneath the watercourse or, on the right bank, under the footpath. Where the watercourse enters the spillway beside the dam, a culvert on the left bank carries water for 2 miles from the Ballinascorney and Ballymaice Streams.

The spillway is a noble piece of engineering. The right-hand bend with its stone weir, pierced by twenty openings, reduces the speed and force of the water at times of high floods. Thereafter, it descends by a series of five cascades — again created to reduce the eroding powers of the flood. In wet weather, the spillway, filled with rushing water, is a fine sight — probably the biggest waterfall in the county.

At the foot of the dam, an area of level ground is interrupted in places by concrete channels which act as traps for the gravel brought down by the floods. Pipes and valves lurk in a little tunnel in the dam nearby. A little way downstream is the beautiful Superintendent's House and all around are trees and shrubs. These were originally planted by order of the Town Commissioners who wanted their waterworks to be a thing of beauty. To this day, the grounds are lovingly maintained by the local workforce.

In the 1990s, a car park was laid out at the head of the upper lake, on the right bank at Castlekelly Bridge. Larch and willow trees shade it and there is a wealth of wild flowers there. These are at their best in late summer when the purple loosestrife is in bloom — or perhaps in May when gorse and broom make splashes of yellow, contrasting with the white of hawthorn in the hedges.

The footpath from the car park crosses the Dodder before coming to the gate which keeps cars and livestock out of the precincts of the reservoir. The river is dammed just over a mile upstream to divert it into the Cot Brook and the Artificial Watercourse. Reduced to a trickle in dry weather, the river, when in flood, flows directly to the lake and, in the course of more than a century, the floodwater has deposited quantities of sand and gravel to create a delta. Free from grazing and disturbance of any kind, this provides an area of natural vegetation with willow and alder and a fringe of reeds and yellow flag. Heron, mallard and moorhen are regular inhabitants of the waterside. Besides robins and chaffinches, small birds such as long-tailed tit and redpoll are frequent visitors.

The path leads to the dam, with hedges of hawthorn, black-thorn and occasional guelder rose to the right and, above them, the steep green slopes of Piperstown and St Anne's. St Anne had nothing to do with the region, other than being mistaken for St Senctan who founded a monastery there in the distant past. A holy well on the hillside is still venerated, and a cemetery marks the site of the religious settlement which flourished for many centuries.

The little granite tower stands directly above the foot of the dam and houses controlling valves. Below the embankment, Scots pine and larch trees have been planted and give an impression of how the valley might have appeared in the days when Fionn and the Fianna hunted deer there. It is only an impression because, although pine might have grown there, larch certainly did not. The lower part of the valley may be reached adventurously by walking down the slope of the dam or, sedately, by crossing the lake and taking the footpath beside the spillway.

Waterworks masonry at Glenasmole

The Upper Lake in Glenasmole

A road, accessible to cars, leads down the valley from the Superintendent's House and follows the lower lake. Across the water, the hill slope is officially recorded as a woodland area of 'Regional importance' and described as:

> *One of the highest drift-filled valleys in the country with naturally developing hazel woodland on the east side which contains an interesting flora and fauna.*

The final historical feature of the waterworks is downstream of the lower dam where the water flows through the 'miller's weir' — a measuring device to allow the mill-owners to see that they were in receipt of a fair share of the water supply.

A mile farther downstream, the roadway passes between granite gateposts, from the reservoir property of Dublin Corporation to the public domain of South Dublin County Council.

Grid O1020, Sheet 50 (Castlekelly Bridge car park). This is the most convenient stopping place for cars. Bus 49 goes to within half a mile of the lower entrance. Buggy- and wheelchair-friendly in parts, dogs on leads; a delightful and safe walk for all ages. Wonderful picnic spot — otherwise food and drink are far away.

The Dodder

There is a book called *Down the Dodder* and it is very strongly recommended. The river of the name is a true Dubliner — only the merest traces of some of its small tributaries seeing fit to cross the border and accept a little water from County Wicklow. The main stream measures all of 18 miles and almost exactly half of that length lies within the city and suburbs of Dublin. The source of the Dodder is on Kippure (see p. 51) and, with the help of tributaries and aqueducts, it forms the delightful lakes of Glenasmole (see p. 264). This chapter advances the claims of the suburban section to deserving the attention of a citizen. Energetic souls could walk the nine miles on a single day — but reasonable people are more inclined to take it in smaller pieces.

In 1941, a 'planning report commissioned by County Borough of Dublin and Neighbourhood' was prepared by the Scottish town planner, P. Abercrombie. Among many other far-reaching proposals, he recommended that 'linear parks' be developed along the Dodder and the Tolka rivers. The scheme was that the local authorities, whenever possible, would acquire riverside properties to preserve, or develop as parkland. The ideal was to have a footpath by the water all the way from Oldbawn to Ringsend.

Partly because some buildings and private gardens already extended to the river bank, and partly for reasons of financial stringency, that ideal has yet to be fully realised. But by far the greater part of the river bank is freely accessible to the public, their dogs and their buggies.

The name of Abercrombie is known to few. His vision has had a profound effect on Dublin and secured in the Dodder Valley a wonderful line of green. The foresight of the councillors and officials who agreed to retain his services, as well as the determination of others who have made sure that his ideas would be translated into action, have also played their part. Houses, factories, bridges and other interruptions divide the riverside walk into five pleasant entities, beginning at Oldbawn and wandering downstream to Ringsend.

Oldbawn to Firhouse

Oldbawn Bridge, a fine, single span, was built in 1840 as a fairly remote rural crossing and it was widened in the 1990s to accommodate intense commuter traffic. In common with many of the bridges and walls in the valley, the greater part of the masonry is limestone, quarried nearby in the lowlands. But the decorative coping and string courses are of granite, from the mountains. The arch is supported by 'pyramidal abutments' of limestone which have served their purpose well, keeping the bridge in good shape for 150 years.

Downstream of the bridge, the land on the left bank is maintained as playing fields and rolling open space for serious relaxation. The playing fields occupy the level ground of a former flood plain of the river, which meandered at that height after the end of the ice age. It then broke through some barrier and set to work to create a plain at a lower level. The present-day bed of the river is yet lower. Further development of these 'river terraces' has been a matter for human control since the thirteenth century when Maurice Fitzgerald, Justiciar of Ireland, saw to the construction of the great weir at Firhouse.

There was probably a milldam at the spot long years before. Fitzgerald's requirement was for a high weir to divert the water from the Dodder to the nearby Poddle. The Poddle is a much smaller river, but it flows past Dublin Castle and was the principal supply of water to the medieval city. As the city grew, this supply proved inadequate and so the ingenious scheme of diverting the Dodder was set in action. The splendid stone weir that now stands on the spot is eighteenth-century work. The 1990s were a time of prodigious roadworks when it became necessary to bring the M50 across the valley. When the work was completed, South Dublin County Council developed a waterside park centred on the weir.

Firhouse to Rathfarnham Bridge

Downstream of the roadworks, the river flows for a while at the bottom of a small gorge. On the left bank, a line of pine trees marks the course of the City Watercourse, as the diversion to the Poddle was named. An old two-storey building — in rough-cast on the lower storey, and yellow brick on the upper — was once the engine house of a flour mill, the first of nine powered by the Watercourse. The green fields on the right bank are the upper regions of Cherryfield Park which extends for a mile by the riverside until it meets the Firhouse Road.

Once again, the level ground has been set aside for contact sports, while the land by the margin of the river is well-supplied with footpaths, and screened from the athletes by lovely old hedges. The people in the Parks Department of the County Council are justly proud of the Cowslip Field. Cowslips thrive in limestone land where the grass is cropped at just the right time. If it is cut or grazed too early, the flowers perish. But they can't survive either if the grass is never cut. Haymaking in the old days suited them well, because cattle were kept off the meadows, but the grasses were cut after the cowslips had flowered. Lawn-mowers have replaced the cows, but the Field is left uncut until high summer. It is a particularly fine sight in May when the cowslips bloom. The same maintenance rule also favours many other wild flowers, and the park contains a small, but beautiful, reminder of the meadows enjoyed by past generations.

Across the river from the grounds of Cherryfield, the house with the high-pitched roof is called Spawell. Built between 1712 and 1730, it was the centre for medicinal waters which, until 1750, rose from a spring nearby. A most fashionable watering place for the citizens of the time, the Spawell even published a newspaper for its patrons.

Templeogue to Rathfarnham

Just downstream of Austin Clarke Bridge, the Dodder flows over a high weir and loses itself for a brief space between back gardens. Public access becomes possible again at the end of Washington Park, 500 paces down the road from the bridge, on the right bank. The valley has gently sloping sides on this stretch, and the path looks across the river to the charming crescent called — with startling originality — Riverside Cottages. The river flows beneath Springfield Bridge, and the footpath changes to the left bank, offering a choice of a walk beside the river with a high stone wall on the left, or of penetrating the wall through one of a number of gates, and enjoying the many attractions of Bushy Park. The walk outside the park permits a free rein for dogs and gives a glimpse of an outcrop of the limestone bedrock, which is usually hidden beneath the glacial till.

The park was originally part of a large country demesne. This was gradually sold by its owners for housing — except for the piece acquired by the City Council, in 1951. In the nineteenth century, the Shaws, who owned the estate, made money by grazing cattle on the level ground of the old flood plain, high above the river. The steep bank and the present flood plain were less productive, however, and this may very well have encouraged the family to keep it as a pleasure garden. They planted an arboretum, built a tea house, which they decorated on the inside with sea shells, and used the drainage water to maintain a series of ponds. Excellent landscaping has since been carried out by the gardeners of the City Council. Although largely artificial, the lowest pond is one of the very best places in the Dodder Valley for wildfowl, with a population of mallard and tufted duck, swan, coot and moorhen.

Above the valley, on the right bank, is Rathfarnham. Its restored 'castle' is just out of sight, but the gable of the old church and the steeple of the new one — built in 1784 — stand out. The

Castle was built as a fortress of the Pale but was later transformed to an elegant country house. The present bridge was built in 1765. It was widened in the 1950s and re-named in honour of the Pearse brothers, Patrick and Willie, who crossed it many times to travel from the city to St Enda's.

Rathfarnham to Milltown

Downstream of the bridge, homes and gardens — spectacular ones on the left bank — divert the wanderer. However, the path returns quickly to the riverside on the right bank. The water runs calm and deep, held back by a milldam which hides a rocky outcrop. Part of the flow was diverted at this point to a millrace which ran along the left bank at a high level all the way to Orwell Road, where it powered a long-departed sawmill.

The river is very firmly fenced and embanked on its left side, but the path on the right looks across to a lovely jungly slope with trees and shrubs and, in spring and summer, a heavenly chorus of bird-song: wren, robin, blackbird, thrushes, willow warbler and blackcap, to name a few of the performers. Shrubs with branches overhanging the water provide perches for the kingfisher — more often seen in the morning than later in the day.

The Nine Arches crossing the Dodder at Milltown

Where the Dodder swerves to the left, a triumphal arch stands, floodlit at night but otherwise rendered uninviting by impenetrable barriers and bricked-up windows. Known as the Ely Gate, it was built by order of Henry, Viscount Ely, in the 1770s, as the lower of two entrances to Rathfarnham Castle, his country seat. The Castle, now restored and in the safe hands of Dúchas, the Heritage Service, welcomes visitors and provides acceptable light meals. It stands out of sight above the valley and can be reached by footpath through the housing estate behind the gate.

A footbridge at this point gives access to a pleasant little park, where a level green lawn lies beyond a building of limestone, and behind it an earthen bank. The lawn was once part of the river's flood plain — the former side of the valley forms a steep hill behind the playing fields. More recently, it served, according to the nineteenth-century 6-inch map, as a 'calico drying green'. The building near the footbridge was a lime kiln and the earthen bank a flood protection.

Downstream of the next bridge, the waters run placidly once more, held back by another milldam, this one a gracefully curved structure. Its raceway ran to Dartry where it drove an enormous water wheel. Up to the 1940s, a tiny house stood by the weir. But much has changed since those days, including the obliteration of the sluices and the lowering of the weir in the interests of flood control. The stream flows over one more weir before it passes the Dropping Well and the splendid nine-arched railway viaduct. At the Dropping Well, the path crosses the river and proceeds by the right bank, to Packhorse Bridge.

Milltown to Ringsend

Packhorse Bridge carried the road from Dundrum to town and is the oldest crossing of the Dodder. Abandoned some years ago, it looks upstream to a weir in which traces of the old controlling gates still survive. These diverted the water by a stone channel, under a special arch in the bridge, to Clonskeagh Ironworks. Most of the works have vanished, but traces of its water supply remain in the form of a small brick arch, now half-covered with cotoneaster.

From Clonskeagh, the footpath manages to keep beside the river, down Beaver Row to Anglesey Bridge, at Donnybrook. For more than 600 years, this was the site of great summer fairs which were eventually overcome by Victorian gentility.

The ancient weir at Firhouse, rebuilt in the eighteenth century

A footbridge, downstream of the final rapids, leads to a sheltered terrace and to Eglinton Road which, with Donnybrook Road, effectively bars access to the river. Eglinton Terrace, a lane to the north-west of the football ground, leads into Herbert Park and another pleasing riverside walk. Here, the river is flanked by playing fields and the charming park with its duck pond and pergolas. The exit to the park leads across a patio between the bright new hotel and an apartment block, to Ballsbridge.

Here the Dodder meets the tide. In years long past, it wove its way between sandbanks, but retaining walls were built and the land on either side reclaimed. It is now used for housing, and for a variety of sporting arenas — from greyhounds to Rugby football. Compared to the parks upstream, it is a faintly lonely part of the river, but paths are well maintained all the way to Ringsend Bridge. Its single stone arch makes a fair claim to be the most beautiful of the crossings of the Dodder and was the last of many bridges to be built at that spot. The others were either swept away in floods or left standing far from the riverside when the Dodder propitiously changed its course.

Beside the three great locks of the Grand Canal, the Dodder joins with the Liffey to run to the sea. It was not always a tributary, however. Before the south quays were built it entered Dublin Bay directly; but the Dodder had the last laugh. Unbeknownst to the canal engineers, it was engaged in depositing silt just in front of their magnificent locks — so effectively that the scheme of trans-ferring merchandise from lighters in Dublin Port to the canal barges in the basin never achieved success.

The entire nine miles are shown on the OS Dublin City Map (16th ed.) Oldbawn, bus 49, 49A, is in grid square T7; Ringsend Bridge, bus, 1, 2, 3, is in square K16. Buggy- and wheelchair-friendly all the way. Most of the parks demand poop scoops; Bushy Park is strictly about dogs-on-leads, as is the garden-and-pond section of Herbert Park. Picnicking possible in the parks.

The Royal Canal

Inland Waters

A canal that should never have been built provides many a mile of secluded footpath through city and suburbs in a narrow landscape, rich with birds and wild flowers. Suitable all year, occupies an hour or two.

The construction of the Royal Canal was a mistake — and a very costly one. Conceived in a fit of pique, its life began with twenty-seven years of delays and cost-overruns. Some thirty years of successful trading followed from the date of its opening, in 1817. Then came the railways, always faster and generally more efficient; but the canal did carry commercial traffic until 1951 and remained officially open up to 1966.

Twenty years of decay were followed by a new lease of life when the Office of Public Works released the waterway from the transport authority. The canals had become heavy burdens to the freight companies, but the OPW, to be succeeded by Dúchas, the Heritage Service, was entitled to cherish them as priceless public amenities. So they go from strength to strength, carefully tended and restored where necessary. They form delightful walks for all the populace and their dogs, as well as being places to fish or propel boats for the specialist minority.

The nether regions of the Royal Canal lie amongst wasteland in the vicinity of Sheriff Street; the junction of the canal with the Liffey was actually cut off from the waterway by a railway line being built across it. Purists who wish to follow the towpath all the way, may begin on North Wall Quay, where the second of the two splendid lifting bridges on the north quays stands idle. However, the canal becomes more inviting in the vicinity of Croke Park. Swans sometimes nest near Mountjoy Jail. Mallard and moorhen are ubiquitous, and tufted duck — black with white flanks — sometimes come to visit. In summer, swallows fly to this area — the only ones to live within the confines of the inner city.

One of the major problems faced by the canal in Dublin was that it had to climb to — in canal terms — a great height in a short distance, before reaching the slightly elevated plains of Fingal through which it makes its way. The sixth lock is 115 feet above sea level and the canal has only 2 miles in which to get there. Attaining this level required deep excavations and the building of high embankments, together with the construction of the six locks. The excavations and embankments are largely a one-off capital cost. But the passage through six locks is a permanent financial disincentive because of the long delays it causes in navigation. One positive point about the double lock at Cross Guns Bridge, was that the head of water was sufficient for a power supply, and Shandon Mills, beside the locks, availed of this for many years.

The level stretch of canal which follows runs along the crest of a ridge. At the end of the last glaciation, this was part of a wide plateau. However, the Liffey to the south, and the Tolka to the north, carried the glacial soil away on either side, leaving only the ridge. It is too steep and narrow for houses, so they stay away on the south side, while the railway climbs slowly out of the valley to the north. These factors lead to the existence of an extraordinarily isolated walk, between bridges, for a good mile in the midst of a largely built-up area. The soil is rich in lime and bright with wild flowers.

The next lock is at Ashtown where a further mile of secluded walkway begins. In contrast to the previous stretch, with its view of urban or industrial development, this one feels decidedly rural. Well-grown hedges shield it from the nearby railway and the Navan Road to the south. To the north, open fields and the occasional farmhouse, or affluent dwelling, have resisted the Developer's intentions right into the twenty-first century.

However, the rural refuge is dramatically transformed where the canal enters the spectacular civil engineering works of Junction 6, on the M50. The motorway runs at the bottom of a deep cutting which the canal crosses by way of an aqueduct, and its companion, the railway, runs on a viaduct close by. A further aqueduct, in the form of a large pipe, carries purified Liffey water to the west. Above all of these is the roundabout where the Navan Road crosses the entire complex and allows interchange with the motorway.

Upstream of the junction, the canal reverts to its traditional appearance and there is a delightful little reach between the next two bridges at Blanchardstown. The twelfth lock there lies a little below the 60-metre contour and, from that point onwards, the canal remains level until it crosses the county border and enters Kildare. But it does this at a considerable cost. The next reach sets out between the railway to the south and the back gardens of Roselawn Road to the north. Then comes a dramatic change: the banks on either side rise higher and higher until they completely block out the suburbs — with the exception of one tall television antenna.

This, the Deep Sinking, extends over 2 miles and involved excavation through rock to a depth of 8 metres. The cost at the time was £40,000. But the cutting was a necessity because the Duke of Leinster had ordained that the canal should pass conveniently

Broom Bridge on the Royal Canal — where Hamilton set down his formula for quaternions

close to his demesne at Carton. In the interests of economy, it was kept as narrow as possible and confined to the passage of one barge at a time. The tow-path had to stay well above the water — up to 30 feet in places. The cutting even witnessed a shipwreck when, on a night in November 1845, a packet boat struck a rock, and sixteen of its passengers perished. Today the banks, for the most part, are shaded by ash and hawthorn, except in places where the limestone bedrock appears above the water.

The canal, with its partner the railway line, continues for 4 miles from Kirkpatrick Bridge to the county boundary. It then follows a particularly interesting reach for some 2 miles through County Kildare to Louisa Bridge. Here, the Valley of the Rye Water is crossed by a massive aqueduct, an earthen embankment, pierced by a stone tunnel through which the river flows 110 feet below the canal. It took 6 years to build and cost £27,000 — all for the sake of that grand old duke. Allegedly healing waters were discovered in the course of the work, and traces of the spa which flourished there have been excavated. The damp ground, with water rich in lime, has a fine show of wild orchids in late summer.

The canal walk from the Liffey to Louisa Bridge is 13 miles, and that leaves 78 miles to traverse to its end by the Shannon. Many books have been written about the waterway and its history. For detail, consult Peter Clarke's; for a brief, but more discursive, guide, Ian Bath and Ruth Delany's booklet is recommended.

Grid 15K to 1F on OS Dublin City Map (16th ed.) Buses, including 11, 13, 16, 27, 31, 38, 40 and many others cross the canal. The canal is approachable at many points where pleasant, old, stone bridges carry the roads across it. The towpath runs all the way except in the extremities of the docklands. A delight for dogs, wheelchairs and buggies. Picnic spots a bit limited in the absence of open spaces. Car parking on roadside near most of the bridges.

The Grand Canal

Inland Waters

The successful canal, created as an industrial undertaking, but always with an eye to amenity — a perfect place for a short or long walk.

The Grand Canal runs on the southern outskirts of Georgian Dublin, and the most delightful historical fact about it is the enlightened attitude of its supporters. In 1766, the Pipe-water Committee of the City Assembly of Dublin made the following observation:

> ... the canal would be a pleasing recreation as well as a salutary walk to the inhabitants of Dublin, if trees were planted on the banks of the canal, for that purpose..... your committee contracted with Mr Patrick Edgar to supply 400 trees, thirty feet high, matched fair and straight, at 3s 3d a tree, including all expenses of planting.

Those trees have long since passed away, but the authorities have planted many more, and the banks are delightfully shaded by poplars, London planes and weeping willows.

The canal originally ran in the direction of the city centre, not far from St James's Gate, where it was extended to the City Basin to contribute to the public water supply. There were plans for a steep descent from the Basin to the Liffey but they were fortunately abandoned at the suggestion of one of the canal engineers,

William Chapman. In 1785, he published a pamphlet on the *Advantages of bringing the Grand Canal round by the Circular Road into the River Liffey*. There was good utilitarian thinking there, but Chapman also insisted that the canal would be an amenity for the people and would add to the beauty of the city. Two hundred years later, nobody who walks the canal bank, or sits beneath its trees, could disagree.

The building of Dublin's two Circular Roads — north and south — had commenced in 1763, and the planned canal route lay just beyond the South Circular, on the outskirts of the city. The Ordnance Survey map of 1849 shows built-up areas to the south of the canal between today's Rathmines Road and Ranelagh Road. But, to the east, the greater part of the land lay in open fields. The area west of Portobello Bridge has undergone dramatic changes since that time when it comprised a substantial reservoir with canal docks and, next to it, Portobello Gardens, a park rather larger than Fitzwilliam Square. For the most part, they have been covered over by office blocks, a factory and town houses with gardens. A little area of paved park with shrubs occupies part of the canal harbour which was functional into the 1940s.

Now lined with hotels and expensive townhouses and clinics, Charlemont Mall and Charlemont Place on the left bank are both named on the 1849 map. However, there were extensive open spaces farther downstream, except between Baggot Street and Upper Mount Street where the beautiful houses — which for the most part have survived — were already in place.

The canal continues to provide a salutary — indeed delightful — walk for the inhabitants of Dublin. The truly inner-city reach, from Portobello to the docks is the best for strolling thanks to the broad verges which give an element of relief from the traffic. They occupy the old tow-paths where, in bygone days, big, beautiful draft horses ambled along drawing barges. They enjoyed a brief resurrection during the Second World War, after which internal engines made them finally redundant.

The stone bridges, with their single arches, are works of art. Each bears a medallion with the name of a director of the Canal

Company — La Touche, Charlemont and others. In artistic terms, the greatest bridge is the one dedicated to the barrister, Joseph Huband; it spans the canal opposite Upper Mount Street and St Stephen's Church, and is the most lavishly decorated.

The land at Portobello — or La Touche — Bridge is 75 feet above sea level, and the canal must descend that far in the course of a mile and a half before it reaches the Liffey. It accomplishes this through eight locks, the majority of them furnished with magnificent wooden beams to give the operator the leverage needed to open the gates. The exceptions are at Lower Mount Street and Charlemont Bridge where there is too little space for the beam arrangement and a winch-and-pulley system replaces it. Each lock gate is furnished with two small sluice doors near the bottom, opened and closed by a rack and pinion system. They are opened to allow the lock to fill, or to drain, gradually, and bring a vessel gently up or down.

Some of the locks are usually left empty, with the lower gates open and the water cascading over the upper ones. This has an interesting effect on the vegetation by keeping the walls more or less moist. Many wild plants thrive there, rooting in the old mortar in the crevices. At Charlemont lock, there is a luxuriant growth of mother of thousands. Green, with tiny leaves, it was introduced to Ireland originally as a greenhouse plant but it later escaped and spread to many unlikely places.

Reeds grow by the canal verges, rooting in the silt and growing tall and graceful above the water. A slender species named *Glyceria* is the most abundant, and a canary grass grows with it. These two were the only reeds present in the 1970s when inner Dublin was subjected to an intense botanical survey. Since Peter Wyse Jackson and Micheline Sheey-Skeffington, helped by fellow members of the Dublin Naturalists' Field Club, published their book in 1984, two additional reeds have appeared. One is the 'common' reed, tall and strong and distinguished by big feathery tufts of flower heads. It is rapidly expanding its range and has taken over substantial stretches of canal verge from the former species. The second is the bulrush, bearing flowering spikes faintly resembling frankfurters, but bigger and browner. It grows in just one place, on the right bank about a hundred paces downstream of Portobello Bridge.

The fields, where the canal was built, formed a flank of the Liffey valley and sloped gently down to the sea. But even the gentlest slope is unacceptable to a canal barge, so the system of level stretches and locks is required wherever the route goes up- or downhill. This was achieved by a succession of embankments and cuttings and explains some of the features of the canal path. Grand Parade runs along the edge of the embankment, while Dartmouth Square, behind it, is so much lower that it is approached by a flight of steps.

Patrick Kavanagh remembered on the banks of his beloved canal

Wilton Terrace and Mespil Road make a claim to border the most attractive reach of the canal in the city. For some reason, perhaps because there are more office workers to throw crumbs, the greatest congregation of mallard and black-headed gulls gathers there. Some of the mallard have a tendency to species impurity — possibly because of cross-breeding with the occasional white domesticated duck that lives with them. Sporting patches of white plumage, which no true mallard should countenance, they are tolerated by the pure race and have been present for many generations. Just downstream, on the edge of another embankment, memories of past canal-lovers, Patrick Kavanagh and Percy French, are preserved in bronze and stone.

The canal at Herbert Place is in a cutting, so the tow path has to run under the bridge well below the level of the road. There is another deep cutting at Clanwilliam Lane, and then the canal goes beneath the railway bridge and opens into its inner dock. To the east, the former Boland's Mills building towers above the water, while on the left bank sits the delightful Waterways Visitor Centre, with its exhibition of relevant history and natural history.

The larger portion of the Grand Canal Docks was, for many a year, a run-down district with an unusually interesting wild garden of buddleias and other blow-ins. However, it has rapidly risen in status, with the old warehouses transformed to affluent dwellings or refined businesses. The crystal-clear water of the dock is a refuge for the city seagulls as they relax between foraging expeditions. The docks communicate with the Liffey through three magnificent stone-built locks, each boldly carved with the names of such dignitaries as the Lord Lieutenant, and the date 1796.

Grid 13M (Portobello) to 15K (Grand Canal Docks) OS Dublin City Map (16th ed.) Buses, including 7, 12, 14, 15, 45, 46A and many others cross the canal. Car access and parking on a Sunday is almost unrestricted. As the canal has two sides, a circular walk is possible, its length endlessly adjustable thanks to the numerous bridges. Buggy- and wheelchair-friendly, a delight for well-controlled dogs. Picnic spots a bit limited in the absence of open spaces.

 Epilogue

The Grand Canal happened, by chance, to be the fifty-second recommendation for a Dubliner's Sunday. But the canal — and more particularly its dockland — makes a good place to end the story, as it is something of a microcosm of Dublin and its surrounding counties. Mountains are the sole missing entity. There is flowing water, still water, and the tide. Birds and wild flowers abound. The canal locks provide an offering from the realm of archaeology. The buildings present some of the best of ancient and modern architecture. Above all, there is space — the greatest gift that we can leave to posterity.

References

Anon., *The Howth Peninsula*, Dublin: Howth/Sutton 2000, 2000.

Anon., *National Heritage Inventory*, Dublin: An Foras Forbartha, 1981.

Anon. *Exploring Glendalough Valley*, Dublin: Office of Public Works, 1990.

Anon., *Exploring Glendalough*, Dublin: Heritage Service, 1997.

Bath, Ian and Delany, Ruth, *Guide to the Royal Canal of Ireland*, 3rd ed, Dublin: Office of Public Works, 1994.

Bhreathnach, Edel and Newman, Conor, *Tara*, Dublin: Stationery Office, 1995.

Clarke, Peter, *The Royal Canal: The Complete Story*, Dublin, Elo Publications,1992.

Clinch, Phyllis E.M., 'Botany and the Botanic Gardens' in James Meenan and Desmond Clarke, *The Royal Dublin Society 1731–1981*, Dublin: Gill and Macmillan, 1981: pp 185–206.

Colgan, Nathaniel, *Flora of the County Dublin*, Dublin: Hodges Figgis, 1904.

Craig, Maurice, the Knight of Glin, and Cornforth, John, 'Castletown, Co. Kildare', Reprinted from *Country Life*, 1969: 99, pp 722, 798 882.

Craig, Maurice, *Dublin 1660–1860*, London: Cresset Press, 1952.

de Courcy, J.W., *The Liffey in Dublin*, Dublin: Gill & Macmillan, 1996.

Durand, John F,. 'The Evolution of State Forestry in Ireland', PhD thesis, National University of Ireland.

Farrington, A., *Glacial Lake Blessington*, *Irish Geography*, 1957: 3, pp 216–222.

Gardiner, Piers R.R. and Robinson, K.W., 'The Geology of Ireland's Eye: The Stratigraphy and Structure of a Part of the Bray Group'. *Geological Survey of Ireland, Bulletin* 1970: 1, 3–22.

Gilligan, H.A., *A History of the Port of Dublin*, Dublin: Gill & Macmillan, 1988.

Goodwillie, Roger, *Powerscourt Waterfall: Guide and Nature Trail*, Enniskerry: Powerscourt Estate.

Harbison, Peter, *The High Crosses of Ireland*, Bonn: Rudolf Habelt, 1992.

Healy, E., Moriarty, C., and O'Flaherty, G., *The Book of the Liffey*. Dublin: Wolfhound Press, 1988.

Jeffrey, D.W. (ed.), *North Bull Island Dublin Bay — a Modern Coastal Natural History, Dublin*: Royal Dublin Society, 1977.

Joyce, Patrick Weston and McCarthy, Muriel (ed.), *The Neighbourhood of Dublin*, Dublin: Hughes & Hughes, 1994.

Keane, Rory, Hughes, Anne, and Swan, Rónán, (eds), *Ardgillan Castle and the Taylor Family*, Dublin: Ardgillan Castle, 1995.

Kennedy, P.G., *An Irish Sanctuary — Birds of the North Bull*, Dublin: Three Candles Press, 1953.

Kirk, Frank, *Nature in the Phoenix Park*, Dublin: Stationery Office, 1993.

Leask, H.G., *Irish Castles*, Dundalk: Dundalgan Press, 1951.

Leask, H G., *Glendalough*, Dublin: Stationery Office, 1977.

McConnell, B. and Philcox., M.E., *Geology of Kildare and Wicklow*, Dublin: Geological Survey of Ireland, 1994.

McNeill, T.E., 'Trim Castle, Co. Meath, The First Three Generations', *Archaeological Journal*, 1977: 147, pp 308–336.

Mitchell, Alan, *Powerscourt Tree Trail*, Wicklow: Powerscourt Estate, 1990.

Mitchell, Frank, *The Shell Guide to Reading the Irish Landscape*, London: Michael Joseph/Country House, 1986.

Moriarty, Christopher, *Down the Dodder*, Dublin: Wolfhound Press, 1991.

Nelson, E. Charles, and McCracken, Eileen M., *The Brightest Jewel: A History of the National Botanic Gardens Glasnevin, Dublin*, Dublin: National Botanic Gardens, 1987

Ó hÉailidhe, P. 'An Unrecorded Wedge-Tomb at Killakee, County Dublin', *Journal of the Royal Society of Antiquaries of Ireland*, 1978: 108, pp 101–103.

O'Brien, Jacqueline, and Guinness, Desmond, *Great Irish Houses and Castles*, London: Weidenfeld & Nicholson, 1992.

Pearson, Peter, *Between the Mountains and the Sea: Dún Laoghaire–Rathdown County*, Dublin: O'Brien Press, 1998.

Powerscourt, 7th Viscount, *A Description and History of Powerscourt*, London: Mitchell and Hughes, 1903.

Praeger, R. Ll., *The Way that I Went*, Dublin: Hodges Figgis, 1937.

Raftery, Barry. 'Drumanagh and Roman Ireland', *Archaeology Ireland,* 1996: 10, 1, pp 17–19.

Reilly, P.A., and McCullen, J., *Wild Plants of the Phoenix Park. Dublin*, Stationery Office, 1993.

Slavin, Michael, *The Book of Tara*, Dublin: Wolfhound, 1996.

Sollas, W.J. 'A Walk along the Glacial Cliffs of Killiney Bay', *Irish Naturalist*, 1894: 3, pp 13–17.

Sweetman, David, *The Medieval Castles of Ireland*, Cork: Collins Press, 1999: p. 28.

Taylor, John, *John Taylor's Map of the Environs of Dublin (1816),* Dublin: Phoenix Maps, 1989.

Warren, William P. X., *Wicklow in the Ice Age*, Dublin: Geological Survey of Ireland, 1993.

Wyse Jackson, Peter, and Sheehy-Skeffington, Micheline, *The Flora of Inner Dublin*, Dublin: Royal Dublin Society, 1984.

Index

Celtic church, 92

Chaffinch, 266

Chambers, SirWilliam, 125

Chapelizod, 176

Chapman, William, 283

Charlemont lock, 284

Charlemont, Earl of, 125

Cherryfield Park, 272

Chester Beatty Galleries, 87

Chesterfield, Earl of, 163

Chiffchaff, 155

Chippindall, T. H., 203

City Watercourse, 272

Clarendon, Frederick Villiers, 101

Clarke, Peter, 281

Clarke, Tom, 83

Clements, Nathaniel, 163

Clinch, Phyllis, 147

Clock Tower Building, 88

Cloghoge River, 68

Clonskeagh Iron Works, 275

Clontarf, 228, 234

Coal Harbour, 209

Colgan, Nathaniel, 204

Collins Barracks Museum, *see* National Museum

Collins, Michael, 77

Colonnades, 91

Conolly Folly, 113

Conolly, Lady Louisa, 111

Conolly, Speaker William, 47, 112, 126

coral, 221

Corbet, Myles, 120

Corrig Mountain, 51

corydalis, 204

cotoneaster, 275

Cowslip Field, 272

crab, 238

Craig, Maurice, 112, 125

crinoid, 221

Croke Park, 279

Cromwell, Oliver, 85

Croppies' Acre, 83

Cross Guns Bridge, 279

Cross of Cong, 80

Cross-leaved heath, 52, 66

crowberry, 52

Cruagh, 60

curlew, 211

Curragh, 178

cycad, 150

Cypress, Monterey, 170

D

Dalkey Hill, 200, 201

Dalkey Island, 238

Dalkey Sound, 241

Daly, Denis, 118

Dargan, William, 96, 97

Dargle, 68, 169

Dartry, 275

Darwin, Charles, 104

de Courcy, J.W., 82, 175

de Lacy, Hugh, 35

Huband Bridge, 284
Huxley, T.H., 104

I
Iapetus Ocean, 43
Iona, 93
Ireland's Eye, 250
Irish National Stud Company, 180
Irish Volunteers, 80
Iron Age, 79
Islandbridge, 175

J
Japanese Gardens, 178
Jeffrey, David, 228
Johnston, Francis, 163
Joyce Museum, 208
Joyce, James, 206
Joyce, Patrick Weston, 190
Joynt, Rachel, 88

K
Kavanagh, Patrick, 285
Kennedy, P. G., 228
Kilkenny coal fossils, 104
Killakee House, 48
Killegar, 153
Killiney, 190
    Bay, 195
    Hill, 200
Kilmainham, 175
Kilmashogue, 57
King's River, 64, 69

kingfisher, 275
Kingstown Baths, 206
Kippure, 51
Kirkpatrick Bridge, 281
Kirwan, Richard, 101
Kish, 206
kittiwake, 252
Knights Hospitallers, 32, 163
Knights Templar, 163
Knocksink Wood, 152
Knot, 217
Knowth,.25
Koran, 90

L
Lady's bedstraw, 242
Lake Mareoticus ,21, 41
Lambay porphyry, 197
Lanice, 216
Laoghaire, King, 30
Laputa, 243
lapwing, 217
laurel, 170
Leask, H.G., 15, 36
Leeson, Joseph, 116
Leinster House, 77, 96, 101
Leske, N.G., 101
Lhwd, Edwin, 27
lichen, 191
Liffey, 55
Liffey Head Bridge, 64
limpet, 238
ling, 45, 52, 61, 66

National Museum
    Kildare Street, 77
    Collins Barracks, 82
National Print Museum, 106
National Stud, 178
Natural History Museum, 100
Neolithic, 25
Newgrange, 25
Newman, Conor, 32
Nimmo, Alexander, 263
Niven, Ninian, 150
Noble fir, 49
North Bull, 229
North Wall, 229
North Wall Quay 279
Norway spruce, 29, 34

O

O'Byrne, Seán, 131
O'Connell, Daniel, 32
O'Curry, Eugene, 264
O'Kelly, M. J., 26
O'Reilly, Seán, 125
O'Ríordáin, Seán P., 31
Oak, 18
Oisín, 264
Old Red Sandstone, 247
Oldbawn, 270
Oldhamia, 189
Orwell Road, 274
Owendoher, 50
oyster, 220
oystercatcher, 212

P

Packhorse Bridge, 275
Palaeolithic, 78
Pale, 151
Parnell, Charles Stewart, 143
Parnell, Tom, 143
Pearce, Edward Lovett, 112
Pearse brothers, 274
Pearson, Peter, 203, 209
People's Garden, 166
peregrine falcon, 18, 254
Periwinkle, 238
Phoenix Park, 162, 182
piast, 71
pilgrims' way, 70
Piperstown Gap, 49
Pipe-water Committee, 282
Poddle, 272
Pollaphuca, 151
Polypody, 202
Polystichum, 70
Pooka, 263
Poolbeg, 229, 237
Poolbeg Lighthouse, 209
Pope John Paul II, 166
poplar, 282
Portmarnock, 220
Portobello Gardens, 283
Portraine, 223
Portraine sandstone, 156, 190, 197
Powerscourt, 45, 168
Powerscourt, Viscounts 168